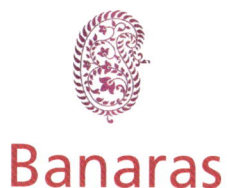

Banaras

For my father Som Majumdar (1942 – 2003)

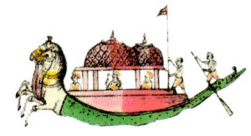

Lotus Collection

© Nandini Majumdar, 2014

First published in 2014

The Lotus Collection
An imprint of
Roli Books Pvt. Ltd
M-75, Greater Kailash II Market, New Delhi 110 048
Phone: ++91 (011) 4068 2000
Fax: ++91 (011) 2921 7185
E-mail: info@rolibooks.com
Website: www.rolibooks.com
Also at Bengaluru, Chennai, & Mumbai

Cover: Panorama of Banaras © British Library / Parts of
this panorama also appear as chapter openers.
Design: Bonita Vaz-Shimray & Shrabani Dasgupta
Editors: Priya Kapoor & Neelam Narula
Pre-press: Jyoti Dey
Production: Shaji Sahadevan

ISBN: 978-81-7436-916-1

Printed at Thomson Press, New Delhi

Banaras

Walking Through India's Sacred City

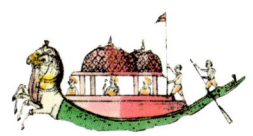

NANDINI MAJUMDAR

Photographs by
CONSTANTINO SCHILLEBEECKX

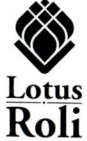

Lotus
Roli

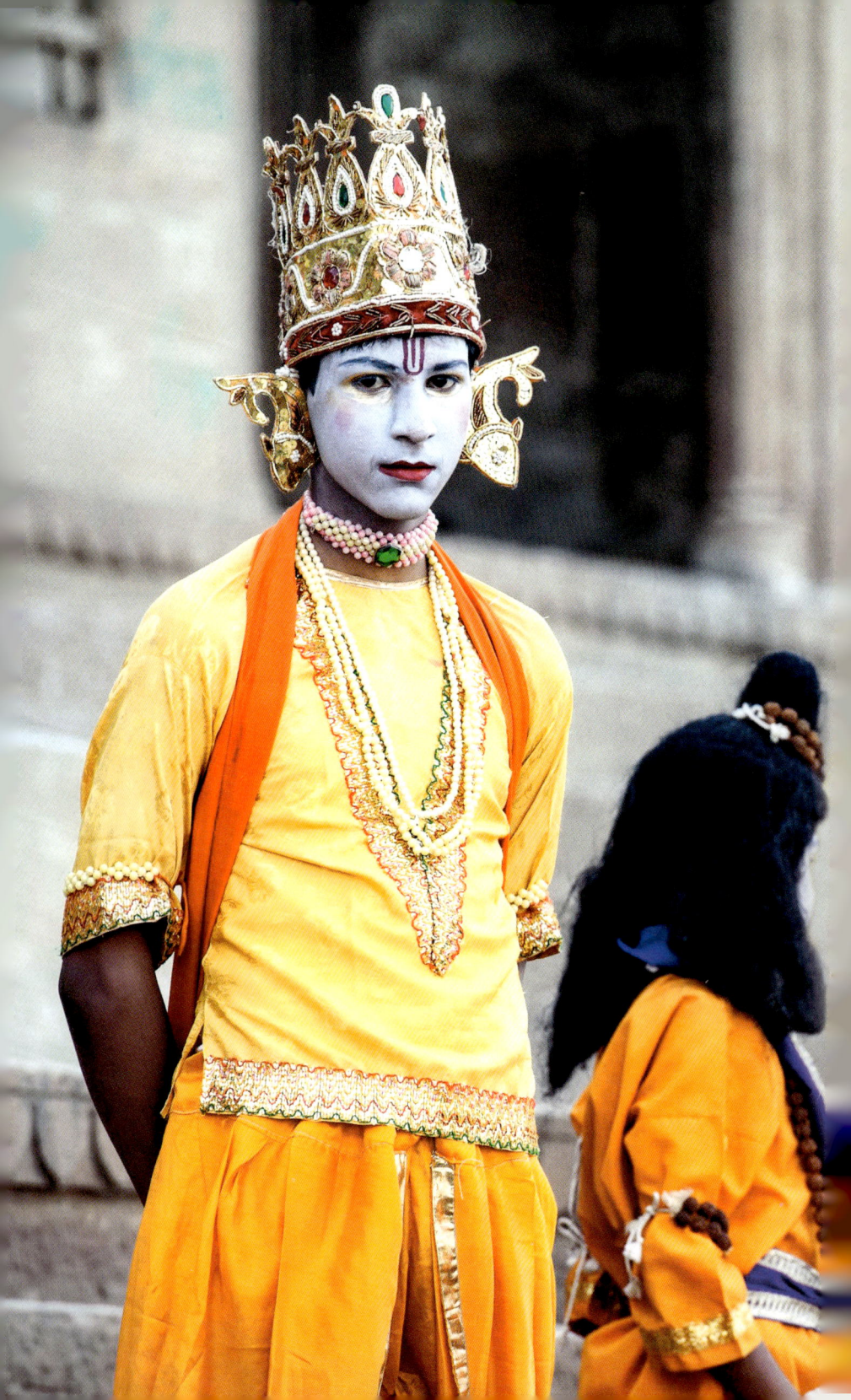

Facing page: Banaras, India's pilgrim capital, is also famous for the spectacular theatrical genre called Ramlila, in which children play the gods.

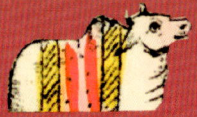

ACKNOWLEDGEMENTS

Thank you to the charming and generous Banarasis I met while exploring the city, for their stories and philosophical insights.

To Tara Prasad ji and Vinay Pandey ji, for helping to sort through the mountains of maps at the Varanasi Development Authority, for travelling through sweltering May afternoons to the far north of the city to have the maps copied, and for printing blueprints in their free time at home.

Thank you to Anjan Chakrabarty and Naval Krishna, for his valuable suggestions, and to Sheila Pinkel for her hours of guidance.

Thank you to the individuals who read the walks, went on them and gave me their input, including the children of Vidyashram – The Southpoint School.

I wrote this book based on original fieldwork and research, through talking to the residents of Banaras and walking the lanes of the city. The book is also indebted to the work of the following scholars, to whom I extend my gratitude: L. Corre, Steven G. Darian, Diana Eck, Sandria B. Frietag, Anuradha Kapur, Christopher R. King, Rai Anand Krishna, Nita Kumar, Philip Lutgendorf, Jonathan P. Parry, Pravin S. Rana, K. Rotzer and Rana P.B. Singh.

And finally, for their love and support, thank you to: Irfana Majumdar, with whom the idea of a book of walks through Banaras was first sown and the first photographs taken, Nawal Kishore Singh, who accompanied me on seemingly aimless meanderings and helped manually measure the lanes of Shivala, and Nita Kumar, who gave me a love for the city's free spirit and a thirst to wander and discover.

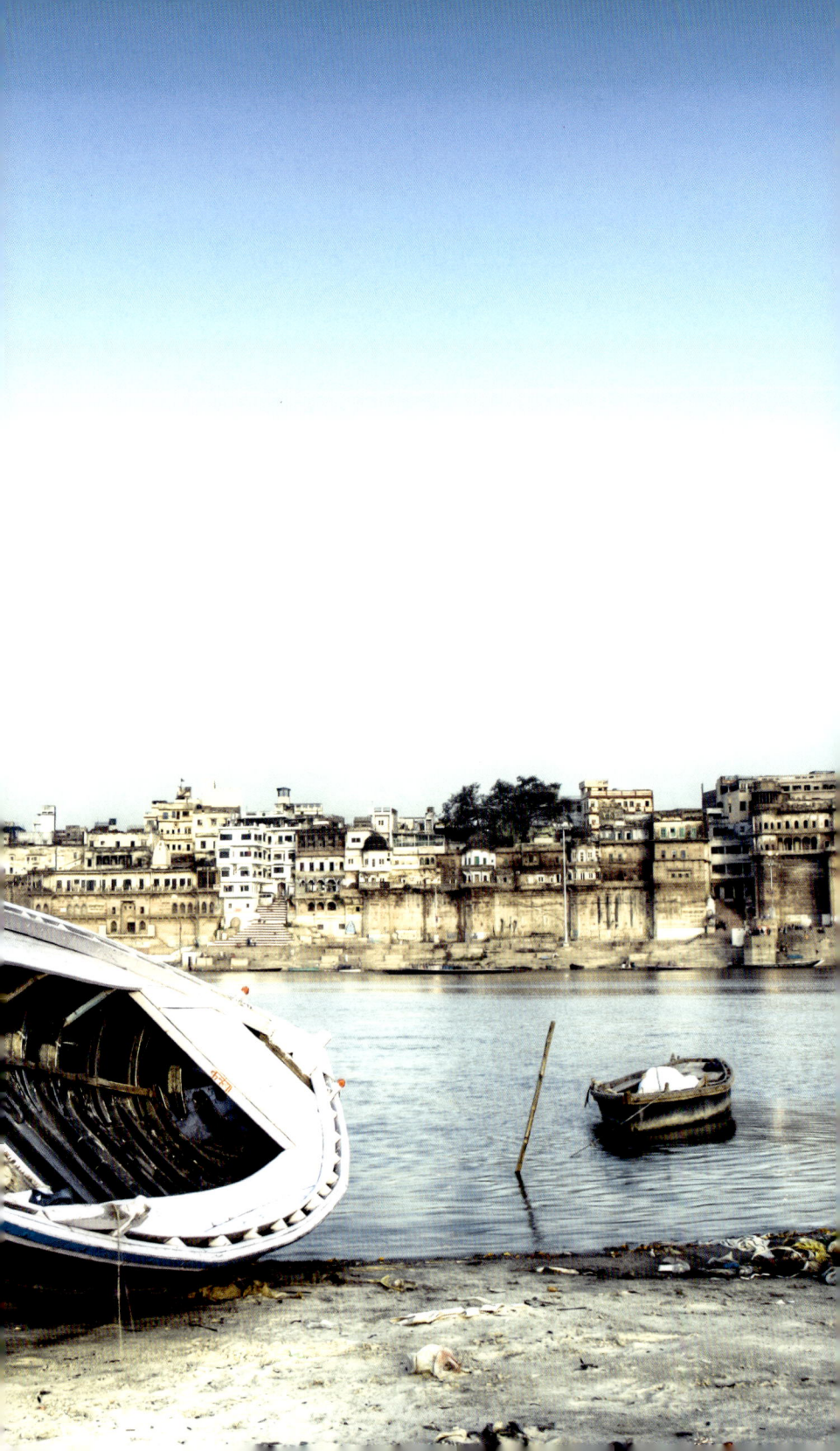

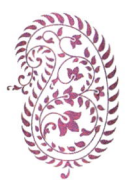

INTRODUCTION

The lanes of Banaras form a maze parallel to the river, running between homes, palaces, and places of worship. They run serpentine or jagged, rarely at right angles to each other, and only those born within them know their eccentricities by heart.

They are paved with fine-grained sandstone quarried from the nearby hills of Chunar. Walking through them, you lose your sense of time, place, and self, and are accompanied by a constant sense of discovery. The stone slabs play with scents and light, your senses and psyche. The air, moving through the lanes of stone, shifts from stillness to breeze. Sometimes the buildings breathe down on you. Other times, they seem to cradle you, slowing your breath, the pace of your thoughts.

Within rooms facing the street, artisans work at handlooms and lathe machines. Wooden shuttles clatter as they weave silken threads into warp and weft. At crossings, shopkeepers lay out spirals of betel leaves and jars of savoury snacks. They pour steaming tea and ladle chilled yoghurt into clay cups. You move past squares and old wells. Sometimes you flow along in a stream of people and animals. Other times, you are alone, save for a pillar that is centuries old, but continues to stand in its original form.

As you walk, you encounter the Hindu gods and goddesses in their countless forms. Idols of Shiva, Vishnu, and Devi frame doorways and crowd the roots of peepal trees. It is said that Banaras is home to 330 million gods. This extended family of gods and goddesses are related to one another through an enormous corpus of mythology, which finds material expression in the city's sacred sites and spaces.

Of all the gods, you meet Shiva the most. Shiva, the god of death, destruction, and dance, defies all categories and conventions. He is a mountain ascetic, a dweller of the cremation ground, and a bridegroom dressed in brilliant silks. He wears, at different times, a garland of skulls and the crescent moon in his hair. His name means 'auspicious', 'blessed', 'gracious', but he reveals himself in the inauspicious and terrible. He bestows blessings and wields weapons. Banaras is *Rudravasa*, the city of Shiva (also called 'Rudra', 'the wrathful'), resting on the middle prong of his trident. It is also *Avimukta*, the city 'never forsaken' by him. Other gods and goddesses make room for at least one Shiva *linga*, Shiva's symbol, in their temples. There is a saying in Banaras, '*Kashi ke kankar me Shiva shankar!*' or 'Lord Shiva is in every pebble of Kashi'. So Shiva is not just in shrines and temples, but in every particle of dust in Banaras.

As you walk, you will also encounter mosques and Sufi shrines. These are significant parts of Banaras, making it an important Islamic city even while it is known as a Hindu one.

Through the lanes, you can walk from the southernmost to the northernmost tip of the city. Or, head east at any point and you will, around a corner, following a twist, reach the river.

Here by the river, the lanes give way to stairs that sweep down to the water's edge, interrupted by landings, called ghats. You stand on the topmost step, looking across the wide,

Facing page: Banaras offers many breathtaking panoramic views of India's most sacred river, Ganga.

floodlit Ganga to the quiet other shore. The buildings behind you form a stone facade famous the world over, dotted with old trees, bamboo umbrellas, and temple spires. At dawn and dusk, the panorama of the riverfront curving north is illuminated like nothing else in the world.

The river, ghats, and lanes make up the fabric of Banaras. Over the centuries, religion, commerce, and the arts have given birth to a special spirit that moves through the city's lanes. This spirit is a *joie de vivre* called *mauj* and *masti*, or abandon and craziness. You achieve it through a glass of frothy *thandai*, a dip in the Ganga, a nap under a tree, an unannounced stop at a friend's, an open-air music session, or a trip to the local saint's tomb. It reflects the Hindu belief in balancing *kama, artha, dharma,* and *moksha*. *Kama* means sensual pleasure, intensity of emotion, and aesthetic enjoyment, found in temples and in the arts, but also in the smallest gestures and actions. *Artha* is practical action rooted in the material world. *Dharma* is relevant action, the right thing done at the right time, sometimes translated as 'duty'. *Moksha* is release from the worldly cycle of reincarnation. The key to happiness is achieving a balance between the four life goals effortlessly, with the blissful freedom characteristic of the long-haired Shiva dancing bare-chested in his leopard skin.

Many scholars call the city 'pre-modern', for Banaras has escaped industrialization. The city's main industries are home-based crafts – weaving, embroidery, stonework, metalwork, and woodwork. And so, comparatively, homes here are humble, concerns simple, and lives carefree. It is no coincidence that home-based production has produced a culture of freedom and pleasure. One anthropologist writes about a much-loved metaphor among the people of Banaras, that of *khulapan*, or openness. What *Banarasi*s value is a *khula dil* (an open heart), a *khula mijaz* (an open nature), and *khuli bat karna* (speaking openly). They equally treasure the little bit of open space, the *khuli jagah*, in the heart of their neighbourhood. For them, happiness is the easy movement through the layers of the self and the world.

So, how can we understand the spirit of the city? Banaras is an open place. All one must do is step out into its lanes.

Mark Twain quipped, 'Benares is older than history, older than tradition, older even than legend, and looks twice as old as all of them put together!'

In the 1940s railroad constructors working on a high strip of land in northeast Banaras accidently unearthed the brick remains of an ancient city. Two decades later archaeologists excavated pottery, implements, and seals, which they dated to the 8th century BCE. This was one of the oldest settlement sites in the world, as old as Jerusalem and Athens.

Let us go back to the start of this fascinating story. We can only wonder if ancient Kashi was the base of an Aryan tribe called Kashi or perhaps the capital of the Kashi kings who fought in the famous war described in the Sanskrit epic, Mahabharata. We do know, from the Mahabharata, the ancient Hindu texts called the Puranas, and the Buddhist Jataka tales, that between the 8th and 6th centuries BC, Kashi was one of the sixteen great kingdoms of the Aryans, along with Magadha to its east and Koshala to its north. Magadha and Koshala competed repeatedly for power over Kashi, for Kashi was situated strategically on the Ganga and along the largest trade route in India at the time, which connected eastern India to the north-west. Kashi was already an important commercial centre. The Jataka tales and the Puranas describe the city's abundant wealth, the productivity of its workshops, and the quality of its products, particularly its fabrics.

Not just the city, but the entire area of the city and its environs, called 'Kashi', was coveted by the gods and humans alike from that ancient time. *Mahatmya*s, or poems of praise, found in the ancient texts the Puranas describe in rich detail the area surrounding the gated city.

Kashi was *Anandvana* or the 'Forest of Bliss', lush with silver, slender *kasha* grass (from which, perhaps, comes the name *Kashi*). It was thick with groves and gardens and filled with birds and bees. The Forest of Bliss remained this way, open and lush, into the 19th century. The accounts of travellers and the maps of James Princep, an East India Company cartographer, capture its geography over the centuries. Kashi was divided into five forest tracts and laced with lakes and streams that drained into one another, swelling and sinking with the rhythms of the river. Residing in the Forest of Bliss three millennia ago were pre-Aryan, local deities called *gana*s, *ganesha*s, *naga*s, *yaksha*s, and *devi*s. These were mostly associated with ponds and trees, their presence honoured simply, with a swathe of red thread around a tree trunk or a daub of vermillion on a stone. They were popular heroes, serpent gods and goddesses, and mother goddesses.

The Forest of Bliss attracted worshippers of these ancient local dieties. It also attracted religious seekers and seers, who challenged the Vedic religious system and its emphasis on Sanskrit texts, the power of priests, and elaborate rituals. Instead they focused on introspective wisdom (*gyan*) and new perspectives (*darshan*). The forests and streams of Kashi were ideal for hermitages and tempted the most radical new gurus. Gautam Buddha was one of these teachers. A prince by birth, he had travelled far from his kingdom, seeking enlightenment. At Banaras, he identified his first five disciples and delivered his first sermon. In the centuries following the Buddha, other great teachers lived and taught in Banaras – the grammarian Patanjali, the philosopher Shankara, and the theologian Ramanuja.

It was from the local deities of the Forest of Bliss that the great gods of Hinduism, Vishnu and Shiva, and the goddess, Devi, arose and established themselves in Banaras. The Buddhist Jataka tales, the epics Mahabharata and Ramayana, and the Puranas record the development of Hinduism and Mahayana Buddhism. Over the next millennia, Vishnu and Shiva gathered as entourages and incarnations the various local deities. Some *gana*s and *devi*s became independent gods and goddesses, like Ganesh, Sitala, and Kali. Others became consorts of the great gods, like Parvati. The concept of bhakti or devotion developed, as rituals of worship evolved from ancient practices. The Mauryas in the 3rd and 4th centuries BCE and the Kushanas in the 1st century CE were patrons of Buddhism. The war-weary Mauryan emperor Ashoka converted to Buddhism and travelled to the township of Sarnath, outside Banaras, where the Buddha first attained enlightenment under the Bodhi tree. Ashoka developed a Buddhist town there with monasteries and temples. His famous lion capital stands in the Sarnath museum today. Then in the 4th century CE the Bhara Shivas and the Guptas ushered in a glorious age for Hinduism. They built temples and sanctioned religious texts to be written. By the end of Gupta rule in the 6th century CE the Hindu pantheon was firmly established and devotional movements of all kinds flourished.

These centuries were also a time of considerable architectural and sculptural achievement. Under the Mauryas, the first images of the Buddha were sculpted, along with images of the Hindu pantheon, and evolved into an increasingly sophisticated aesthetic. And from the accounts of travellers we know of the city's tall temples, its lanes and avenues, and the surrounding forests, which continued to attract traders and merchants, gurus and students, pilgrims, and the wealthy.

When Banaras rose to political power, its reigning dynasty, the Gahadvalas developed it as a stronghold for both Buddhism and Hinduism. They developed a new Buddhist monastery in Sarnath, built numerous shrines, demarcated three sacred zones in the area of Kashi, created networks of pilgrimage routes, and built rest houses for pilgrims all along the riverfront. As pilgrims poured in, Kashi's reputation as a powerful tirth, a sacred pilgrim site, grew, as an earthly place where one could 'cross over' from the material world and the cycle of reincarnation to the 'far shore' of liberation.

Squabbles between the Gahadvalas and their neighbours tempted the Afghan invader Muhammed Ghuri and his general Qutb-ud-din Aibak to snatch power from the Gahadvala King Jayachandra. In 1194, Qutb-ud-din razed the Rajghat Fort and demolished the city's most important temples. Following him, the Sharqis and the Lodis in turn destroyed parts of the city and constructed mosques on the foundations of temples.

The Mughal emperor Akbar ascended the throne at Delhi in 1556. Akbar was liberal and syncretic in his religious views and imperial approach. He collaborated with the Rajputs and Marathas, who ruled over vast portions of the subcontinent, by appointing Rajput and Maratha kings to administrative posts. Two of his senior ministers Man Singh and Todar Mal rebuilt demolished temples and paved sections of the riverfront in Kashi. The Shiva temple Vishwanath was re-built after being demolished twice before. It is the city's most important temple today.

Akbar's great-grandson Aurangzeb inherited the throne in 1658. Following the dictate of a good Muslim ruler, Aurangzeb tried to superimpose an Islamic city over Hindu Banaras named 'Muhammadabad', by erecting *idgah*s, or mosques for special Id worship, on the foundations of razed temples. The most striking was the Alamgiri Mosque, whose soaring minarets were the tallest and slenderest in Mughal architecture to date. The mosque remains a majestic landmark on the city's skyline.

These centuries, from the 12th to the 17th, have often been depicted by historians, amateur and professional alike, as a time of destruction and tumult under 'Muslim rule'. However, some of the city's most beautiful monuments, both secular and religious, were built during this time. Banaras also remained an unparalleled centre for commerce, religion, and intellectual life. Royal families and states from all over India wanted to establish their presence in the city. They poured in their wealth and built up large complexes along the riverfront, complete with a ghat, a palace for retreats, a temple, a pond or well, a rest house for pilgrims, a school, and an *akhara* or gymnasium. Homes of sandstone had become numerous, standing shoulder-to-shoulder in shady lanes. In courtyards and street corners, wealthy families erected personal shrines. The concept of the mohalla or separate neighbourhoods crystallized, with each neighbourhood protected by gates. Migrants streamed into the city. As communities from west, south, and east India grew, Banaras became a cosmopolitan centre, the city that encompassed all India.

Specialized markets developed: Khojwa for grain, Raja Darwaza for baskets, Thatheri Bazaar for etched brasswork, and Kunj Gali for silk. In their workshops, Muslim and some Hindu weavers produced yards of silk and gold brocade. Metalworkers hammered dazzling brass and silver objects into creation. Trade flourished. Barges carrying goods from all over the country and from England sailed down the wide and fast-flowing Ganga, docking at ghats along the riverfront. In exchange, Banaras traded spices, wood, stone slabs, perfumes, jewellery, and the most exquisite of silks, all products in high demand.

Treatises on religious duty and manuals for rites and rituals were written by the scholars of the city, who were patronized by wealthy migrants from other parts of India. The literary Bhakti movement swept through north India with Banaras as the stronghold of its development. Poet-saint Ravidas wrote iconoclastic and anti-caste poetry filled with sombre, home-spun truths. An 'untouchable', he wrote of how before god all humans are corrupt or 'untouchable'. Kabir attacked organized religion with gentle wit and wry humour and called only the body, not temples or mosques, the place of worship. Later, in the 13th century, Tulsidas adapted the classic Sanskrit epic the Ramayana into the vernacular. His accessible Ramcharitmanas is the most widely-read version of the epic today and is divided into episodes and performed annually mostly at street corners. The songs of these poet-saints are known to all.

By the turn of the 18th century, the centralized Mughal Empire weakened, with the Marathas and the British East India Company gaining power and tussling for control. As central power weakened, local administrators grew virtually independent. Through a series of leases, the political responsibility for Banaras passed from the hands of the Nawab Wazir of Awadh to a local Brahmin landowning family. This line of local kings continued to serve as administrative middlemen for the British after the fall of the Mughals. They were powerful in the city, regarded as incarnations of Shiva by the people and greeted publicly by his names: '*Har har Mahadev!*'

This was a time of new alignments of local power. Merchant bankers drawn to Banaras for its commercial opportunities formed a tightly-knit oligarchy known as the 'Naupatti' ('society of nine sharers'), which became the pinnacle of complex business networks. They managed their establishments deep within the lanes. Trading centres began to compete with one another, using devious strategies to keep their systems secret. Behind the busy trade networks were an order of mendicants called Gosains. They were monks turned traders and soldiers. As they moved on pilgrimage routes, they traded goods and developed strong military skills to protect themselves.

The collaborations between the merchant bankers, Gosains, and Rajas of Banaras gave birth to a unique urban style. An elite community grew out of the traders, merchants, and moneylenders. These aristocrats patronized music and dance, theatre and literature, arts and crafts. They raced their horse-driven carriages down the streets and sailed king-sized houseboats down the river. They financed elaborate fairs and festivals and partook in the political life of their city. They regarded themselves with pride as 'cultured' and *shaukeen* or 'full of passion'. The spirit of the city, the soul of Banaras, arose out of the confluence of religion, trade, and political power in these centuries and the previous three millennia.

By now the city resembled the Banaras we know today, the city of dense stone quarters cut through with lanes, the city of the soaring riverfront. The Marathas, who had long wanted control over north Indian cities of religious and commercial importance but had never managed to control Banaras, financed much of the city's 18th century construction of temples, palaces, and pilgrim resthouses. British administration also gave shape to modern Banaras. Two broad roads were cut through the city, running south to north parallel to the river. Streams were drained and converted into streets, ponds into parks. Forests were razed for habitation. The ancient Banaras, the Forest of Bliss, was no longer visible. But woven into the dense fabric of Banaras one can find all the threads of its long and rich history, starting three millennia ago.

For gods and humans alike, Banaras has always been the object of desire. The city itself has always come first. Today, Banaras retains its flavour, its *Banarasipan*, with fervour. It continues to be a city of lanes and workshops, places of worship, and spaces for leisure. Its people still value, above all, freedom and abandon.

But for a variety of reasons, Banaras is changing. Literally and figuratively, the old Banaras is being broken down. Its love for openness and modernity's more individualized spaces do not always coexist creatively and harmoniously.

One of the wonderful and unique qualities of Banaras is that it demonstrates how the culture of a place is not coterminous with its religion. The culture of a city is hopefully not coterminous with a historical period either. Change is of course natural and inevitable. But change can be steered into desired directions. This book is an effort to preserve the most beautiful parts of Banaras, written with the hope that its readers will discover and celebrate it.

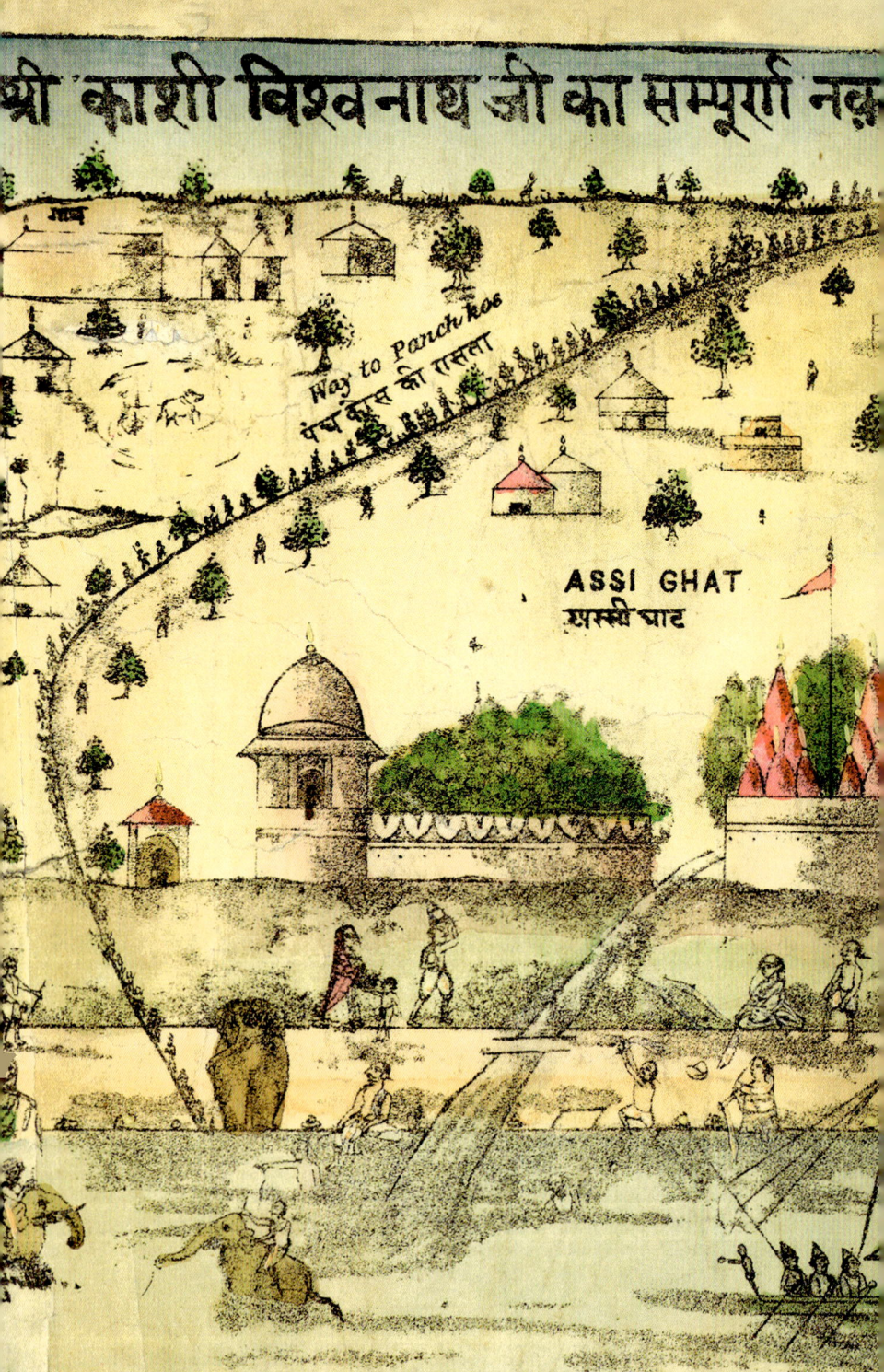

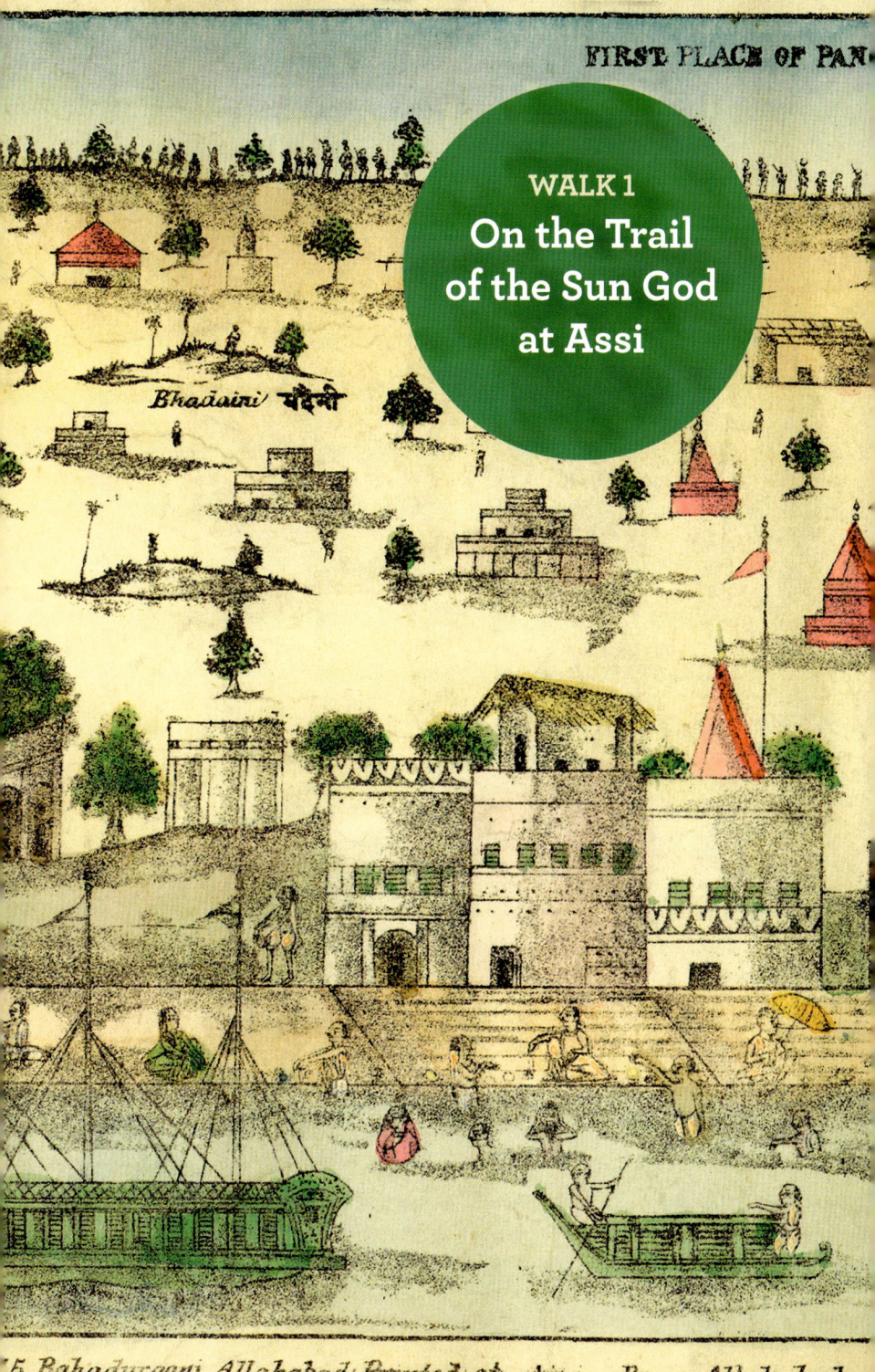

WALK 1
**On the Trail
of the Sun God
at Assi**

Bhadaini चंदैनी

5 Bahadurganj Allahabad, Printed at Aina Press Allahabad,
गंज में है ऐनी प्रेस में छपा सितम्बर १९०१ पहली दफा

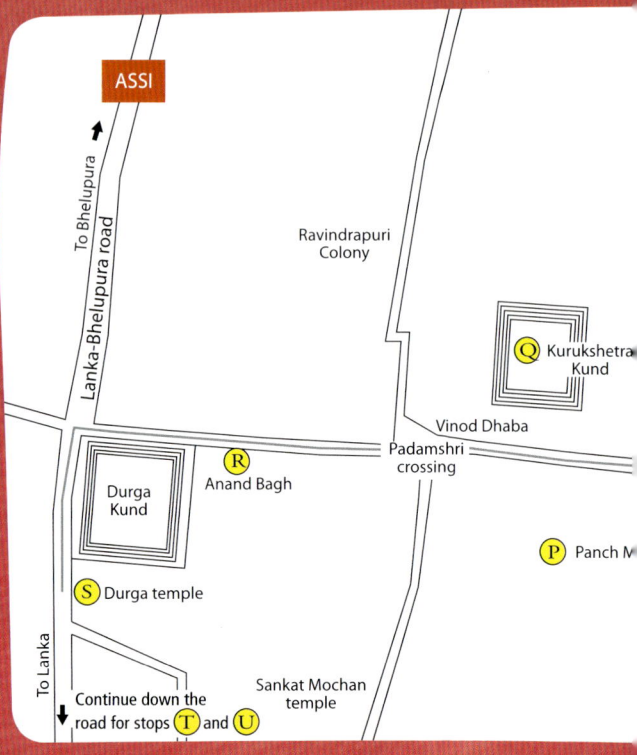

Explore charming buildings, indulge in riverfront activities, visit an ancient water reservoir dedicated to the Sun God, and temples devoted to the demon-slayer goddess, Mahishasurmardini, the poet-saint, Tulsidas and Hanuman.

THINGS TO SEE
- A pond dedicated to the sun god mentioned in the Mahabharata
- Temples of the wrathful goddess, Durga, gentle Hanuman, blue-skinned Krishna and the popular 16th-century poet-saint, Tulsidas
- A traditional banarasi gymnasium

ALLOW
Three to four hours, or two to three with the exception of the last three stops

WALK ITINERARY
Jagannath Mandir I Assi Ghat I Panchameshvara Temple I Asi Sangameshvara Temple I The Assi lane - Tulsi Ghat - Swaminath Akhara I The House of Tulsi I Lolark Kund I Durga Temple I Tulsimanas Temple I Sankat Mochan Temple

The last three stops can be combined to form a separate trip

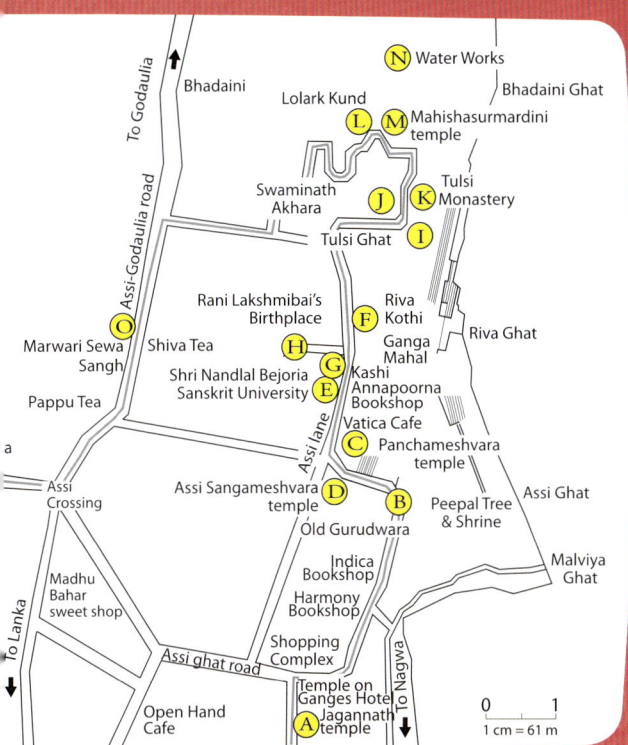

To Godaulia
Assi-Godaulia road
To Lanka
a

Bhadaini
Lolark Kund
N Water Works
Bhadaini Ghat
L **M** Mahishasurmardini temple
Swaminath Akhara
J **K** Tulsi Monastery
Tulsi Ghat
I
Rani Lakshmibai's Birthplace
Riva Kothi
F
Riva Ghat
C
Marwari Sewa Sangh
Shiva Tea
H
Ganga Mahal
Pappu Tea
Shri Nandlal Bejoria Sanskrit University
G
E
Kashi Annapoorna Bookshop
Vatica Cafe
Assi lane
C Panchameshvara temple
Assi Crossing
Assi Sangameshvara temple
D
B
Peepal Tree & Shrine
Assi Ghat
Old Gurudwara
Malviya Ghat
Indica Bookshop
Harmony Bookshop
Madhu Bahar sweet shop
Shopping Complex
Assi ghat road
To Nagwa
Temple on Ganges Hotel
Open Hand Cafe
A Jagannath temple

0   1
1 cm = 61 m

GETTING AROUND ASSI

Assi is an intimate neighbourhood, far south along the river. Its northern boundary stretches to the Shivala neighbourhood. Go south down the road to reach the famous Banaras Hindu University and the neighbourhoods of Nagwa and Samneghat.

VISITING ASSI

A popular neighbourhood among international tourists, Assi consists of hotels, cafés, music stores, yoga centres and a well-connected international community. It is also a favourite neighbourhood among local Banarasis. Lovers of art, philosophy and politics spend hours ruminating by the river or chatting in the many tea shops that crowd Assi's lively crossings. Within the shady lanes, boatmen lead quiet lives with their families.

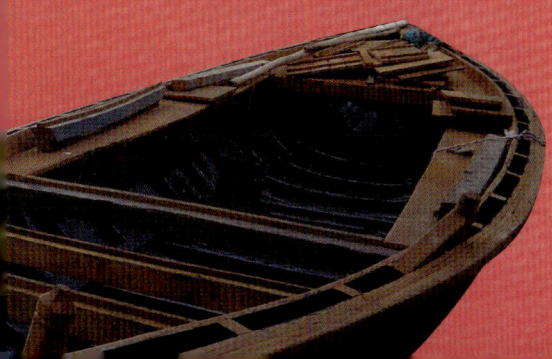

THE HISTORY OF ASSI

Three millennia ago, the Forest of Bliss stretched towards the south and west from the far northern plateau of Rajghat. The neighbourhood that is today called Assi lay at the edge of Kashi (the larger area of Banaras and its environs, today it is a pious name for the city), where the rivulet Asi met the Ganga. This far southern region was well-forested and laced with streams and ponds. There were few signs of habitation, only mansions of the wealthy, some isolated *ashrams* where gurus led disciplined lives with their pupils, and Lolark Kund, the ancient water tank, dedicated to the sun god, mentioned in works as early as the Mahabharata. With the rise of the Gahadvalas and the turn of the first millennium AD, the ancient northern city was destroyed, and in the process of reconstruction began to spread southwards. During the reign of the Gahadvala king Govindcharan, Queen Kumara Devi took sacred baths at Lolark Kund. By the 16th century, the poet-saint Tulsidas had established a monastery, a temple and a ghat next to Lolark Kund.

The epic Mahabharata and old Buddhist tales refer to the city as 'Varanasi'. One explanation is that the name comes from the river Varana, which flowed into the Ganga at the site of the ancient city on the northern Rajghat plateau. But many people also believe that the name comes from joining Varana and Asi. Asi was the name of the rivulet that flowed into the Ganga in the southern region of what has today come to be known as Assi.

There are many myths and passages in the Puranic texts that explain the name 'Varanasi'. Diana Eck writes that, according to one myth, the gods created two rivers to protect the city from evil. They named the southern river 'Asi', which means 'the sword', and the northern river 'Varana', or 'the averter'. Another text explains that both rivers originated from the feet of Purush, the primordial man created at the beginning of time – Varana from the right foot and Asi from the left. And yet another text describes the rivers as the veins of the metaphorical body of the city. These stories illustrate the textured nature of the sacred geography of Banaras, or, using the terminology of a number of scholars, how the layers of 'microcosmos' and 'macrocosmos' mesh together.

Ⓐ JAGANNATH MANDIR
Chariots of the God

→ *Directions to Jagannath Temple: Turn right down the Assi road from the Assi crossing. Take the second right at 'Hotel Temple on Ganges'. Turn into the pastoral compound on the left. Walk through the compound, past a peepal tree, temple, and small man-made pond, and through a tunnelled walkway. A statue of the eagle Garuda, who helped Ram in the* Ramayana, *faces the temple.*

What to Know The English word 'juggernaut' was supposedly derived from the huge chariots of Jagannath, such as the one stored in this temple. Jagannath is another name for Vishnu, the 'preserver', one of the Hindu trinity of Brahma, Vishnu and Shiva.

Jagannath Mandir was built by Queen Dulari Radhakunvar in the 19th century. It is named after Jagannath Temple in Puri, Orissa, in eastern India. The temple in Puri houses Krishna, an avatar of Vishnu,

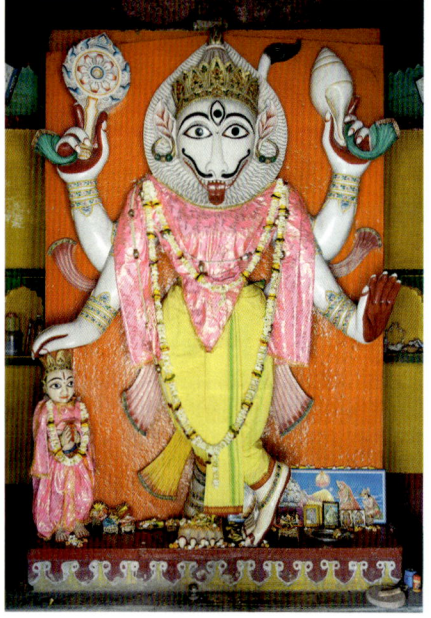

Narsimha at Jagannath Temple.

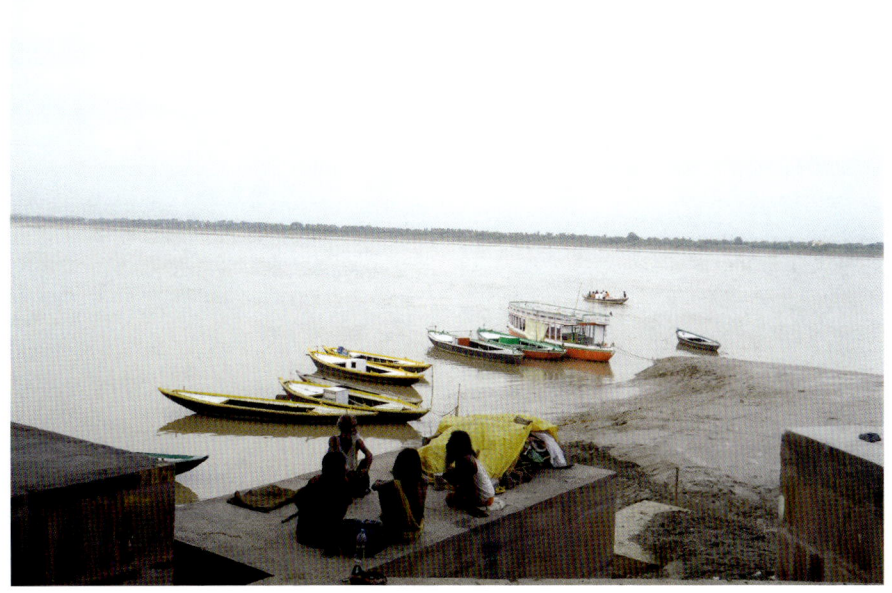

Relaxing by the river at Assi Ghat.

and is one of India's largest and most famous temples.

The Jagannath Temple of Banaras has a pastoral, ruined atmosphere and could hardly be called one of the most impressive temples of Banaras. But its wild delicacy charms and its openness gives one a sense of the older forested Banaras, the Banaras of clay, grass, stone and water flowing freely into one another.

What to See The images of Krishna, his brother Balaram, and sister Subhadra in the inner sanctum are made of fragrant sandalwood. Along two walls of the temple compound there are rooms for the Jagannath chariot and the temple priests. Another temple dedicated to Narasimha, Vishnu's man-lion form, forms the southern wall of the compound.

What to Do Every year in the Puri temple, during the first monsoon month of Asharh (June-July), Krishna and his two brothers are taken out on a 'chariot pilgrimage' or a procession called the 'Puri Rath Yatra'. The Puri Rath Yatra festival is replicated in Banaras as well. As part of the festival, an enormous rath or chariot begins its journey from the Jagannath Mandir at Assi. Crowds follow Krishna and his brothers through the entire city to the Rath Yatra crossing in the northwest, which is named after this very function. There a mela or fair takes up the

---

THE MEANING OF DHAMA

The sacred geography of Kashi replicates, and in doing so, is believed to actually contain, the sacred sites of all India. In Diana Eck's words, Kashi is like a crystal, gathering and refracting divine light. These sacred sites are called tirthas (literally, 'crossings'), where one might 'cross' from the material world to the 'other' shore of liberation, and dhamas, the 'abodes' of the gods.

The word dhama may be translated in a variety of ways. It essentially means a place where divine power is concentrated. The four dhamas of India are: Badrinath in the Himalayas, Rameswaram at the southernmost tip of the country, Dwarka on the western coast of Gujarat and Puri in Orissa in the east. These sites were defined as dhamas by the spiritual guru Shankaracharya in the 9th century. The Jagannath Temple of Kashi represents the eastern dhama of Puri.

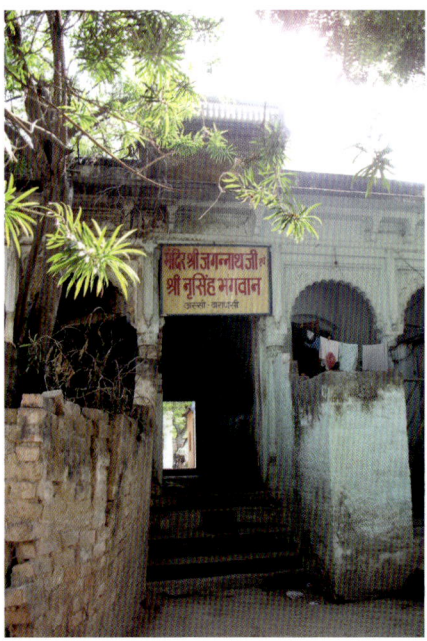
Entrance to the Jagannath Mandir.

entire street. Hawkers sell clay images of gods, wooden toys, balloons and useful items such as mirrors and combs. Carts with high stacks of nan-khatai roll into the Rath Yatra crossing by the hundreds. *Nan-khatai*, a flaky, melt-in-the-mouth biscuit, available in many flavours, is baked especially for the Rath Yatra fair in home-based workshops all over the city and in nearby villages. The wonder is that it remains crisp even in the humidity of the monsoons. Slowly, amidst these festivities, the Jagannath chariot circles back to its temple in the south.

Ⓑ ASSI

The Eightieth Ghat

→ *Directions from the Jagannath Temple to the river: Walk back through the compound and turn right into the lane. Turn right on the Assi*

road and follow it straight down to the river, turning left past the hotels and bookshops.

What to Know Assi means 'eighty' and ghat refers to the stone steps and stretches that descend to the water's edge. Assi Ghat is supposedly the eightieth ghat in Banaras, and one of the city's most popular. For school children who want to fly kites, couples on a date, young men who love to loiter, or the artist trying to hone his skills, Assi is an all-day getaway. It offers both privacy and socialization.

What to Do Throughout the year, music concerts are held on the wide flight of stairs of the ghat. In the season of Ashwin (September-October) the ghat serves as a stage for the *Ramlila*, the spectacular theatrical enactment of the Ramayana that takes place over nine days leading up to the festival of Dussehra.

What to See Until recently, the ghat was unpaved (*kachcha*). The main buildings on the ghat were built by the Marathas in the 18th and 19th centuries. The last construction took place in the 2000s. The two prominent old buildings on the ghat are Ganga Mahal, straight and slender, and Riva Kothi, its rounded pylons rising past carved windows to rooftop latticework. Sit on one of the wide steps and admire the city skyline curving northwards. The Malviya bridge marks the northernmost neighbourhood, Rajghat. A low 'pontoon' bridge marks the southernmost neighbourhood, Samneghat. Pontoons are large cylindrical buoys that keep afloat wooden planks that together make a bridge.

Assi Ghat is one of the most important riverfront stretches from a religious point of view, along with the ghats Manikarnika, Panchganga, Dashashwamedh and Adi Keshav. It is a stop on several pilgrimages such as the Haridwar pilgrimage, the Char-Dham pilgrimage ('pilgrimage of the four *dhamas*'),

DIWALI

Diwali is the spectacular 'festival of lights' in the season of Ashwin (September-October), celebrating Lord Ram's homecoming after his thirteen-year exile in the forest. People decorate their homes with dozens of little clay lamps in celebration. The ghats are a particularly good place to admire the dazzling panorama that Banaras becomes on the night of Diwali.

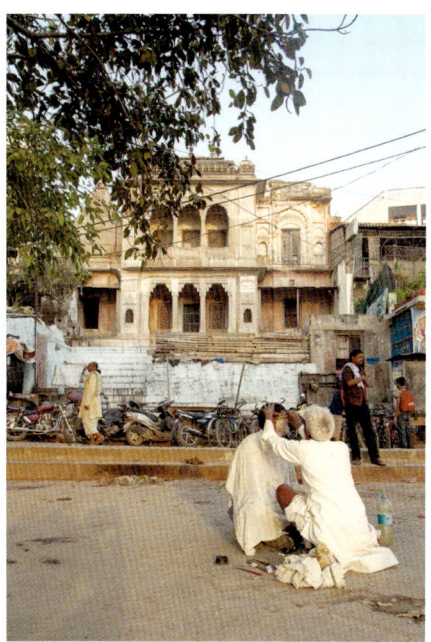

A barber in front of the old Gurudwara at Assi Ghat.

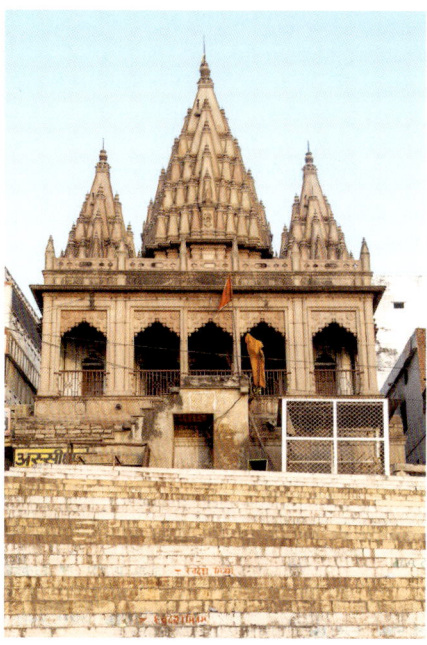

Panchameshwara Temple at Assi Ghat.

and the Panchatirth (a pilgrimage of the five special ghats, which are Assi, Dashashwamedh, Manikarnika, Panchganga and Adi Keshav).

Pay attention to the large peepal tree. Peepal (Sacred Fig or Ficus Religiosa) is a species of the banyan fig native to parts of South and South

East Asia and a member of the fig or mulberry family. It is sacred in Hinduism, Jainism, and Buddhism, and a much loved and protected tree in Banaras. Under the peepal tree at Assi, boatmen wait for customers, sitting in a row. There are small images of Shiva, Durga, and Hanuman, and a large enclosed one of Hanuman, covered in vermillion. Residents of Assi highly revere these images and visit them throughout the day. You may notice that small plaques or engravings accompany many images. These record the name of the image's donor or the person in whose honour or memory the image has been donated. An individual may choose to donate or establish an image, a bell, or even a slab of stone, under a neighbourhood peepal tree or in an existing shrine or temple, in memory of a beloved family member or to mark an important personal event. Other family members and neighbours learn of the donation, begin to visit the spot, and in turn make donations of images, bells, or stone slabs. This process transforms the worshipped tree into a neighbourhood shrine, the shrine into an enclosed temple, or the neighbourhood

FOOD

In the shopping complex, at the corner of the Assi Ghat road and the path down to the river, you can find **ice cream** in the Amul store and **coffee** in Page Break Café.

On Assi Ghat, there are stalls of tea, cold drinks, ice cream, freshly roasted peanuts and favourite **sweet and savoury snacks** such as chat, samosas and bhelpuri.

The city's only **pizzeria** can be found on Assi Ghat. Very popular with tourists, Vatika Cafe serves fresh, tasty pizzas, as well as a range of other basic Italian dishes. Please note that like most other food establishments in Banaras they only serve vegetarian food.

A few minutes walk away, Open Hand Cafe serves excellent coffees, cakes, and sandwiches.

temple into a larger one known city-wide. This localized form of devotion, truly 'popular' in that it is 'of the people,' has wonderful examples all over Banaras. The Assi peepal tree is one such example.

Directly opposite the tree, above a flight of stairs, stands a charming two-storey stone building. Until at least a century ago, this was a gurudwara or Sikh temple and housed a copy of the *Guru Granth Sahib*, the book of the teachings of the Sikh gurus. Today, it is a private home.

Ⓒ PANCHAMESHVARA TEMPLE
Banarasi art aficionados & temple deities
→ *Directions from Assi Ghat to Panchameshvara Temple: Ascend the wide flight of stairs overlooking the river to the elevated, five-spired temple at the top.*

What to Know Panch means 'five' and 'ishvar' means 'lord'. This five-spired temple has five deities, one under each of its five spires. In the inner sanctum there is an image of Lakshminarayan, or Vishnu (also called Narayan) and his consort Lakshmi. At the four corners connected by verandahs there are Shiva, Radha and Krishna, Ram and his wife Sita, and his brother Lakshman.

What to See Paintings of gods and goddesses adorn the top of the doorway to each shrine. Notice Ganga riding a crocodile in one painting and a tortoise in another. This style of painting using vivid colours and natural dyes is the typical Banarasi style of wall painting, replicated on cloth curtains and wooden, stone and glass figurines, beads, and toys – products that are sold in fairs and during festivals. Many painters live in the neighbourhood of Khojwa (see Walk 8; pages 122-29). You may also see giant wheels of crosshatched bamboo stored along the temple's verandahs. These rustic discs form the tops of the umbrellas that dot the riverfront in the summer, completing the quintessential Banarasi river panorama.

Ⓓ ASI SANGAMESHVARA TEMPLE
The union of the holy rivers
→ *Directions to the Asi Sangameshvara Temple: Go down the temple steps and turn right down the narrow lane. Turn left just before the enclosed yard at the crossing to reach the tiny Asi Sangameshvar Temple.*

What to Know 'Sangam' means 'union' and Asi Sangameshvara means 'lord of the confluence at Asi.' The confluence at Asi refers to the confluence of the Ganga and the Asi rivers, the Asi river today being a rivulet.

What to See The marble plaque on the wall quotes passages from *Kashi Khanda*, an ancient text in which Kashi is described and praised extensively. Inside, the largest *linga* is believed to be ancient although the temple itself is a modern construction. This *linga* is a 'Baneshvar' *linga*, or the *linga* of the 'Lord of the Forest'. Water drips slowly onto all the *lingas* to keep them cool. In the niches surrounding the *lingas*, there are images of Ganesh, Vishnu, Surya the sun god, and Annapurna, goddess of nourishment.

Ⓔ THE ASSI LANE
A glimpse into riverside lives
→ *Directions from Asi Sangameshvara Temple to the Assi lane: Turn left outside the temple, going past the enclosed yard, and at the small crossing, turn right down the Assi lane.*

What to Know This lane is the nerve of the Assi neighbourhood. The old houses here have been owned for generations by the same residents, mostly small businessmen, boatmen and snacks stalls' owners. Students, professors, artists and international tourists also live here in the many rooms available for rent.

What to See Admire the old-fashioned homes that line this lane. Looking down side alleys and into doorways gives you interesting glimpses into the lives and work of the residents of Assi.

Ⓕ RIVA KOTHI
Music & History
What to Know Riva Kothi, built by the king of Riva (in present-day Bihar), marks Riva Ghat on the riverfront. Strains of tabla and sitar escape the windows of the building. Today, the building serves as a hostel for music students of Banaras Hindu University.

What to See Many of the students who live in Riva Kothi offer private lessons to music

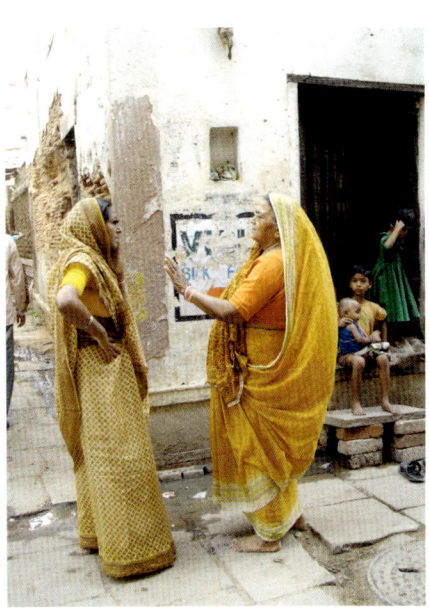

Local residents in the lively Assi lane.

enthusiasts, including international tourists. If you befriend one of them, you may be lucky enough to tour the interiors of Riva Kothi. The numerous staircases offer fun escapades and the roof a wonderful view of the river.

Ⓖ SHRI NANDLAL BEJORIA SANSKRIT COLLEGE
The life of an ancient language
→ *Directions from Riva Kothi to Sanskrit College: Opposite Riva Kothi, the building with ornate metal balconies houses the Sanskrit college 'Shri Nandlal Bejoria Sanskrit Mahavidyalaya'.*
What to Know Amazingly, Sanskrit is still taught in scores of special schools in Banaras, although it is otherwise a 'dead' language like Latin. The students study ancient Sanskrit texts such as the Vedas, grammar, philology, and philosophy. They graduate to work as teachers, commentators and specialists in rituals and discourse.

Ⓗ RANI LAKSHMIBAI'S BIRTHPLACE
Remembering a queen's valour
→ *Directions from Sanskrit College to Rani Lakshmibai's Birthplace: Rani Lakshmibai's birthplace is housed within the tall metal gates to the right of Sanskrit College if you are facing it.*

What to Know Rani Lakshmibai (1835-58) was the queen of the Maratha-ruled princely state of Jhansi (in present-day Uttar Pradesh). She was named Manikarnika at birth, after the earring that Shiva dropped at Manikarnika Ghat. She was renamed Lakshmibai when she got married, after the Goddess Lakshmi. During the Indian Mutiny of 1857, she was one of the main rebel leaders, fighting against the British alongside other rebel forces, including the likes of the legendary Tatya Tope. She was killed in battle wearing full warrior regalia, and is a celebrated figure for her valour.

What to See Adjacent to the Nandlal Bejoria Sanskrit school is an enclosed compound with an impressive statue of Rani Lakshmibai, commemorating the spot where she was born.

Ⓘ TULSI GHAT
Hanuman's abode
→ *Directions to Tulsi Ghat from Assi lane: Continue in the same direction down the lane until it forks, one fork turning left and the other continuing uphill. Take the uphill fork and follow it to the small square.*
What to Know Three Shiva shrines, an old peepal tree, and a large balcony overlooking the river mark Tulsi Ghat. The balcony is a marvellous place for resting and surveying the riverfront. Early in the morning, bare-chested men come to practice yoga on the balcony. In the afternoon, monkeys frolic in the shade. At the base of the tree, images and Shiva *lingas* cluster together.
What to See The white building with a narrow verandah is the ancestral home of Vishwambhar Nath Mishra, the current head priest of Sankat Mochan, a Hanuman Temple that has become immensely popular in the past few decades. His is a hereditary position. The other two buildings are the guesthouse of the Sankat Mochan Foundation, and the laboratory for the Swatcha Ganga Foundation, which conducts research on water pollution and spearheads attempts to clean the river Ganga.
What to Do
Dhrupad Festival
Every year within the Sankat Mochan Foundation guesthouse campus, a free public music festival takes place over three nights. It

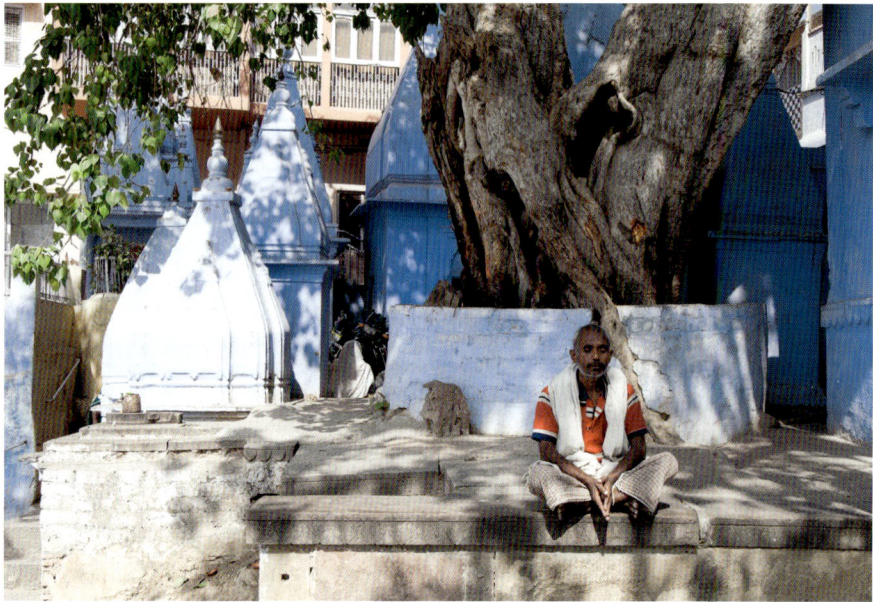

Shrines to Shiva at Tulsi Ghat.

celebrates one of the ancient musical styles of India, dhrupad, and is called Dhrupad Mela. Artists of the *pakhawaj* (dhrupad drum) and dhrupad singers are invited from all over India to participate in this esteemed event. Some of the most famous Dhrupad artistes include Jiyafariddudin Dagar, Jiyasayuddin Dagar, Jiyafahiyuddin Dagar, Umakant and Ramakant Gundecha, the Mallik brothers and Ritwik Sanyal (a vocalist from Banaras).

Ⓙ SWAMINATH AKHARA

The Banarasi love of the body

→ *Directions from Tulsi Ghat to Swaminath Akhara: Step through the gate opposite the late Veerbhadra Mishra's residence.*

What to Know Today, there are few akharas for a variety of reasons. But one type that continues is the gymnasium, of which the Swaminath Akhara is an example. The Swaminath Akhara was founded by the poet-saint Tulsidas (1547-1623), who also established a Hanuman temple, a monastery and the Tulsi Ghat.

An akhara is a club with open membership, organized activity, and a guru. In the Banaras of the past there were akharas of music, poetry, sword fighting, religious teaching, and working out.

Nita Kumar writes (*The Artisans of Banaras*) that we find the first mention of wrestling in India in the ancient Hindu epics, the Ramayana and the Mahabharata. In the 14th century, the Mughal emperor Babur brought central Asian styles of wrestling to India. The succeeding Mughals were extremely fond of the sport. During the reign of Akbar (1556-1605), central Asian styles merged with indigenous ones, evolving into a new form of wrestling called *kushti*, from the Persian word *kusht*, which means to wrestle. In Banaras, akharas and akhara practice came to acquire a cosmopolitan character, as did many aspects of the city's culture, reflecting characteristics of south, west and east India. Akharas are open to all ages, castes and religions. All akhara-goers are men and most akharas are segregated by mohallas, including mohallas with Bengali, Marathi or Bihari residents (each goes to their own). However, there is no rule about it, and the odd person could wander into

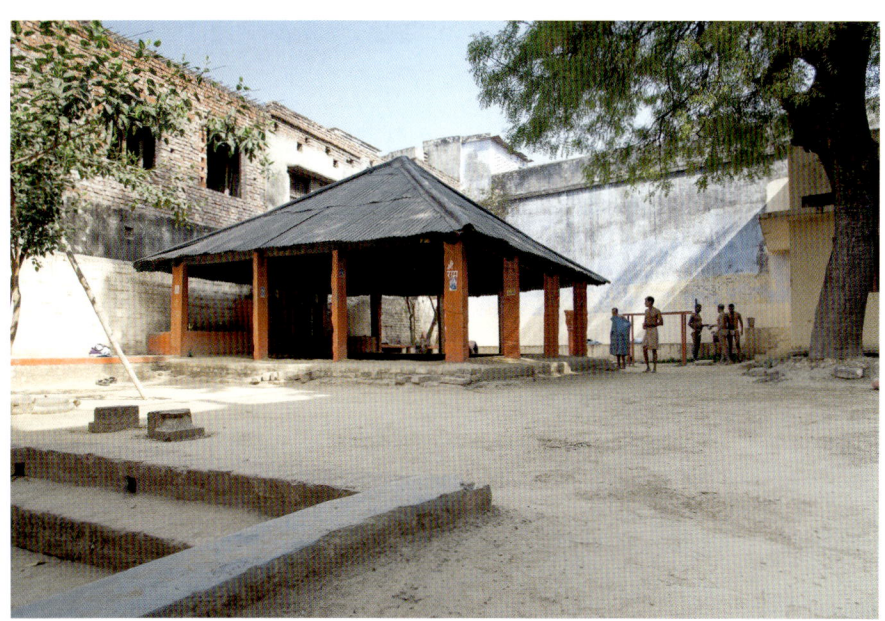

Wrestlers at Swaminath Akhara.

another neighbourhood's akhara and become a regular patron of it, and be totally accepted. Bodybuilders of varying ages, incomes and education, arrive before sunrise. They bathe and massage their bodies with oil. Then they exercise, practice old routines and learn new ones from their guru or seniors. They do *dand-baithak* or sit-ups, *jori phirna* or turning the *jori* (a pair of wooden cylinders tapering at one end, filled with iron or concrete), yoga routines such as *suryanamaskar*, and push-ups. Popular weights include the *gada*, a round stone attached to a stick; the *jori*, and the *nal*, a wheel-like disc with a grip in the centre or a hole for the neck. In the Hindu epics, Hanuman and other heroes used versions of the *gada*. After their exercises, members of the akhara rest under the shade of the neem, peepal and mango trees in the akhara compound, wearing their *langots* (underwear) or *gamchchas* (loose cloth wound once around the waist). They drink water, and, if they like, prepare and consume bhang. Bhang is an intoxicant prepared from the Cannabis plant and a special favourite in Banaras, resulting, when consumed, in a spirit of *mauj* or carefreeness. It can be had in many forms, dry, mixed with spices, or ground and mixed in a drink called *thandai*. Wells in every akhara are equipped with a sculpted stone for mixing bhang with spices.

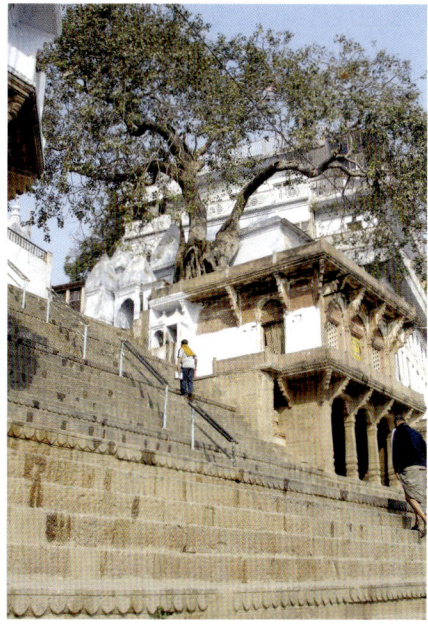

Stairs leading up to the Tulsidas monastery above.

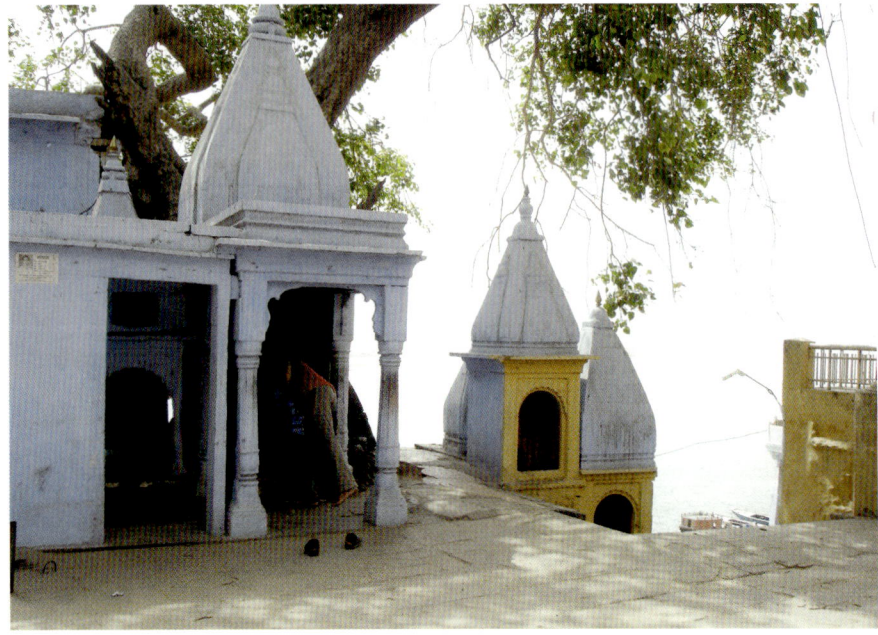

Shrines adjoining the Tulsidas monastery, of Hanuman and Shiva.

The wrestlers allow the mud to dry on their bodies. As it turns to *dhul* or dust, it resembles the *bhasm* or ashes on Shiva's body. The *mitti* or mud of every akhara is smooth and soft, having been brought especially from the river. This *mitti* acts as a natural remedy for sprains and wounds. It is sometimes enriched with healing compounds such as turmeric, mustard oil, salt, and lime juice, with camphor added for fragrance. Every akhara has a unique lineage. Legends about prized wrestlers and *jori* swingers are commonly heard in Banaras. Often, the akhara will keep a picture of its founder, which its members will garland and revere. Members feel devoted to their teacher, to the history and the mud of their akhara. Akharas are places of leisure and pleasure. Caring for the body, nurturing and pampering it, constitutes an essential part of *Banarasipan*, or the ethos of Banaras.

What to See Inside the Swaminath Akhara, there is a covered sandy space for wrestling and an open space with a clay floor for working out. You may see some of the wrestlers' weights, such as the dumbbell or *gadai*, lying around.

Ⓚ **THE TULSIDAS MONASTERY**
A famous poet composed

→ *Directions to the house of Tulsidas from Swaminath Akhara: The tall building houses the home of the late Veerbhadra Mishra on the ground level floor, the Hanuman Temple on the middle floor, and Tulsidas monastery on the top floor. Enter through the narrow door opposite the Swaminath Akhara.*

What to Know Tulsidas (1547-1623) is celebrated as one of the great poet-saints of the Bhakti movement, along with Kabir, Meera and Ravidas. The Bhakti movement spread as a popular, people's movement that challenged the old Brahmanical, Sanskritized version of religion. It was characterized by a new wave of devotional poetry in the vernacular. Like the other Bhakti poets, Tulsidas wrote in Awadhi, a language spoken by the masses, rather than Sanskrit. But unlike the other Bhakti poets, Tulsidas lived during the reign of the Mughal emperor Akbar, who strove to be a patron of all the religions in the subcontinent (primarily Hinduism, Islam, Christianity, and Jainism) and who created his own syncretic religious doctrine called *Din-I-Ilahi* (Persian, 'divine

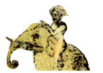

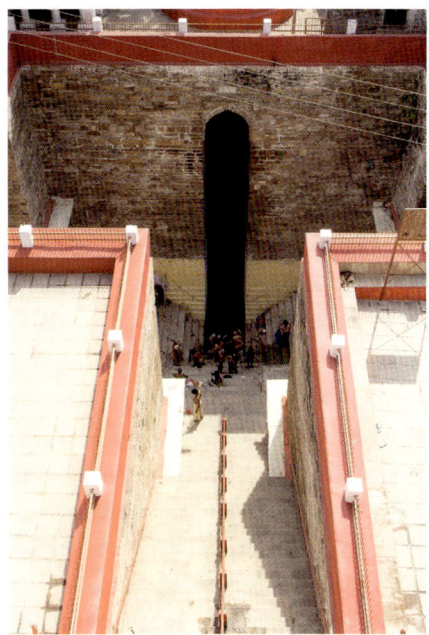

Lolark Kund reservoir.

faith'). Akbar rebuilt many of the city's oldest and most elaborate temples, such as the Vishwanath Temple. Tulsidas's poetry is a wonderful example of the syncretism that characterized Akbar's reign. Most famously, Tulsidas translated and adapted the Sanskrit epic Ramayana into the vernacular, as the more accessible *Ramcharitmanas*, which gained instant popularity with the people. It continues to be the most widely read version of the epic today.

Tulsidas' *Ramcharitmanas* is prefaced by a 40-verse long poem in praise of Hanuman, called the 'Hanuman Chalisa' (chalis means forty). Tulsidas was a Vaishnav and a bhakta or devotee of Lord Ram. Consequently, Tulsidas greatly respected Hanuman, Ram's monkey-protector and friend in the Ramayana. The efforts of Tulsidas popularized the devotional worship of Hanuman in Banaras. He established 12 Hanuman shrines in the city, including the southern temple of Sankat Mochan and a small

A *kund* is a deep man-made water reservoir with stone steps cascading down on one or more sides to the water. Kunds have been an essential part of both Hindu and Muslim urban and palatial architecture.

shrine at Tulsi Ghat. He is also believed to have begun the Ramlila in Banaras. The Ramlila is a month-long theatrical enactment of Ram's story, which takes place every September-October, in Banaras.

What to See Upon entering, one finds oneself in a marble-floored hall with an enclosed Hanuman image. A doorway on the left leads out to another Hanuman temple established by Tulsidas. The poet's wooden clogs are neatly arranged before the friendly, vermillion-smothered image of Hanuman. There are usually a few priests and worshippers gathered quietly here. A tunnel-like stairway leads upstairs to the monastery where Tulsidas lived and worked. The monastery is bare and not particularly interesting. On the highest floor, though, barred windows provide picturesque views of the river. Tulsidas' legendary wooden cot sits enclosed on one side.

What to Do Every month, the Kashi Sangeet Sabha ('Kashi Music Society'), an organization run by the Sankat Mochan Foundation, organizes a free public music concert in the Hanuman temple in Tulsidas' monastery. Typically featuring Banarasi musicians and attended by the city's close-knit musical community, these concerts are intimate and very atmospheric.

Ⓛ LOLARK KUND
Sacred waters of an ancient reservoir

➝ *Directions from Tulsidas' monastery to Lolark Kund: At the door of Tulsidas' monastery turn right. The narrow lane twists and turns to Lolark Kund. The route takes one past several small temples, opening into a large compound with the reservoir and adjoining temples of Mahishasurmardini and the nine planets.*

What to Know Lolark Kund is an ancient water reservoir dedicated to Surya the Sun. In Kashi, Surya divided himself into twelve parts called *adityas* (see Shiva's Tale, page 28). Lolark is the name of the most important of these *adityas*. Lolark Kund is very likely one of the oldest sites in Banaras. It is mentioned in works as early as the Mahabharata. 'Lolark' refers both to the

SHIVA'S TALE

A long time ago there was a drought on Earth that lasted 60 years. Brahma, the creator, saw the havoc it created. He sought out someone to restore order, and identified the sage Ripunjay as the only one fit for the job. Ripunjay agreed to assume kingship over Earth on the condition that the gods would not interfere in his rule. He ordered the gods to leave Kashi and return to their homes in heaven. Then he took on the name Divodas (which means, ironically, 'servant of the gods') and set about his business.

Under the just and good Raja Divodas, perfect order was restored. But Shiva, who had been banished to Mount Mandara, yearned to return to Kashi. He spent all his time with his wife Parvati discussing how they could return. They decided to ask the 64 goddesses called *yoginis* for help. The *yoginis* took on disguises – some became hairdressers, others acrobats and ascetics – and went to Kashi. But they were unable to tempt the king and disturb his rule.

Now Shiva had to turn to someone else. He chose Surya, the sun, who agreed to help. When Surya first set his eyes on Kashi, he trembled with excitement. The place where he dropped his semen came to be called Lolark Kund – it is said that bathing here guarantees conception. But Surya, like the *yoginis* before him, failed to disrupt Raja Divodas' rule. Ashamed of his failure and enraptured with the brilliant city, he settled down in Kashi, dividing himself into 12 parts called *adityas*. That is how Kashi came to be the home of the *adityas*.

tank and to the sun disc etched into the tank wall near the water's edge. Diana Eck writes of two inscribed copper plates recording the patronage of the Gahadvala kings and queens, who bathed and worshipped here in the 11th and 12th centuries. For centuries before their time, however, villagers probably travelled to the ancient reservoir in the Forest of Bliss. Eck suggests in her book, *Banaras, City of Light* that much before Vishnu and Shiva emerged as the great gods of Kashi, Lolark Kund was probably a place of nags (serpent deities) worship as well as sun worship.

The Lolark Chhat Festival

On the sixth day of the waning fortnight, during every season of Bhadrapad (August-September), a mela called the Lolark Chhat takes place here. *Chhat* means 'sixth'. Until the 1940s, this monsoon fair was one of the most popular in Banaras. Informal stages for music and dance would be set up. Thousands would pour in from nearby villages to bathe, worship and enjoy the festivities. The climax of the fair was the singing, dancing, and worshipping at Kinaram Sthala, the monastery of Aughar saints. The Aghori panth (panth meaning 'way') is one of the most popular and beloved in Banaras. Kinaram, their founder, preached a different kind of social transaction in which there were no rules barring anyone or anything,

from lepers and untouchables, to courtesans and drugs. The basic philosophy held by the Aghori ascetics is that the realization of non-duality is the path to moksha (liberation from the cycle of reincarnation). All 'opposites' and conventional categories are illusory. The Aghori ascetics are devotees of Shiva. Because Shiva dwells in everything, every animate creature and inanimate object is perfect: nothing is 'impure' or 'polluted'. The headquarters of the Aghori panth 'Krim Kund', also the location of Kinaram's tomb, is located in the Ravindrapuri Colony close to Assi and makes for an interesting visit.

Ⓜ TEMPLE OF MAHISHASURMARDINI

Home to the slayer of demons

What to Know Mahishasurmardini is the 'slayer of the demon Mahish' (*asur* means 'demon'). She is a wrathful aspect of Devi, the Great Goddess, and is closely associated with the terrible Kali. She is often shown wearing garlands of skulls and baring bloody fangs. In her temple here she is depicted as a dark black goddess with round, red eyes.

Ⓝ VARANASI WATER WORKS

British architectural influences

What to Know The elegant brick towers visible belong to the Varanasi Water Works,

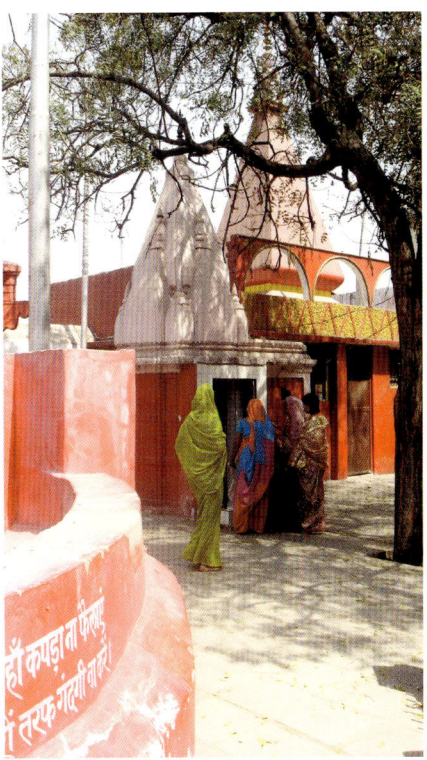

The Mahishasurmardini Temple.

like group that originated in Rajasthan and spread all over India. The Marwari Seva Sangh is an organization run by Banarasi Marwaris that has many social and Hindu activities, including a guesthouse for pilgrims, *goushalas* or homes for cows, a Sanksrit school, and religious discourses.

built by the British in the early 1800s. The British wanted to shift a Ram temple in the area in order to build the water purifying plant. Hindus all over the city protested. Interestingly, many Muslim citizens joined them. This move of solidarity captures the civic spirit that has characterized Banaras over the ages and that overrides other loyalties of caste or religion. For the people of Banaras, 'Banarasi' is a more meaningful identity than 'Hindu' or 'Muslim'.

ⓞ MARWARI SEVA SANGH
India's indigenous capitalists
→ *Directions from Lolark Kund to Marwari Seva Sangh: At Lolark Kund, facing the kund with the Water Works to your left, take the left-hand lane and turn right on the wide lane. Turn left down the main road and walk towards the vegetable shops. Marwari Seva Sangh is on the right, marked by a large gated entrance.*
What to Know The Marwaris are India's indigenous capitalists. They belong to a caste-

ⓟ PANCH MANDIR
Five deities for five shrines
→ *Directions from Marwari Seva Sangh to Panch Mandir: Turn right outside Marwari Seva Sangh if you are facing the road and continue down the Assi road past the tea shops. Turn right at the Assi crossing down the narrow road lane with an Ayurvedic clinic on the left and a tall old house on the right.*
What to Know Like the Panchameshvar Temple on Assi Ghat, Panch Mandir has five separate shrines with deities (*panch* means 'five'). The deities are of Vishnu, Lakshmi, Kali, Durga, Krishna, Radha, Ram, Sita, Parvati, Ganesha, Surya and Ganga, in various groups.

ⓠ KURUKSHETRA KUND
Rani Bhavani's Reservoir
→ *Directions from Panch Mandir: Turn left outside Panch Mandir and go down the roadlane. Kurukshetra Kund is on the right.*

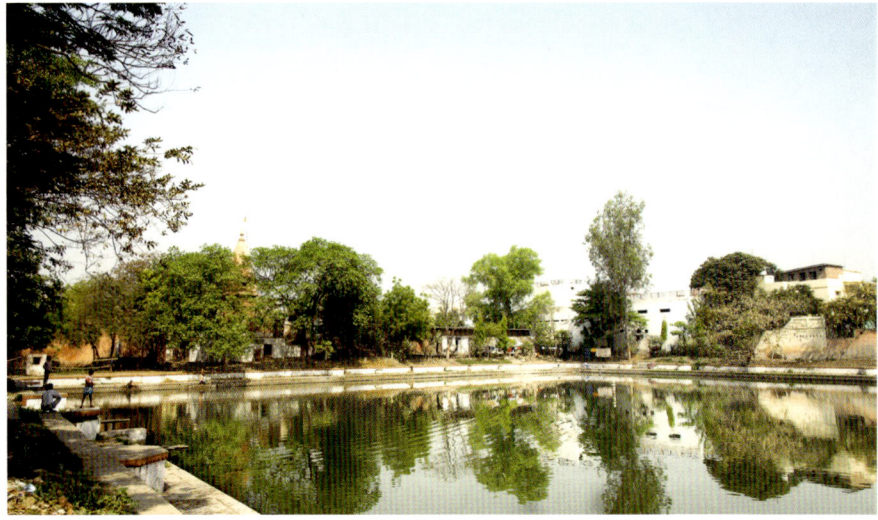

Kurukshetra Kund reservoir.

What to Know Rani Bhavani of Bengal, known for her administrative skills and charity, built the reservoir, Kurukshetra Kund, as a replica of a reservoir in northwestern Haryana that is described extensively in the Mahabharata. Unfortunately, the kund and its adjoining temple are uncared for today.

> **FOOD**
> Under the shade of the peepal tree, there is an excellent **diner** called Vinod (see map on pages 16-17) that serves fresh, hot, and tasty Indian meals.

(R) **ANAND BAGH**

An elegant memorial amidst a garden

→ *Directions from Kurukshetra Kund Panch Mandir to Anand Bagh: Outside the kund compound temple turn right down the road lane. Continue in the same direction past the busy crossing, called Padamshri Chauraha or Ravindrapuri Crossing. After a series of small houses, Anand Bagh is on the left, in a walled compound.*

What to Know This marble memorial to Bhaskarananda Saraswati, a 19th-century Hindu saint, was built in 1910 by one of his disciples. Swami Bhaskarananda wandered all over India for thirteen years before settling in Banaras. He was famous for his miracles of

healing. 'Anand Bagh' means 'garden of bliss'. The cool verandahs of Anand Bagh and its grassy manicured lawn gardens are a popular retreat for neighbourhood children, couples, and students.

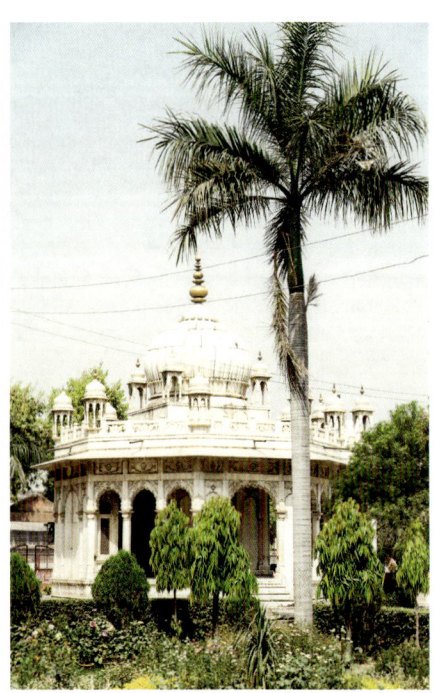

Anand Bagh Memorial.

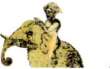

Ⓢ DURGA TEMPLE
She who rides the lion
→ *Directions from Anand Bagh to the Durga Temple: From Anand Bagh, the deep red spire of the Durga Temple is visible. Follow the railing of the water tank counter-clockwise until you reach the gated crimson entrance of the temple, busy with flower sellers and shoe keepers.*

What to Know A flight of stairs takes us to the porch and the inner chamber where Durga resides. She wears a silver mask and tinsel-edged red fabric that shops around the temple sell. Devotees offer a bright red scarf to the goddess along with a coconut.

What to Do *Durga Temple Music Festival* Every year during the season of *Bhadrapada* (August-September), the Durga Temple hosts a three-night classical music and dance festival in honour of the goddess, featuring artists from Banaras and all over India. The central pavilion serves as the stage. The artists perform facing Durga. The audience sits on the verandahs all around. Music enthusiasts and disciples surround the performers on the central pavilion as the music continues all night and into dawn, interrupted only by the chiming of bells as worshippers stream in to catch a glimpse of the goddess. The musical energy is intense and inspiring.

Durga Temple fair Durga is also the subject of honour during every season of *Shravana* (July-August). A large fair is held all along the Assi-Bhelupura road, with rides, snacks and hawkers selling attractive gimmicks from balloons to toy cars. Villagers pour into Banaras for the sacred sight (*darshan*) of not only 'Durga ji' but also Tulsidas and Hanuman in their respective temples further south down the road.

Ⓣ TULSIMANAS TEMPLE
Tulsidas' vision
→ *Directions from Durga Temple to Tulsimanas Temple: Outside the main entrance of the Durga Temple turn left. Walk down the busy Lanka-Bhelupura road, past a crossing and* narrow enclosed grassy plot on the left. Tulsimanas Temple, a white marble building behind tall gates, is on the left.

What to Know *Manas* means 'lake' or 'expanse' in Sanskrit. *Tulsimanas*, or 'the expanse of Tulsi', refers to the persona of the poet Tulsidas in his entirety. Tulsidas' poem is called *Ramcharitmanas*, which means 'the expanse of Ram's character'. His poem recreates Ram in his whole and exists for us to soak ourselves in his character. The Tulsimanas Temple was built by a Kolkata-based merchant in the 1960s.

What to See The modern temple stands like a fortress behind tall gates, surrounded by a spacious, landscaped garden. At the ground-level in three separate groups are the deities Annapurna and Shiva; Ram, Lakshman, Sita and Hanuman; and Lakshmi and Vishnu. There are also miniature electric dolls that depict episodes from the lives of Ram and Krishna. Upstairs, marble slabs on the wall are inscribed with the entire Ramcharitmanas. Within glass display cases, there are editions and translations of the Ramayana into Tamil, Bengali, and other regional Indian languages. The figure of Tulsidas, mechanized and cast in plastic, sits in one corner writing his poem, his head shaking from side to side as he utters 'Ram, Ram' endlessly.

Ramcharitmanas is prefaced by a forty-verse long poem in praise of Hanuman, called the "Hanuman Chalisa" (chalis means forty).

On one level the temple's use of technology is a modern novelty. Villagers hear about it and travel from afar to see it. But, as Nita Kumar notes, on another level, the electric dolls entertain in much the same way that courtesans did in temples in the past. The Tulsimanas Temple is modern, but also continuous with tradition.

Ⓤ SANKAT MOCHAN TEMPLE
Dedicated to the remover of worries
→ *Directions from Tulsimanas Temple to Sankat Mochan Temple: Outside Tulsimanas Temple, turn left and continue down the road, over a bridge. Take the first right after the bridge, where flower sellers sell bouquets. At the end of this lane is the Sankat Mochan*

MUSIC AND DANCE IN BANARAS TEMPLES

Multiple-night concerts take place not just at Sankat Mochan and the Durga Temple, but also at virtually all the major temples and Muslim tombs in the city. It has evolved from the old tradition of entertainment at religious places. In the past, courtesans would regularly perform and local musicians would hold informal gatherings. People had favourite courtesans and singers of *qawwali*, a form of Sufi singing, and of seasonal music, *kajli* in the monsoons and *chaiti* in the spring. Around the turn of the century, Moti Bai and Bari Maina were famous among the courtesans and Rafiq Anwar among the *qawwals*. In temples, this entertainment reflected the concept of *shringar*.

Shringar literally means 'decoration' and refers to heightening the aesthetic and the sensual senses and in taking pleasure in that process. *Shringar* may be done to and through the body, the arts, or the gods. The courtesans of the past and the music and dance festivals that continue into the present are part of the annual *shringar* of the gods.

There have always been reformers who protested about the immorality of mixing religion with the entertainment provided by courtesans. In the mid-19th century, their efforts began to crystallize. At the same time, upper-class patronage of courtesans began to decline. Together, these developments led to the banning of courtesans in 1958. The courtesan street of Dalmandi was vacated and most of its *kothis* or brothels closed. According to all evidence, many of the classical ragas and compositions are taken from 'folk' forms such as *kajli*, *thumri*, and *chaiti*. In the 19th and 20th centuries, a clear demarcation between 'folk' and 'classical' arose for a number of reasons, including among them was the decline of court patronage and the rise of government patronage and its politics. Elite and popular forms always existed, but the categorical division between 'elite' and 'popular' is a modern phenomenon.

In Banaras 'folk' forms of music such as *kajli* and *thumri* would be performed on the same stage as the classical *khayal*, the stage being open to high and low. Banaras remains unique as a 'pre-modern' city with an exceptionally unified culture because vestiges of that 'openness' remain intact. Concerts in Banaras still take place in temples, ghats, and other public spaces, the division between the artist and the audience is blurred, and everyone, regardless of class, enjoys the same music. Quite extraordinarily, classical music transcends class in Banaras.

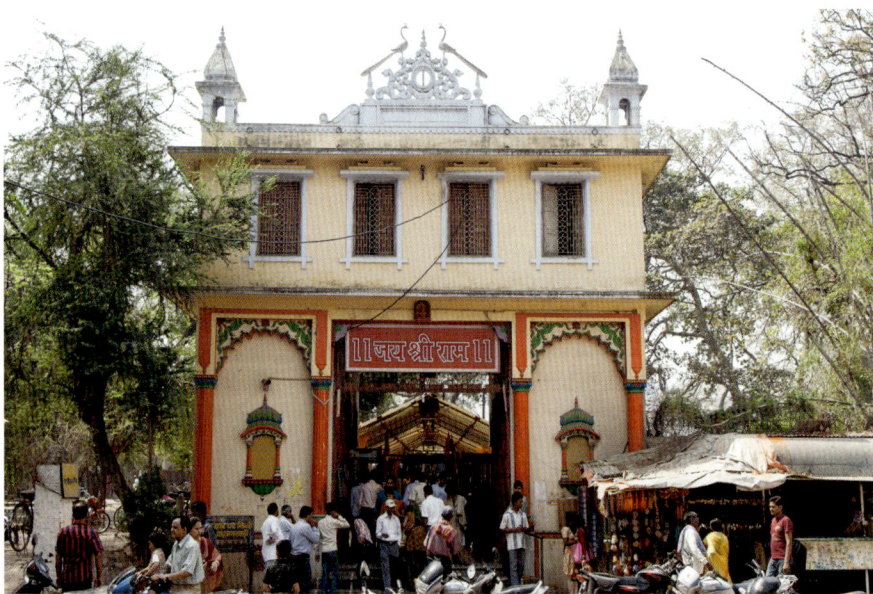

Entrance to Sankat Mochan Temple.

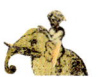

Temple, its entrance marked by flower and sweet shops, a parking lot, a row of lockers, tourist shops, and the large temple gateway with metal detectors.

What to Know Hanuman is Ram's benevolent monkey-helper, servant and friend. In the Ramayana, he and his army of monkeys helped Ram rescue his wife Sita when the demon king Ravan kidnapped her.

Legend has it that in the late 16th century, the poet Tulsidas, who was a devotee of Ram, established a Shiva *linga* under a great peepal tree. This spot became the location for the Sankat Mochan Temple, dedicated to Hanuman as the 'remover of worries'. In the past few decades the popularity of this temple has increased phenomenally.

What to See The temple has a lovely meditative atmosphere. A wooded area skirts its southern border, home to dozens of monkeys. The ancient tree that was visited by Tulsidas shades the temple's paved court. The image of Hanuman, housed within the main sanctum, is friendly and coated thickly with vermillion. The priest sits before him, accepting the flowers and sweets people bring to offer 'Hanuman ji'. On the wall hang images of the previous head priests and of gods and goddesses. Devotees stand at the railing to have the sacred sight (*darshan*) of Hanuman ji. Or they sit by the well that faces the image, believed to contain sacred Ganga water. Many recite the *Hanuman Chalisa*, the 40 verses in praise of Hanuman written by Tulsidas. As they wander around the marble verandahs, they pause to pay their respects to the smaller images in the niches, peer through windows into the main sanctum, or daub vermillion on their foreheads.

What to Do *Sankat Mochan Music Festival* Every year during the waxing moon fortnight of Chaitra (March-April), the Sankat Mochan music festival is held, with local and national artistes performing at this festival. The highest verandah serves as the stage. The audience sits in the inner courtyard and on rooftops. From dusk to dawn, the classical music and dance continues. Those who wish to take a nap or recline are free to do so. People sprawl against the pillars or stretch out in the outer courtyard under the tree. Avid listeners sit at the foot of the stage, keeping time with the music, shaking their heads in meditative appreciation, and calling out 'Vah! Vah!' The artists respond, laughing with each other and the audience, pausing to provide poetic explanations, and performing whatever is demanded of them.

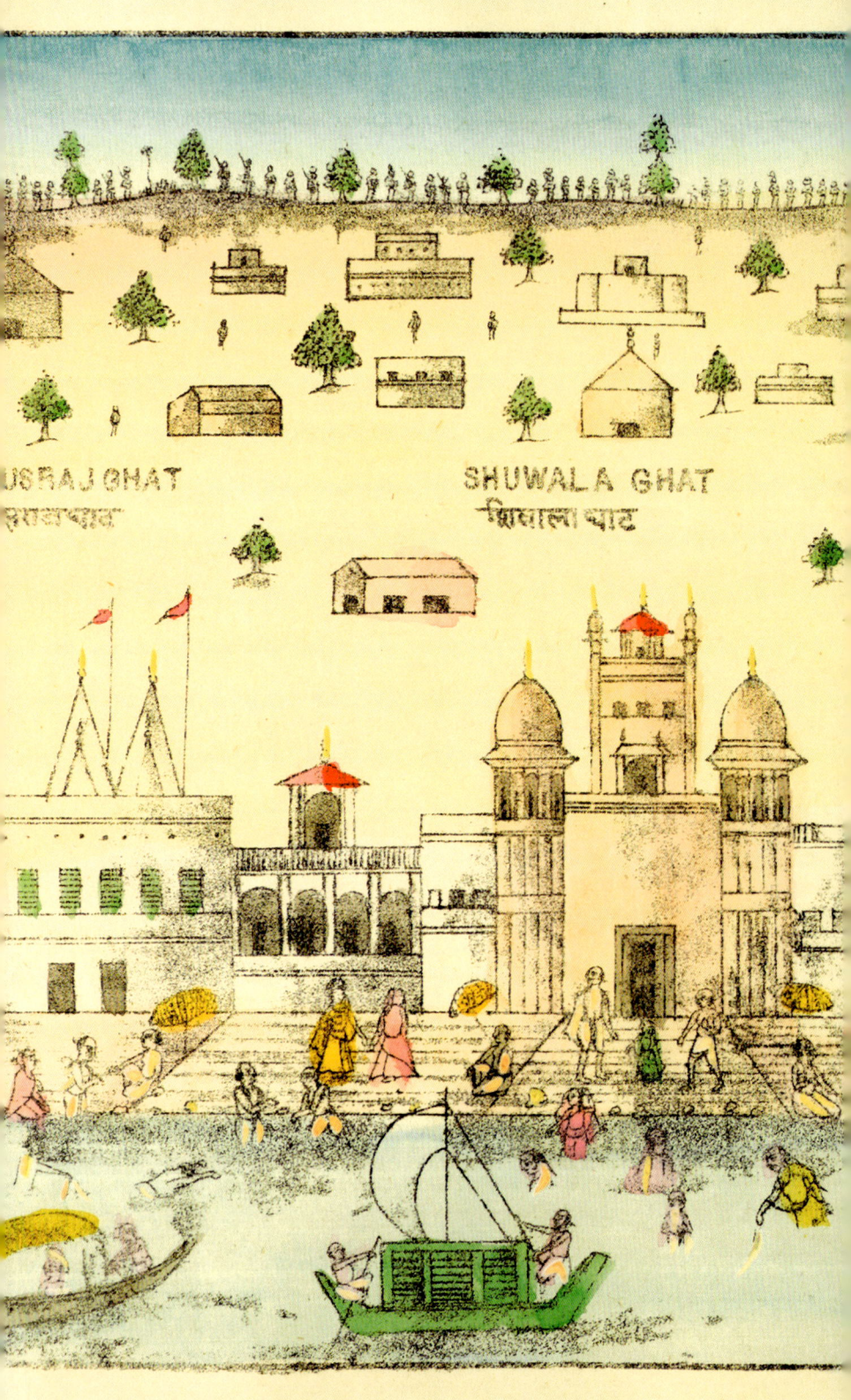

USRAJ GHAT

शराजघाट

SHUWALA GHAT

शिवाला घाट

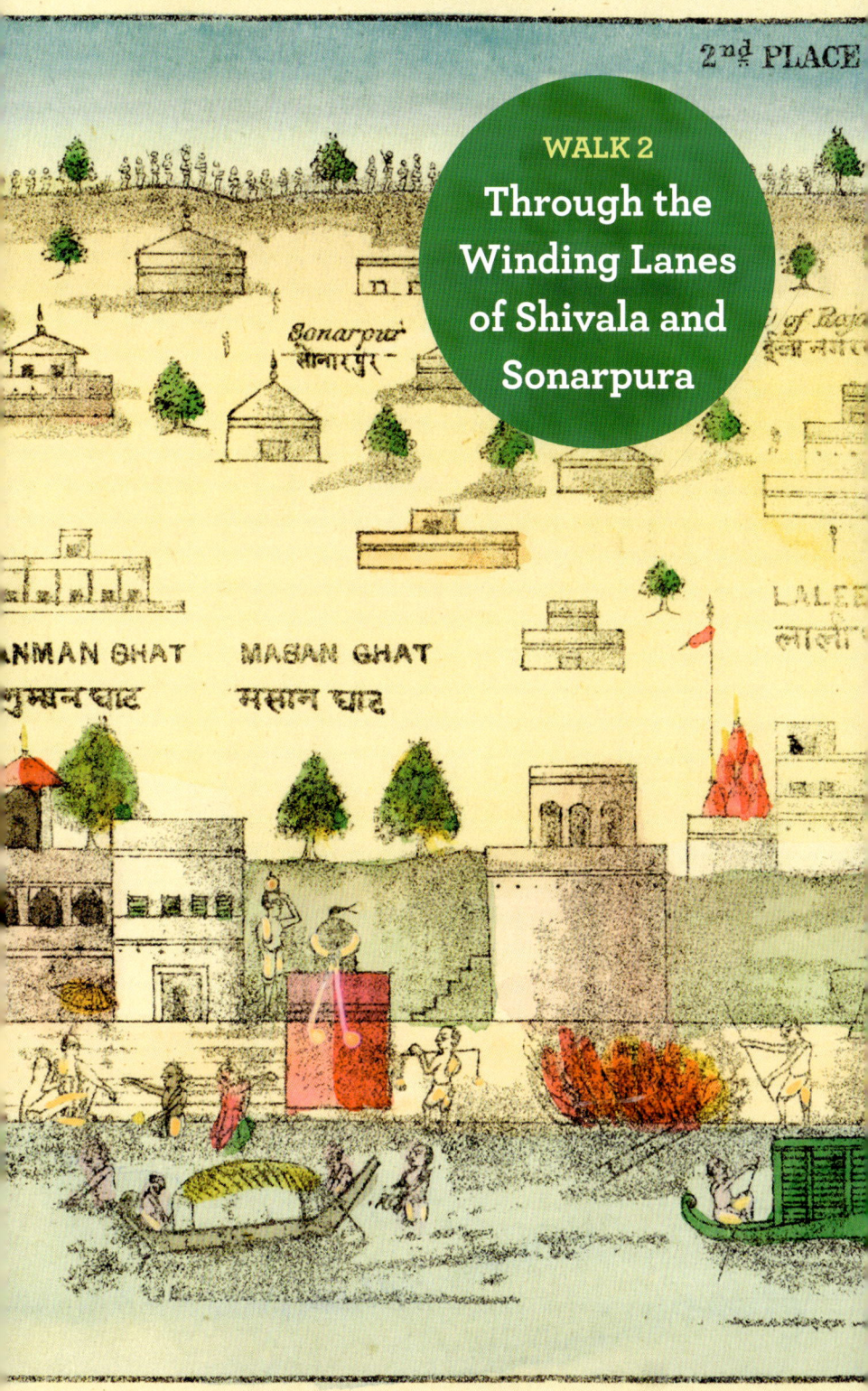

WALK 2

Through the Winding Lanes of Shivala and Sonarpura

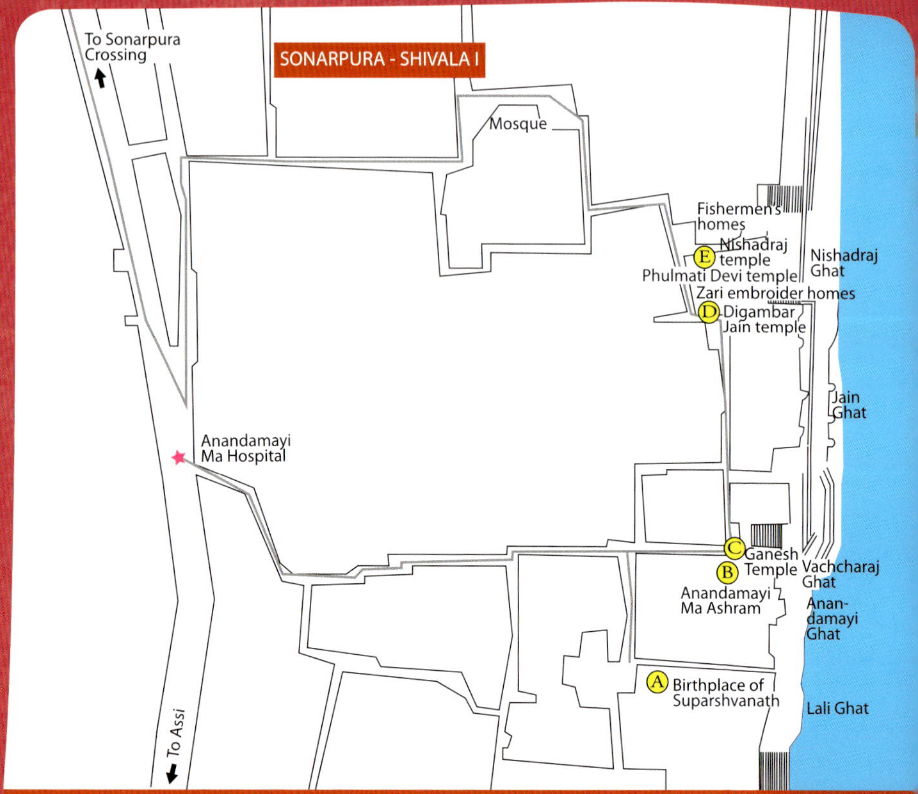

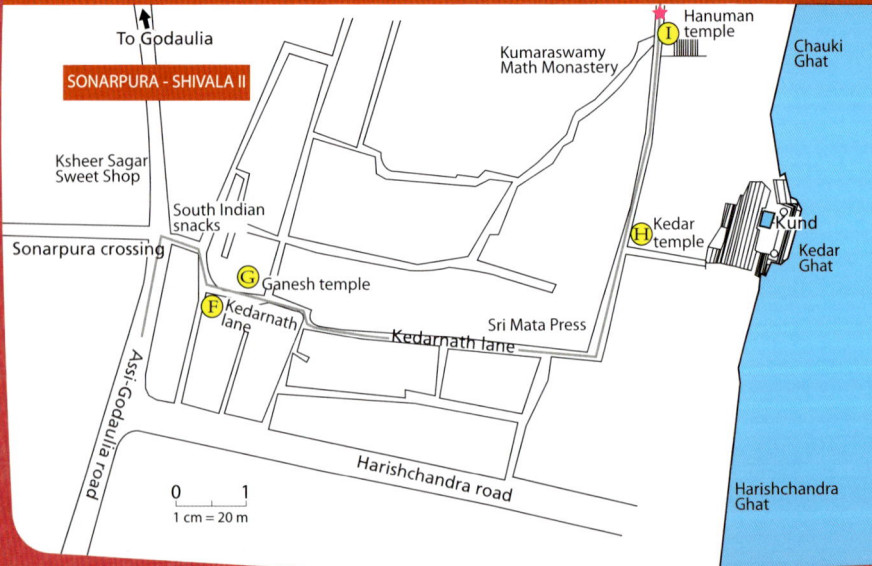

SONARPURA - SHIVALA I

To Sonarpura Crossing

Mosque

Fishermen's homes

E Nishadraj temple

Nishadraj Ghat

Phulmati Devi temple

Zari embroider homes

D Digambar Jain temple

Jain Ghat

Anandamayi Ma Hospital

C Ganesh Temple

B

Vachcharaj Ghat

Anandamayi Ma Ashram

Anandamayi Ghat

A Birthplace of Suparshvanath

Lali Ghat

To Assi

★ Follow the walk trail from Anandamayi Ma Hospital to Hanuman Temple

To Godaulia

Hanuman temple

I

Chauki Ghat

SONARPURA - SHIVALA II

Kumaraswamy Math Monastery

Ksheer Sagar Sweet Shop

South Indian snacks

Kund

H Kedar temple

Kedar Ghat

Sonarpura crossing

G Ganesh temple

F Kedarnath lane

Sri Mata Press

Kedarnath lane

Assi-Godaulia road

Harishchandra road

Harishchandra Ghat

0   1
1 cm = 20 m

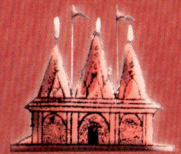

Walk through riverside lanes, stopping at the ashram and memorial of prominent 19th-century saints, temples, embroiderers' workshops, mosques, a Sanskrit school, sweet shops and south Indian cafés.

THINGS TO SEE

- Hermitage of the popular female saint, Anandamayi
- Birthplace and temple of the seventh Jain 'fordmaker' Suparshvanath
- Temples dedicated to goddess Phulmati Devi, chief of fisherfolk Nishadraj, Ganesh, and Hanuman

ALLOW

Two to three hours

WALK ITINERARY

Birthplace of Suparshvanath I Anandamayi Ma Ashram I Ganesh Temple I The Digambar Jain Temple I Nishadraj Temple I The Kedarnath lane I Ganesh Temple I Kedarnath Temple I Hanuman Temple

GETTING AROUND SHIVALA AND SONARPURA

Shivala and Sonarpura form the eastern stretch along the river, entered through one of the lanes on the Assi–Godaulia road. Assi forms the southern limit and Madanpura the northern. This walk can be divided into two separate walks, Anandamayi Ashram to the Phulmati Devi Temple and Kedarnath lane to the Hanuman Temple.

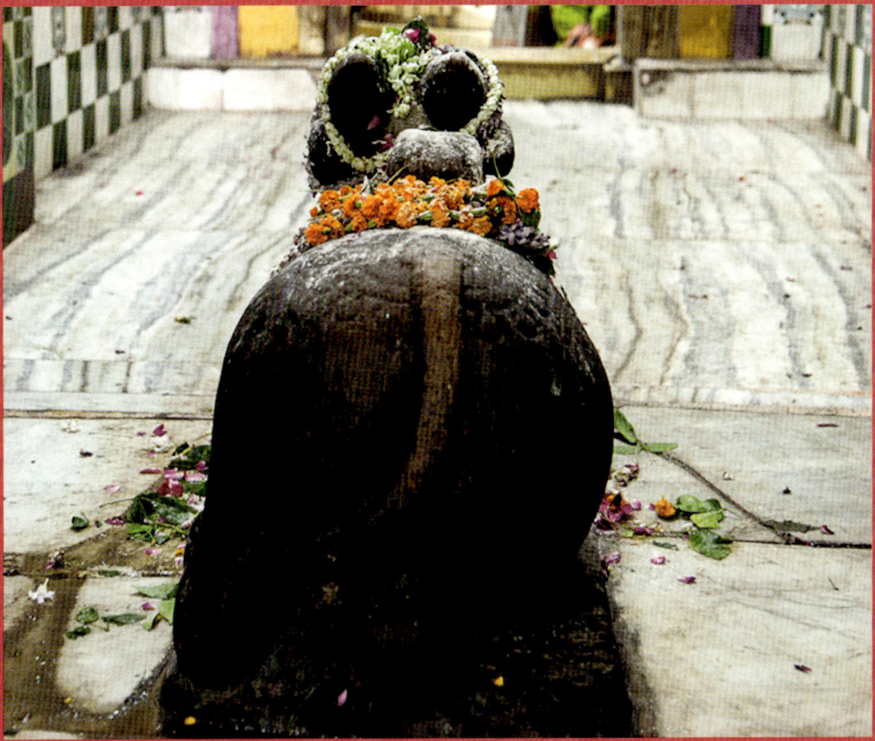

Shiva's bull Nandi guards the inner sanctum at the Kedar Temple.

THE HISTORY OF SHIVALA AND SONARPURA

If you travel north on the Assi-Godaulia road, you will come to a slight climb around the neighbourhoods of Shivala and Sonarpura. This is the hill designated in Hindu history and mythology as Kedar, purportedly the section of Banaras that is situated on the third prong of Shiva's trident. Inside the lanes is the colourful Kedareshvar temple, which anchors this southernmost sacred zone.

As pilgrims, traders and members of the gentry were attracted to the spiritual, aesthetic and commercial vibrancy of Banaras, the city acquired an unusual cosmopolitan character. The different *mohallas* or city quarters came to be populated by distinct ethnic groups, although no *mohalla* was limited to any particular community. In the Chauk area, one was sure to find Marwaris and Gujaratis, who formed the backbone of trade and commerce and continue to do so today. Shivala and Sonarpura became centres of Bengali and south Indian culture. Their lanes were filled with temples, hermitages and rest houses of south Indian sects and pilgrims. As you walk through the lanes, notice a medley of south Indian languages and scripts. Women wearing flowers in their hair and saris in the south Indian style carry brass pots of Ganga water to their favourite local shrines.

Any Banarasi will tell you that most residents belong to the Yadav caste. Yadavs are traditionally milkmen who run *goushalas* ('homes for cows'). They have shops of milk, cream, yoghurt, lassi, and other milk products, and supply milk to households all over the city. The typical Yadav milkman will begin work before dawn and end late at night, spending the day bicycling from house to house, with his shiny metal milk pails weighing several litres, each carefully balanced on his bicycle handlebars. Many of the houses and shops that you will pass on this walk belong to the Yadav milkmen. And one reason for the abundance of cow dung in the lanes of Shivala and Sonarpura is the multitude of cows and *goushalas*.

The Shivala neighbourhood is a wonderful example of how in Banaras, Hindus and Muslims live side by side, often participating in the same activities and businesses. The city's unique history as a centre for trade, pilgrimage, and the arts resulted in the necessary interdependence of religions, classes, castes, and communities in a conscious practice of secularism.

Ⓐ BIRTHPLACE (JANM STHAL) OF SUPARSHVANATH
The seventh Tirthankara

→ *Directions from Anandamayi Ashram Hospital to the Suparshvanath Janm Sthal: The Anandamayi Ashram Hospital lane twists and turns to the river. Take the third right. Follow this lane until you come to the first lane leading towards the river, which ends at a steep and narrow flight of stairs and Lali Ghat. At the top of these stairs to the right is the birthplace of Suparshvanath and a Jain temple.*

The History of Suparshvanath

Around 1000 B.C.E., the luxuriant forests of Kashi fostered ashrams and schools in which new philosophies such as Jainism, Buddhism and Tantra took root and matured. The Jains came to have a long line of spiritual leaders called *tirthankaras*, the 'ford-makers', or *jinas*, the 'victorious ones'. Suparshvanath was the seventh in this legendary line. He was a prince who renounced his princely life in pursuit of nirvana. The first *jina* to be dated was the 23rd *jina*, Parshvanath. He lived in the 8th century B.C. and was succeeded by the famous *jina* Mahavira in the 6th century B.C., who visited and taught in Banaras as a young contemporary of Lord Buddha.

The Suparshvanath Janm Sthal

A small riverside mansion once stood where the Jain temple stands today. Suparshvanath was born in this mansion. He was conceived a little further away, a spot included on this walk and now occupied by another, larger Jain temple.

A terrace with stone railings overlooking the river leads into the marble-floored, stained-glass Jain temple. Inside the temple, Suparshvanath, cast in silver, sits on a pedestal in a meditative, cross-legged pose.

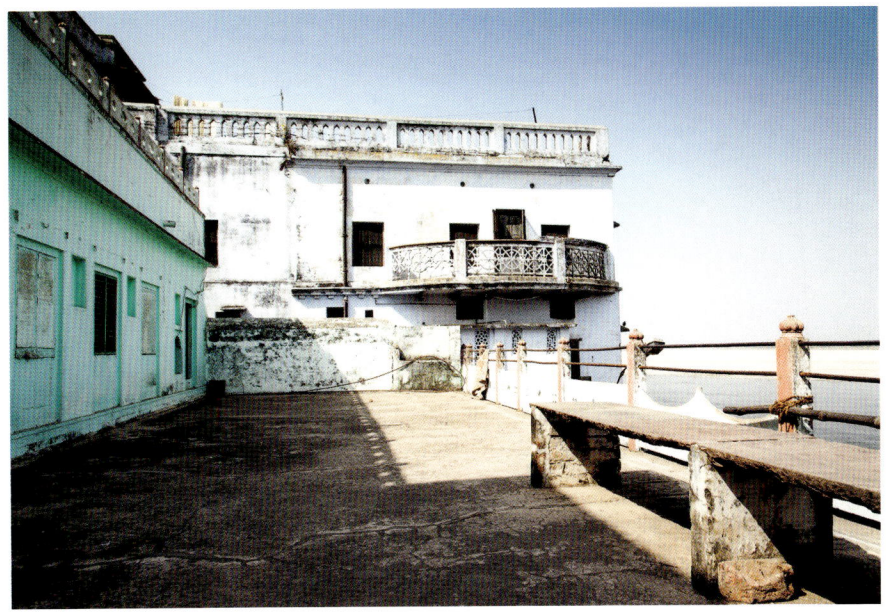

Birthplace of Suparshvanath, the seventh Jain spiritual leader, with Anandamayi Ma Ashram in the background.

In the 14th century, a Jain scholar named Jina Prabha Suri travelled through India, writing about the major Jain tirthas. In his book *Vividha Tirtha Kalpa* he writes about a temple of Parshvanath in Varanasi and praises the city as the shining birthplace of two *jinas*.

ⒷANANDAMAYI MA ASHRAM
A spiritual guru and mystic
→ *Directions from the Suparsh-vanath janmsthal to Anandamayi Ma Ashram: Follow the lane outside the temple to the left. Then turn right until you reach the main Anandamayi Ashram lane. Turn right again. The ashram doorway, with a plaque above it, is to the right just before the lane ends and turns left.*

Anandamayi Ma
Sri Anandamayi Ma (1896-1982), born Nirmala Sundari to parents in present-day Bangladesh, was a spiritual guru and mystic, viewed as neither 'woman' nor 'saint' but as a manifestation of god. During her life, she attracted thousands of followers, including prominent personalities such as the prime minister of India, Indira Gandhi, the physician, Triguna Sen, and the French filmmaker, Arnaud Desjardins.

'Anandamayi' means 'bliss permeated'. The name, given by one of her disciples, refers to her perpetual state of happiness. As a child, she often went into deep trances or spells of ecstasy. She spent much of her life in silence, meditating, or performing complicated yoga positions. She is believed to have possessed an ability to heal through her sheer presence. People suffering from all kinds of physical and mental discomforts reportedly recovered the instant they were exposed to her aura of calm.

> Today, Banaras continues to be a stronghold of Jainism and is recognized as one of Jainism's sacred tirthas.

The Ashram
Mata Anandamayi's first ashram was built in 1929. The ashram located in Banaras, called Mata Anandamayi Kanyapeeth, is a free home and school for girls of any ability and background. The girls live with female teachers, study, do chores and pray. After finishing school, some return to a worldly

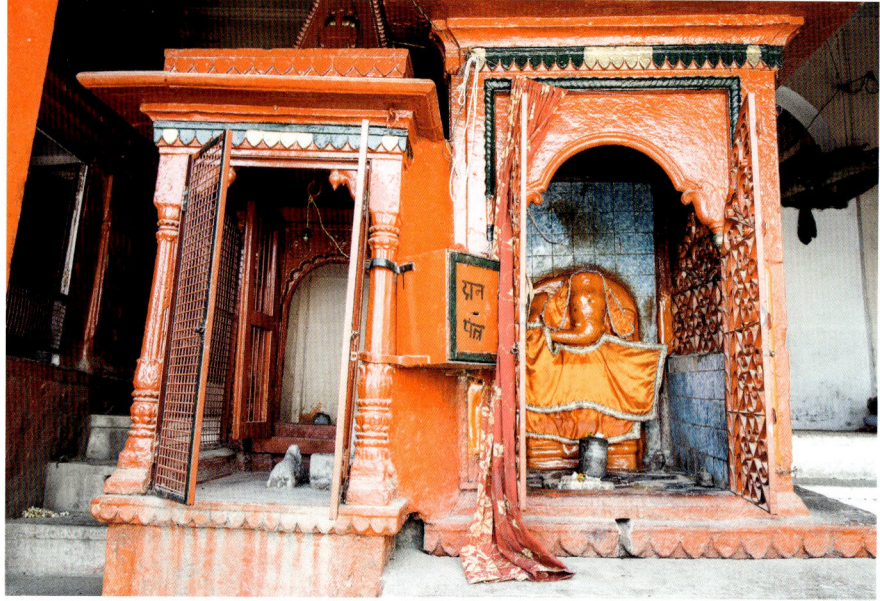

Shrines in the Ganesh Temple.

life, while others continue in the same or another ashram.

The buildings inside the Mata Anandamayi Kanyapeeth comprise mostly classrooms and dormitories that are off-limits to visitors. There is also an office, a library, a bookstore, a balcony overlooking the river, and a temple dedicated to Anandamayi, which visitors can visit. Every evening, the temple hosts bhajan sessions.

Ⓒ GANESH TEMPLE
The lord of obstacles

→ *Directions from Anandamayi Ma Ashram to the Ganesh Temple: Exit outside the ashram and continue straight along the river. Staircases, shrines and temples line this high lane. The first set of small temples to the right is the Ganesh Temple complex.*

What to Know The shrines contain Shiva and Ganesh images. Ganesh is the lord of obstacles and a figure of auspiciousness. He sits at thresholds, at the gates of neighbourhoods and over the doorways of houses. He is worshipped at rituals pertaining to birth and death and at the start of new ventures. Stout, round-bellied and elephant-headed, Ganesha in his present form evolved from the gana group of ancient deities. These ganas, along with their fellow rakshasas, yakshas and devis, were incorporated into Shiva's entourage as his helpers, guards and consorts. Ganesha became known as the son of Shiva and Parvati.

The stone steps leading to the river below the Ganesh shrines is called Vachcharaj Ghat, after a Jain merchant who was pivotal in shaping Banaras as a centre for trade in the 19th century.

What to See In the shrine facing the river, the large saffron Ganesh sits behind the Shiva *linga*. In Banaras, Shiva is the focus even in the temples of other gods and goddesses, and one can be sure to find a *linga* in almost any shrine or temple.

Under the tamarind tree

You may catch sight of the old priest Jeevat Lal washing the Shiva and Ganesh images with water from the Ganga or adorning them with fresh flowers. He is a *kevat* or fisherman by caste and drives a rickshaw for a living. He will tell you how many years ago this spot along the riverfront used to be called 'Imiliya Tale' ('Under the tamarind tree'). There were no buildings here, only a large and ancient *Imli*

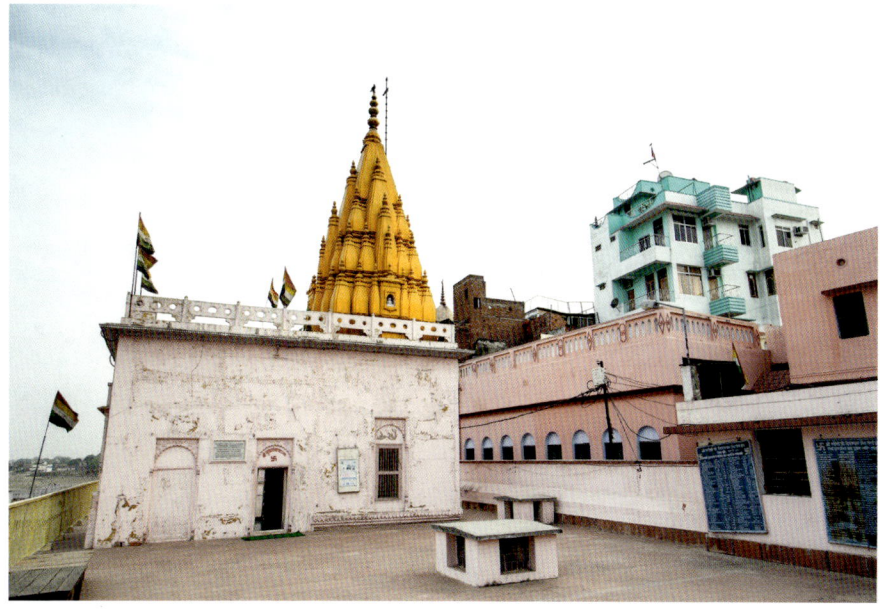

Digambar Jain Temple.

tree. After the tree fell, the ghat was built and *lingas* enclosed.

Ⓓ THE DIGAMBAR JAIN TEMPLE
Dedicated to the seventh Jina
→ *Directions from the Ganesh Temple to the Digambar Jain Temple: Turn right down the lane outside the Ganesh Temple. The white marble doorway of the Jain Temple blocks the end of the lane where it turns left. Go up the stairs to the temple on the roof.*

What to See The large marble building houses a Jain temple on the roof and a Sanskrit school downstairs. The temple contains an image of the seventh *jina* or Jain leader, Suparshvanath. A staircase on the far side of the roof leads underground to the *garbh bhumi* or place where Suparshvanath was conceived. His mother, Padmavati, has been deified here.

Ⓔ NISHADRAJ TEMPLE
Chief of the fishing folk
→ *Directions from the Digambar Jain Temple to Nishadraj Temple and Ghat:*

Outside the Jain Temple, turn right and right again immediately, where the lane is very narrow and lined with doorways. These are the homes of traditional zari embroiderers, the rooms distinguishable by large wooden embroidery frames. The lane opens into a small square with homes, two temples, and a stairway down to Nishadraj Ghat and the river.

In the past, real gold, silver and glass decorated robes and saris for the wealthy. Today, plastic has become the prominent material that is used.

History of zari embroidery
Zari is the gold and silver thread woven into Banarasi saris or used for elaborate embroidery. The Shivala neighbourhood has many workshops and homes of zari embroiderers. Glittering spangles and beads are sewn with silver and gold thread into floral, animal and geometric patterns. A long needle hooked at the end manipulates the thread. Like all the artisans of Banaras, zardoz embroiderers have flexible work hours and days. They mostly have their workshops in their homes and begin learning the craft at a young age. Many are women.

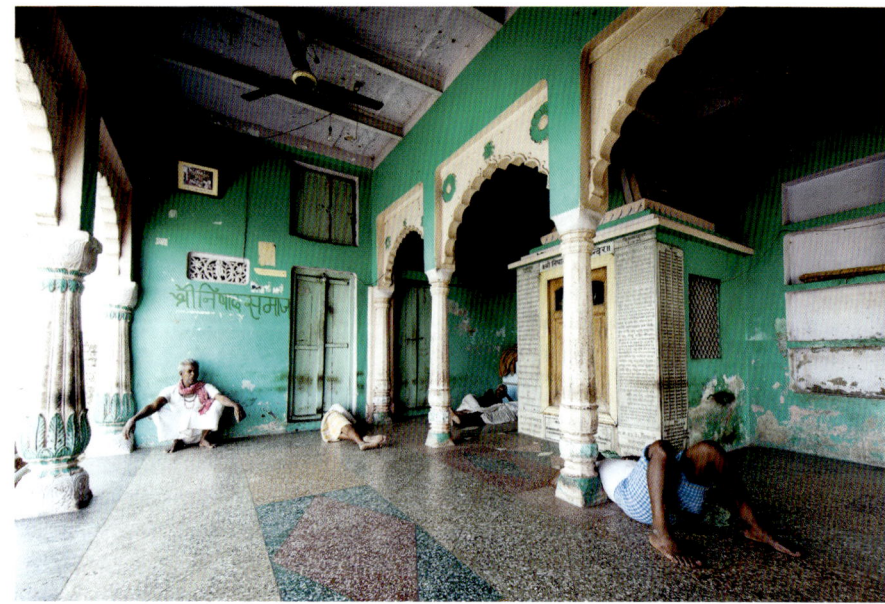

Men taking a nap in the cool environment of the Nishadraj Temple.

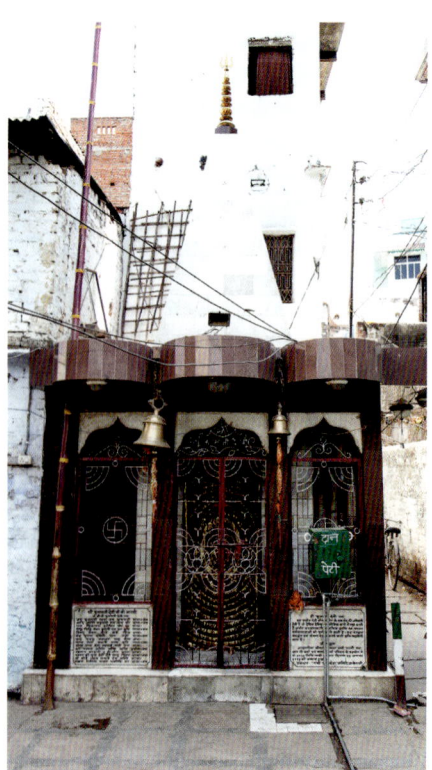

Temple of Phulmati Devi.

History of the Nishad fisher community and Nishadraj

Several thousand fishermen and boatmen live all along the river. They call themselves *Nishad, Kevat* or *Mallah*.

The Nishad caste is traditionally a 'low' or 'backward' caste. About a hundred years ago, there were movements all over India directed at social reform, dealing with issues such as women's conditions, illiteracy and early marriage age. These movements started because of the pressures of colonialism. The colonial government considered certain castes and social practices as backward. The reform movements were caste-based, as each caste tried to 'reform' its practices. The reform efforts included adopting a new 'respectable' name, starting an official organization, holding meetings, publishing a journal and adopting a community ancestor or deity to worship along with rituals and festivals.

The Nishadraj Temple is a product of this effort. Several generations ago, the Nishads of Banaras deified an ancestor, Nishadraj. Nishadraj features in the epic Ramayana as chief of the Nishad fisher-folk, who lived on

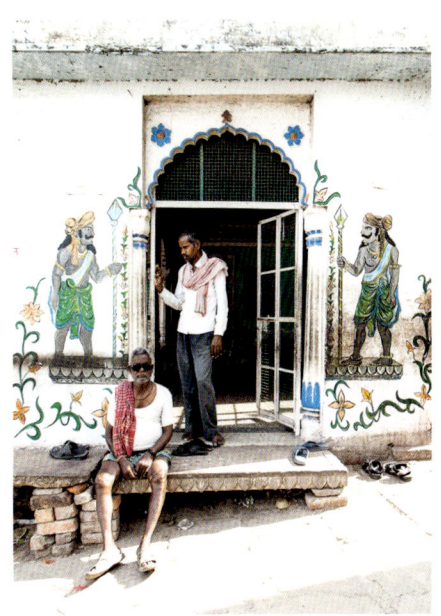

Fishermen outside Nishadraj Temple, Kedarnath lane.

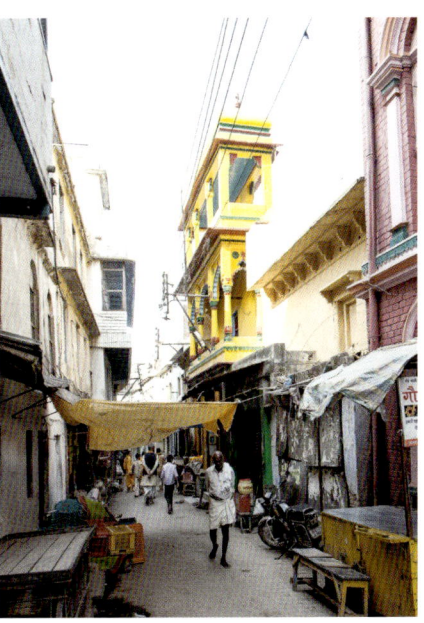

Saint Karpatri's monastery.

the banks of the mythical river, Sarayu. When Ram was exiled to the forest, Nishadraj and his people welcomed him, his wife Sita and brother Lakshman. When it was time for them to move on, the fisher-folk gifted them a boat they had built for them to cross the Sarayu. Nishadraj Temple is also an example of how in Hinduism all sorts of unusual heroes are celebrated and at times even worshipped as honorary gods.

As you walk near the temple, you may notice that children and youth loiter outside their homes or by the river, neither at school nor at work. They will very likely be staring at you since you are an outsider and they have time on their hands. One result of social reform movements was that energies were channelled into ritualized religious activities rather than those that would improve the immediate environment of young people.

EATING IN SONARPURA

All around Sonarpura crossing are **tea shops** and stalls that feature **sweet** and **savoury** snacks. These include the **south Indian idli**, **dosa** and **vada**, made of fermented rice and lentils, and **rolls** of flattened, lightly fried dough wrapped with sautéed and spiced vegetables or meat, a Bengali favourite.

Also at the crossing stands one of the oldest and biggest sweet shops, ***Ksheer Sagar*** ('the ocean of *ksheer*'; see map on page 36). As are all the city's good sweet shops, it is owned by a hereditary milkman who seems to have sweet-making in his very genes. Its specialty is the *rasgulla*, for which it became quickly popular in the year of its establishment – 1965. The shop offers a wide array of sweets apart from *rasgulla*, all delectable, intricately designed and spectacularly presented, many of which are original recipes. The owner, Anup Kumar Yadav, creates and designs many of the sweets himself. The shop uses only natural dyes for food colouring and has done away with the traditional silver foil (*varq*) covering for sweets.

The eateries at Sonarpura crossing become politically active after dusk. They have been the favourite hang-outs of Banarasi journalists for years.

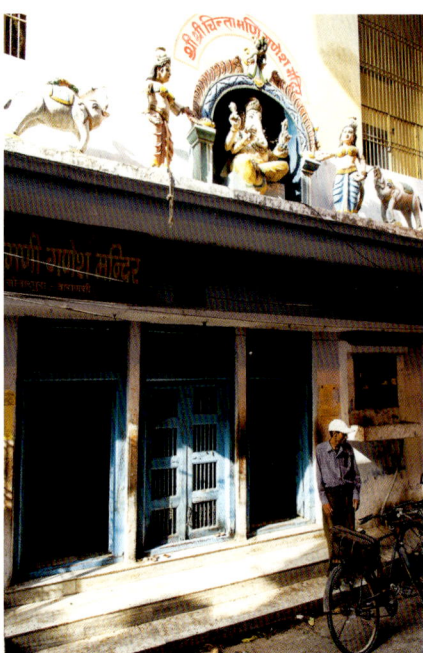

Ganesh Temple.

This continues to the present day, so young people often lack the education and inspiration to work for the economic and social betterment of their lives.

Inside the temple

One side of Nishadraj Temple is open to the river, making it a favourite spot with neighbourhood afternoon nappers. Facing the river is a bright image of Nishadraj.

The temple of Phulmati Devi

Close to Nishadraj Temple is the small temple of Phulmati Devi, a local goddess. Phulmati is an example of the democratic process common in Hinduism through which a prominent or respected personage gets deified locally. An individual or group donates an image and sets it under a tree. Then another worshipper adds a pedestal or a shade. Gradually devotees create an entire shrine or small temple. One can see that the Phulmati Devi temple has been built in stages, the image being established first, followed by the addition of the walls and roof.

Ⓕ THE KEDARNATH LANE
High and elegant columns

→ *Directions from Phulmati Devi Temple to Kedarnath lane: Outside the Phulmati Devi temple, turn right down the lane, continuing in the same direction as before. Follow the lane left, right and left again into a small square with a mosque and homes. At the square, turn left, right and left again until you reach the main Assi-Godaulia road. Turn right on the main road and continue until you come to a busy road on your right and a little beyond, a busy road to your left. This 'broken' crossing marks the beginning of the neighbourhood of Sonarpura. Turn down the lane to your right marked by a colourful sculpted gateway, opposite the busy road to your left.*

What to See As you walk through the lane, look out for Bengali *havelis* or mansions. Many will be red-buffed and high-ceilinged, with tall doors and windows, arches and elegant columns. Each will have an old plaque beside its door with the name of the owner and the house etched in flowery Bengali, sometimes also in English. These Bengali-Banarasis were initially in local-level government jobs, but have evolved to take on various kinds of jobs today.

Typical Bengali titles are Mukherjee, Chatterjee, Chakravarty, Bhattacharya, Bose, Ghosh, Biswas and Roy. Houses are given poetic, affectionate names such as *Anand Kutir* ('cottage of bliss'), *Vrindavan* after the pastures where young Krishna herded his cows and flirted with maidens, and *Saraswati Nivas* ('house of Saraswati' the goddess of learning and the arts). Each home typically has an image of Ganesha painted above the doorway. Designs vary vastly and are quite fascinating to study.

Ⓖ GANESH TEMPLE
The enlightened one

What to Know To your left you will pass a temple of Chintamani Vinayak, the 'enlightened Ganesh'. In Banaras, Ganesh has multiple forms called '*Vinayaks,*' a name that appears in the Puranas and Buddhist Tantras. These 56 Vinayaks are organized in Banaras at the eight directional points in seven concentric circles representing the seven layers of the cosmos, linked by pilgrimage routes.

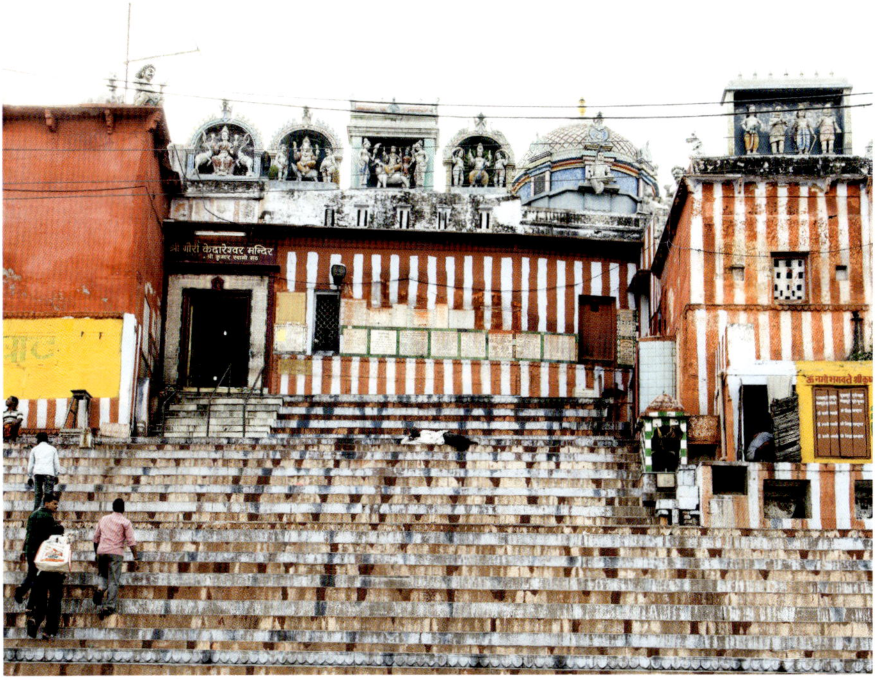

Kedar Temple, in red and white stripes in south Indian style, seen from the river.

Ⓗ KEDAR TEMPLE
Dedicated to Lord Shiva

→ *Directions from Ganesh Temple to Kedar Temple: Outside the Ganesh Temple turn left, continuing in the same direction as before. Follow the lane as it turns left. At the corner where it turns, the building to your left houses a firm called Shri Mata Press that publishes books on spirituality. (All the workers here are monks of the Shri Mata sect, which is a sect that worships Devi or the goddess.) Turn left with the lane. Here, several brightly painted monasteries, most notable that of the popular saint Karpatri, line the lane. The entrance to the famous Kedar Temple is a simple marble doorway on the right.*
What to Know The Shiva *linga* of the Kedar Temple in Kashi is one of the 14 most important as designated by the ancient text, *Kashi Khanda*. It is also a *jyotir linga*, one of the 12 manifestations of Shiva's fiery *linga* of light that pierced the heavens, the earth,

and the netherworld, establishing him as the Great Lord. The *linga* within the temple is not the usual shaft, sculpted out of stone. It is a shapeless rock with a white line running through its centre, because it is a *swayambhu* or 'self-manifested' *linga*.

The original temple of Kedar in India is called Kedarnath and is located high in the Himalayas on the banks of the Ganga. It is one of India's most important tirthas, or sacred spots. There are many stories in the Puranic texts that explain how Shiva, having first established his *linga* in the Himalayas, then did so in Kashi.

The importance of the Kedar Temple in Banaras is undisputed. In the *Kashi Khanda*, a separate chapter is dedicated to its praise. Priests and worshippers claim that the Kedar Temple is older than even Vishwanath, the city's most famous temple, having survived Aurangzeb's destruction that Vishwanath did not. There is some evidence for its antiquity – according

> The Kedar Temple has an entire Sanskrit work called *Kashi Kedar Mahatmya* devoted to its greatness.

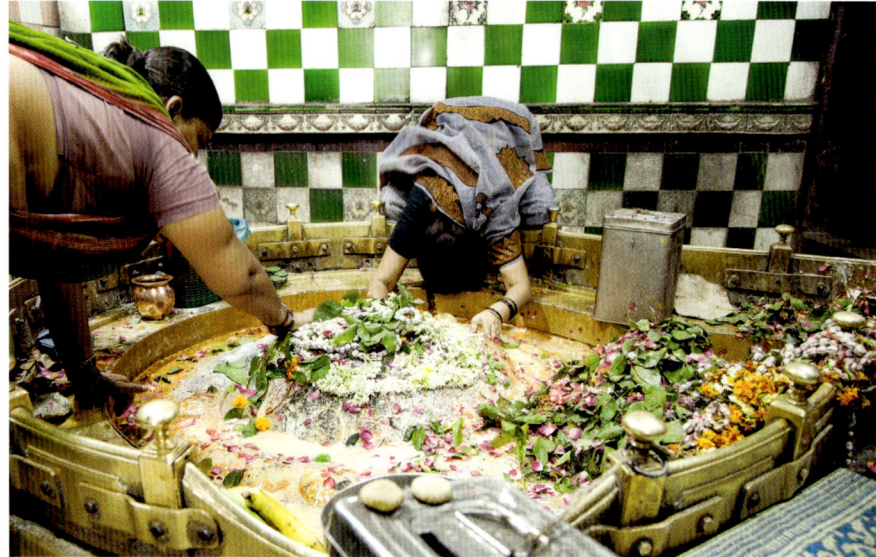

Worshippers at the Kedarnath linga.

to Diana Eck it is mentioned quite early in the Puranas while Vishwanath Temple is mentioned much later.

What to See The temple, dark and damp inside, is lined with marble and filled with images. Each marble slab is carefully etched with the full details of its donor. Shiva's bull Nandi guards the inner sanctum, which houses the famous *linga*. There is also an image of the famous temple of Badrinath in the Himalayas, one of the four *dhamas* or sacred abodes of the gods that are found in the north, south, east, and west of India.

The temple has a red and white striped exterior in south Indian style if viewed from the riverside. A flight of stairs sweeps down from the temple to the ghat, past a shrine of Tarakeshvara, 'lord of the crossing'. On the ghat we find a small water reservoir called Gauri Kund, which is named after an important site near Kedarnath in the Himalayas.

ⓘ HANUMAN TEMPLE
Scriptures and serpent deities
→ *Directions from Kedarnath Temple to the Hanuman Temple and Chauki Ghat: Outside the Kedarnath Temple, turn right and continue until you come to a wide flight of stairs on your right that leads down to the river and Chauki Ghat. The Hanuman Temple is above the flight of stairs, adjoining a small sweet shop.*

A NEIGHBOURHOOD TALE

A single Yadav family owns many of the small businesses in the lane outside the temple, including two sweet shops and a travel agency. Ganguram Yadav, the eldest of the seven brothers, narrates this story about the neighbourhood: A long time ago, there was nothing here, except the peepal tree, the images in its shade, a few large mansions, and open fields. Rani Bhavani of Bengal owned all of the 365 buildings in the area. There was a south Indian saint named Kumaraswamy. He was the only Brahmin in the area who accepted donations from Rani Bhavani. In fact, she gave away one piece of property for each day of the year, until she had nothing left. Because he had accepted donations, Kumaraswamy became ugly. Today, his monastery is a busy place. This is because pilgrims from all over India, including from south India, come to Banaras. Many of them love it so much, they settle down here.

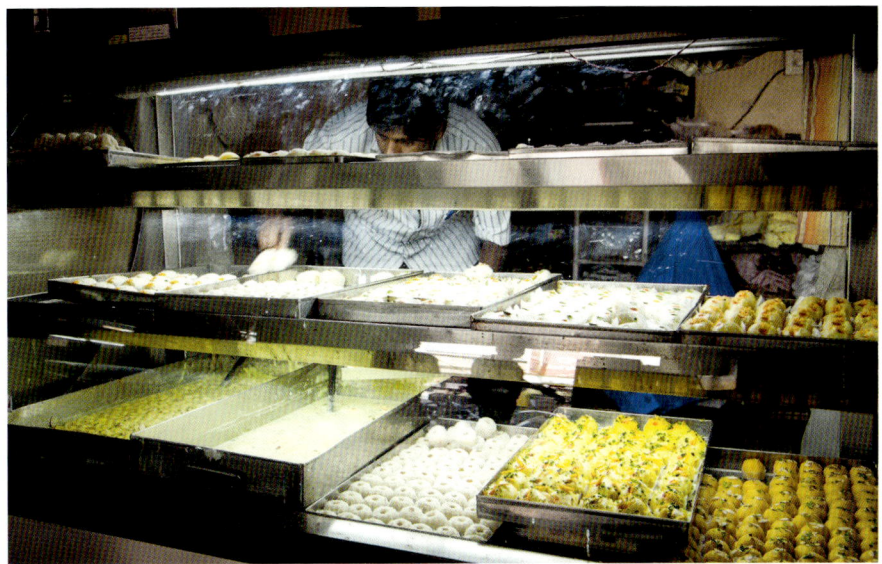

Milk sweets outside the Hanuman Temple.

What to Know The Hanuman Temple at Chauki Ghat has been built around an old peepal tree that shelters a varied collection of Hanuman, Shiva and Naga images under its shade. The serpent deity, Naga, was worshipped along with ganas and yakshas in ancient north India. Ganas and yakshas were local deites associated mostly with ponds and trees that in the 3rd century A.D. began to evolve into the incarnations, entourages and consorts of Shiva and Vishnu.

What to See The small Hanuman Temple, enclosed by a low wall and a gate, is captivating because every inch of it is etched with the names of its donors and with lines from sacred texts. There is also a four-foot high marble statue of Tulsidas, the medieval poet-saint who translated the Ramayana into the vernacular, a version called Ramcharitmanas. The Hanuman Temple is a serene spot, perfect for an undisturbed afternoon of relaxation. Men, young and old, play chess outside.

Exiting Shivala and Sonarpura

Directions from the Hanuman Temple to the Assi–Godaulia road: From the Hanuman Temple, go to the main Assi–Godaulia road via the lane leading away from the river, opposite the temple, past the entrance of the Kumaraswamy Math. Turning right outside the temple takes one to the Dashashwamedh road. Turning left outside the temple takes one back to the Anandamayi Ashram.

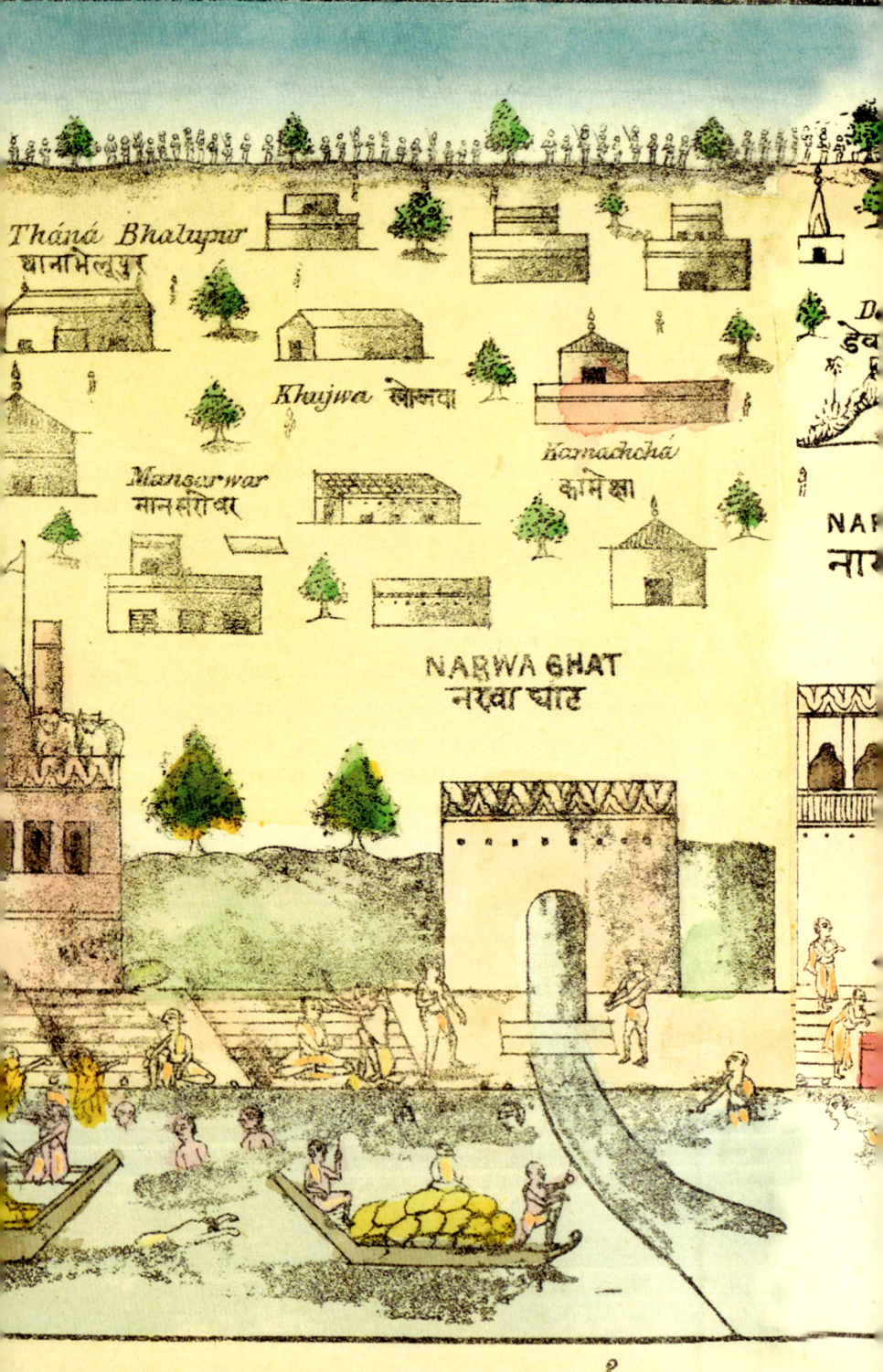

Thaná Bhalupur
थानाभिलुपुर

Khujwa खेजवा

Kamachchá
कामेक्षा

Mansarwar
मानसरोवर

NARWA GHAT
नरवा घाट

D
हे

NA
ना

२

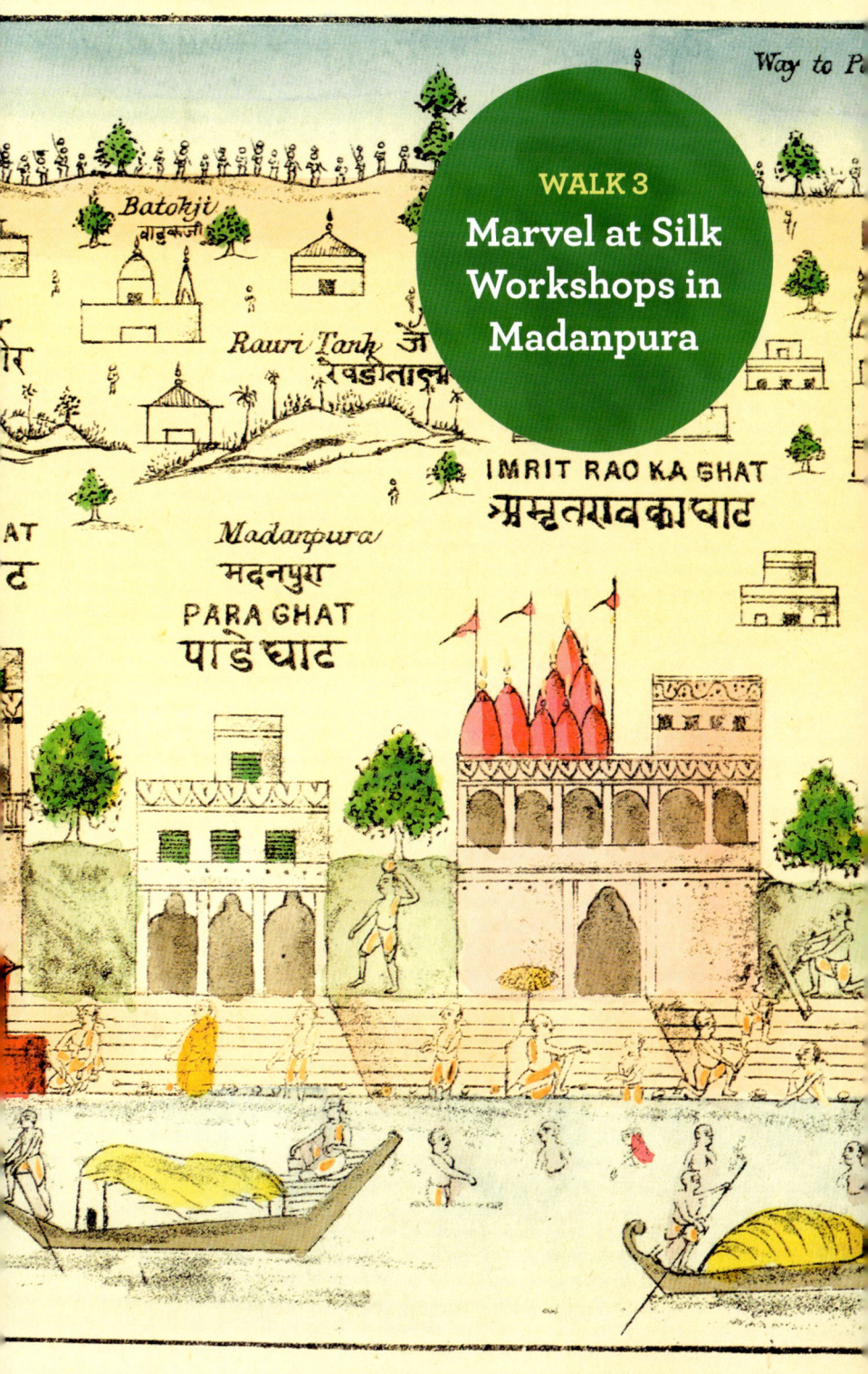

WALK 3
Marvel at Silk Workshops in Madanpura

Batokji
बाबूकजी

Rauri Tank
रेवड़ीतालाब

IMRIT RAO KA GHAT
अम्रतरावकाघाट

Madanpura
मदनपुरा
PARA GHAT
पांडे घाट

Way to P

AT
ट

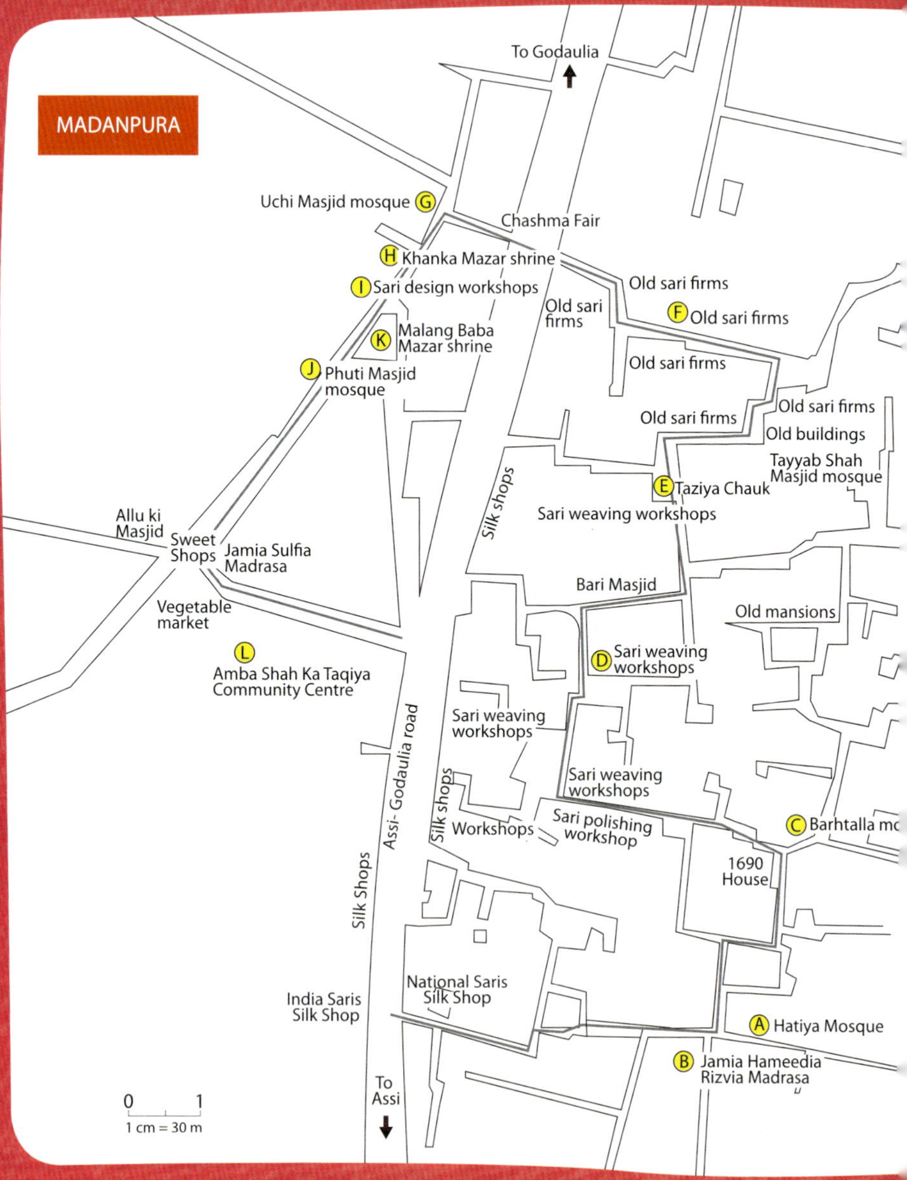

MADANPURA

To Godaulia ↑

Uchi Masjid mosque Ⓖ

Chashma Fair

Ⓗ Khanka Mazar shrine

Ⓘ Sari design workshops

Old sari firms

Old sari firms

Ⓕ Old sari firms

Malang Baba Mazar shrine Ⓚ

Old sari firms

Phuti Masjid mosque Ⓙ

Old sari firms

Old sari firms

Old buildings

Tayyab Shah Masjid mosque

Ⓔ Taziya Chauk

Sari weaving workshops

Allu ki Masjid

Sweet Shops

Jamia Sulfia Madrasa

Silk shops

Bari Masjid

Old mansions

Vegetable market

Ⓓ Sari weaving workshops

Ⓛ Amba Shah Ka Taqiya Community Centre

Sari weaving workshops

Sari weaving workshops

Workshops

Sari polishing workshop

Ⓒ Barhtalla m

Silk Shops

Assi- Godaulia road

Silk shops

1690 House

India Saris Silk Shop

National Saris Silk Shop

Ⓐ Hatiya Mosque

Ⓑ Jamia Hameedia Rizvia Madrasa

To Assi ↓

0   1
1 cm = 30 m

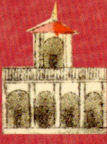

Within the dense lanes of Madanpura, wander past picturesque homes of silk weavers, mosques, Sufi shrines and Islamic schools. Pause at the handloom workshops and silk firms.

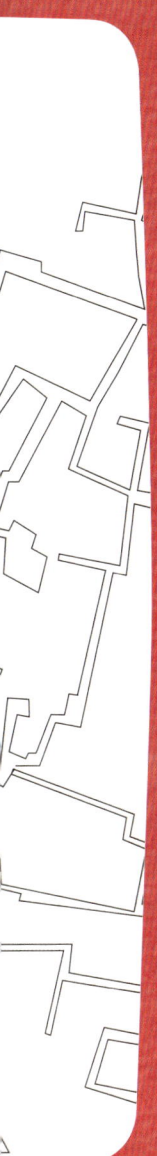

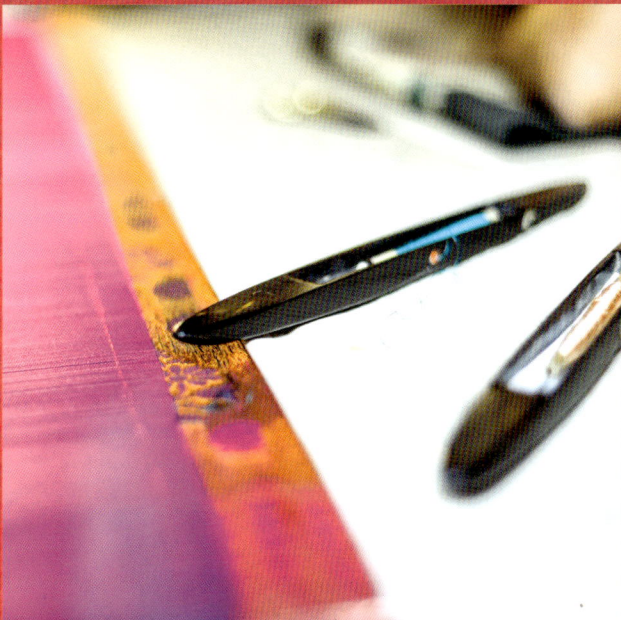

The wooden shuttles that weave warp and weft in a handloom, wound with silk thread.

THINGS TO SEE
- Traditional silk weaving handloom workshops
- Homes and silk firms housed in old mansions
- Mosques and Sufi shrines
- Islamic schools

ALLOW
Two to three hours

WALK ITINERARY
Hatiya Mosque | Jamia Hameedia Rizvia Madrasa | Barhtalla Mosque | Sari Weaving Workshops | Taziya Chauk | Old Sari Firms | Uchi Masjid | Sari Design Workshops | Phuti Masjid | Malang Baba Mazar | Amba Shah Ka Taqiya Community Centre

GETTING AROUND MADANPURA
The lanes of Madanpura are bound on the east by the river, on the west by the Assi-Godaulia road, on the north by Godaulia and on the south by Sonarpura. Madanpura incorporates many smaller neighbourhoods within it, each with its own name.

Along the Assi-Godaulia road, Madanpura can be identified by the sudden preponderance of sari and silk showrooms, such as Enaar Sarees, Taj Baba, Modern Silk Stores and Madani Seraj. From here, any lane heading east may be followed to enter Madanpura.

THE HISTORY OF MADANPURA

Madanpura is known for its mosques and places of worship, saris and silk, and its distinct community atmosphere. However, the city's oldest and most important mosques are not located in Madanpura, but scattered elsewhere in the city.

Madanpura has a preponderance of Muslim residents. But as Nita Kumar points out in her book, *The Artisans of Banaras*, very few in Banaras would call it a 'Muslim neighbourhood'. For a majority of Banarasis, the most relevant identification to evoke is profession. So Madanpura would be described as a weavers' mohalla (bunker) just as Khojwa is a grain market mohalla, not a 'Hindu' one. In Madanpura, there are not only weavers, but also others who contribute to the sari business, such as designers and dyers.

The name Ansari arose from *julaha*, which means 'weaver' and was originally used by weavers themselves. The *Julaha* caste was traditionally considered a low caste, ranked alongside *chamar* (leather-worker) and *bhangi* (sweeper). About a hundred years ago, there were movements all over India directed at social reform, dealing with issues such as women's conditions, illiteracy and early marriage age. These movements occurred as a result of the pressures of colonialism. The colonial government categorized certain castes and social practices as backward. The reform movements were all caste-based, as each caste tried to reform its practices. The efforts at reform included adopting a new 'respectable' name, starting an official organization, holding meetings, publishing a journal, and adopting a community ancestor or deity to worship, along with rituals and festivals. At this time, the *Julahas* adopted the name *Ansari*, which means 'helper of the Prophet'.

The origin of the craft of weaving is of a greater antiquity than many weavers are aware of. There are several theories as to why there are fewer Hindus than Muslims in the trade today. Around 20 or 30 years ago, one weaver compiled the oral histories of Banarasi weavers into a lengthy manuscript: his claim was that Muslim weavers are the descendants of immigrants of A.D. 990, who were already skilled weavers. Another belief is that Muslim weavers are descendants of Hindu converts to Islam.

Until the 17th and 18th centuries, Madanpura was a rural area on the outskirts of the city, skirted by streams and forests. According to some sources, Madanpura was Madanibagh, and was founded in A.D. 1,000. According to others, it was Madandur, and was founded in 380 Hijri, or A.D. 990. Some residents of Banaras today claim that Madanpura was named after a *raees* (member of the elite) named Madan when the area began to urbanize at the turn of the century.

Madanpura is one of the oldest weaving neighbourhoods of Banaras, along with Adampura, Jaitpura, and Bajardiha. It produces silk and brocade that is exported all over the world and that continues to be in great demand within India as well. Even so, the artisans of Madanpura are impoverished, as are other craftsmen of Banaras. The Indian education system fails to provide sufficient and relevant skills for new generations of artisans to rise out of poverty and ensure a brighter economic future for their craft. For artisans and their children, too large a gap exists between schoolwork and home culture for both education and work to happen simultaneously, effectively and happily. Most artisans' children begin to train when they are very young and, as a result, drop out of school at an early age. This fact becomes obvious when walking through Madanpura, you encounter children hard at work in workshops and playing games at street corners.

The Name of Ansari

After 53 years in Mecca, Prophet Mohammad reached Medina. In Medina, he was helped by the people, who were weavers. The term for 'helper' in Arabic is *nasir* and the plural of *nasir* is *ansari*. The first Muslim weavers of Banaras traced their ancestry to the original helpers of Prophet Mohammad. They began to call themselves *Ansari*, a title of respect and dignity.

Today, the term *julaha* is often used for weavers interchangeably with *Ansari*, but only by non-weavers. *Pathan* and *Sheikh* are two other Muslim 'castes' along with *Ansari*, but these have always been thought of as high

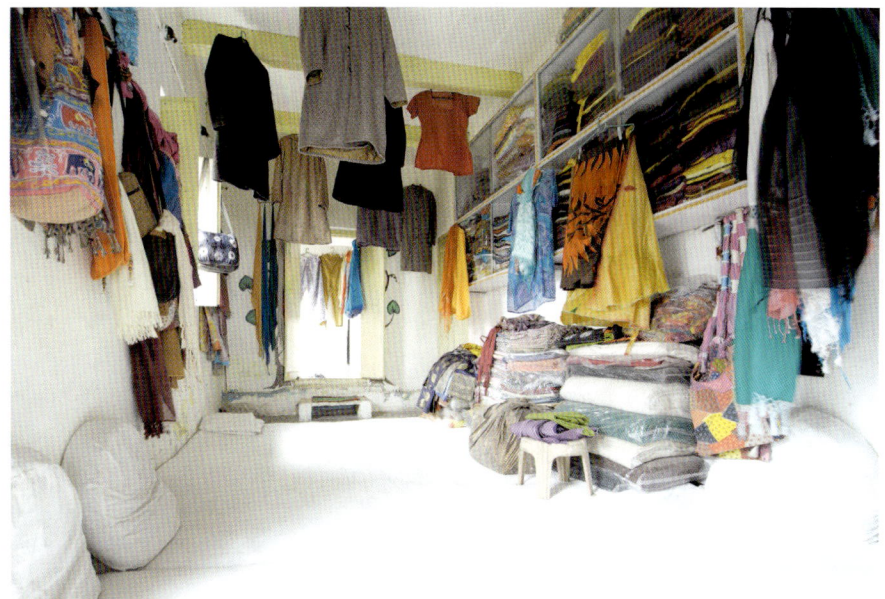

A silk shop in Madanpura.

castes. *Pathans* and *Sheikhs* claim to be the descendants of the original Muslim migrants to India from the Middle East, whereas the low-caste *julahas* were Hindu converts to Islam who took up the craft of weaving. The *Pathan* and *Sheikh* castes can be recognized by two common surnames, Mirza and Khan.

Banarasi silk

From its ancient genesis, Banaras was famous for its fabrics. The earliest Jataka tales describe Banaras as a great centre of trade and manufacture. Later, the Mughals patronized brocade production, decorating their courts with shimmering silk in floral and animal patterns.

Banaras' silk industry is unique in terms of its products and history. Unlike other cottage industries in India and silk weaving elsewhere in the world, it has flourished over the centuries. During the 18th and 19th centuries, policies of the East India Company and the British Raj reduced the manufacture of silk fabrics and encouraged the consumption of foreign-made goods all over India, most notably in Bengal. The silk industry of Banaras thrived through and despite such threats.

There are numerous reasons for its survival. Banaras developed an excellent infrastructure of trade, being strategically positioned on the Ganga, a centre for pilgrimage, and a favourite retreat of the wealthy. Added to this were the matchlessness of the city's muslin, silk and brocade, and the versatility of the products. From the beginning, weavers and designers developed an ability to quickly adapt to changing demands. Their labour was the only input in the production of silk fabric, which gave them direct access to and control over the market. Also, imperial rulers, the Mughals and then the British, were careful never to meddle too much in Banaras' economy and culture, which left the silk industry virtually undisturbed.

By the end of the 19th century, Banaras specialized in two silk products. These were *kamkhwab* or brocade, and plain silk. *Kamkhwab*, the more famous of the two,

> Since the end of the nineteenth century, Banaras has specialized in two products: Brocade and plain silk.

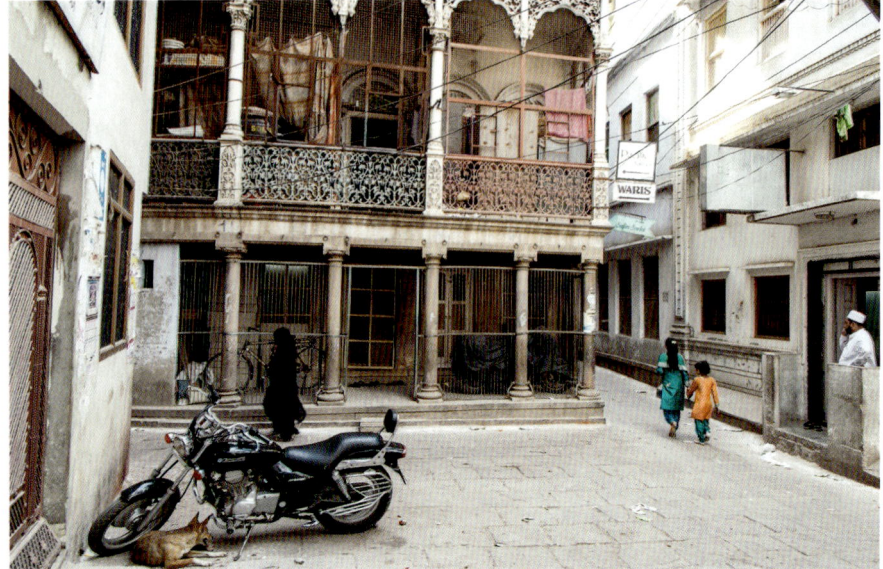

Old homes around a square in Madanpura.

was woven with three to seven layers of warp threads with a silk base supporting intricate silver or gold designs. Plain silk was used for religious and auspicious occasions. There were many varieties of both brocade and plain silk. Initially, only kings and aristocrats bought brocade. At the beginning of the 20th century, the wealth of the nobility reportedly decreased, thereby diminishing the demand for *kamkhwab*, and the sari and plain silk took over in popularity. Today, Banaras manufactures saris and specialized fabrics for ceremonial occasions, for people of all classes.

The homes

All Madanpura homes have similar interiors, even newer and fancier ones. You enter through a low doorway and a dark, narrow hallway, into a courtyard. The stairs, on one side, leads upstairs into the domestic area. Here, the women take care of the children and do the housework. They also do the preparatory work for weaving, such as filling bobbins and spinning yarn.

Many weavers work independently, using their home as the workshop. The rooms for the looms are on the ground floor, adjoining the courtyard. The ground floor thus looks busy and professional, maybe with yarn or sari boxes stored in a corner and a space for making business deals. The upstairs is domestic, chaotic or tidy, depending on the homemaker. Weavers are friendly and ready to invite visitors into their homes. Only women can go upstairs unless you are a relative or a close friend, since the system of *purdah* or seclusion (literally 'curtain' or 'veil') continues to be observed in Madanpura.

The people

We may wonder why the weavers seem so relaxed. Within the workshops or homes, they laugh and chat. The men dress casually in a lungi with a shirt and a *gamchha* (light cotton towel or scarf) thrown over the shoulder. At any odd hour, an Ansari will be chewing pan or betel leaf, his mouth stained red and his cheeks full. The weavers get up frequently from their looms to spit, stretch, or to wander through the *gali* outside.

The work of weavers, as of all Banarasi artisans, is 'pre-industrial'. It contains a high degree of freedom, with flexible working hours and holidays. Weavers choose when and how to work or not to work. They decide whether to weave for 14 hours or whether to spend the day strolling outside and drinking tea.

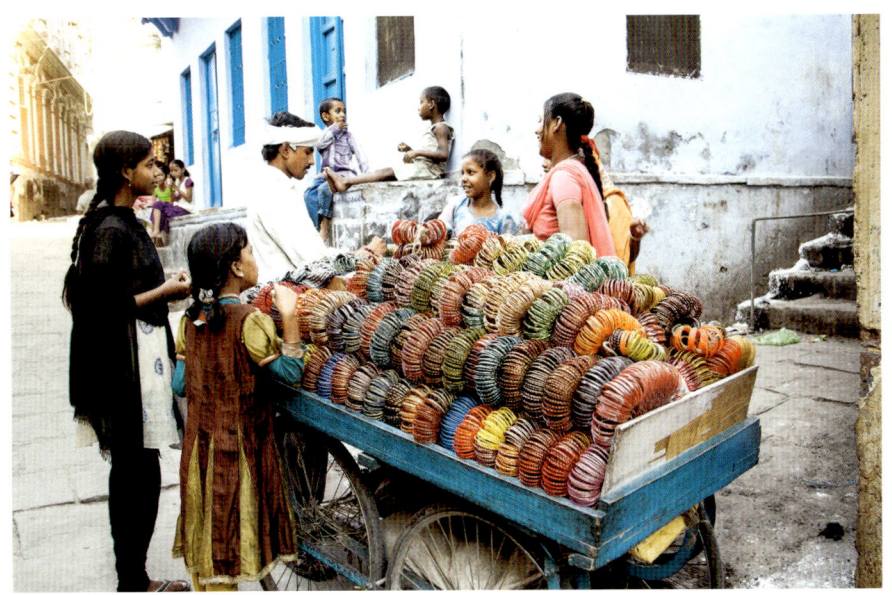

Madanpura residents admire a cart of bangles for sale.

The weavers of Madanpura are proud of this balance between *mehanat* ('hard work'), *aram* ('leisure' or 'idleness'), and *masti* ('fun'). They treasure their freedom dearly. For them, the worst punishment would be to have rules imposed on them. Their work culture is one they have nurtured, cherished and philosophized about for generations.

The main festivals the weavers celebrate are Id-ul-Fitr (commonly known as Id), Id-ul-Zuha (or Baqr Id), Id-e-Milad-ul-Nabi (or Barah Wafat) and Shab-e-Barat. On these occasions, work stops for a week at a time. At Id, the lanes, squares and mosques turn into carnivals of colour and entertainment. The entire family is out of the house, enjoying food and music, dressed in new clothes, visiting friends. At Baqr Id, there is high excitement as sheep, and an occasional buffalo or camel, are ritually slaughtered and the meat is then distributed. Shab-e Barat is in memory of ancestors and the tombs of favourite saints or *mazars* are lit up and weavers along with their families visit them at night.

> Barah Wafat is the most glamorous of all the festivals, with all-night recitations of *nat* or poetry in praise of the Prophet on his birthday, particularly by well-rehearsed children.

Finally, Moharram, though not a 'festival' but rather a time of mourning, is enthusiastically observed in Banaras. Among all the interesting activity are parades carrying *taziya* or replicas of the tombs of the martyrs, Hasan and Hussain. There are also parades with sword and bamboo pole virtuoso displays and processions honouring the horse Duldul, which returned alone after Imam Hussain was martyred.

The weavers have a rich cultural life. The people of Madanpura are proud of their neighbourhood. Their loyalty to their neighbourhood, is reflected in the pomp with which they celebrate their festivals, the enthusiasm with which they compete with other neighbourhoods in wrestling and music competitions, and their confident swagger as they wander through Madanpura's lanes. They describe their neighbourhood as one of the most cultured and sophisticated in the city.

Apart from leisure and festivity, there are times when weavers work long hours, staying at their looms late into the night. They get large orders to complete especially during the weeks and months preceding important festivals.

Ⓐ HATIYA MOSQUE
Madanpura's oldest mosque

→ *Follow the lane opposite 'India Sarees' and adjacent to the 'National Saris' silk shops. Hatiya Mosque and Jamia Hameedia Madrasa are at the first crossroads.*

What to Know The mosques in Madanpura have vaguely known origins and histories. Sandwiched within dense lanes, most are also architecturally unremarkable. That said, the Madanpura mosques are highly loved and used spaces. Most worshippers are the Muslim weavers and sari businessmen who live in the neighbourhood. There are over 20 mosques in the small area of Madanpura. Most are at least four centuries old and were established by a wealthy Muslim resident of Madanpura. They have grown in size and importance over the centuries, and have been renovated several times over.

The Hatiya Mosque is in the smaller neighbourhood of Madanpura called Hatiya. It is also called Masjid Jahangir, after the Mughal emperor Jahangir (1569-1627). It is the oldest of the larger mosques of Madanpura. The *maulana* (Muslim spiritual teacher) Abdul Hamees built it in the mid-19th century. The mosque belongs to the Barelwi sect or school of Q'uranic teaching. Differences between the three sects are ritualistic and difficult for the outsider to grasp. All mosques are similar in their structure and functioning. Like all mosques, the Hatiya Mosque belongs to the Wakf Board, which means that it is a charitable and religious organization owned by Allah. The donor is known as the *wakif*. A caretaker is chosen from among members of the community and is known as the *mutwalli*.

Ⓑ JAMIA HAMEEDIA RIZVIA MADRASA
A leading Islamic school

→ *Directions from Hatiya Mosque to Jamia Hameedia Madrasa: Opposite the Hatiya Mosque, the tall building with ornate windows houses the Islamic school called Jamia Hameedia Rizvia Madrasa.*

What to Know The Islamic school called Jamia Hameedia Rizvia is one of the three main Islamic schools or madrasas in Madanpura. It belongs to the Barelvi sect of Islam.

What to See Like other madrasas, Jamia Hameedia Rizvia functions in an old-fashioned, whitewashed building with tall walls on the outside. Inside, there is a central courtyard with modern offices and classrooms all around. Younger children sit on the floor while older ones work at desks and chairs. Modern blackboards and textbooks are used. The main difference is that in a madrasa, children learn Urdu, and it might be the primary medium of education for the first few years. They also learn Arabic and the Q'uran, totaling the number of languages they need to know to five. Madrasas typically do not teach sports or the arts, and are separate for boys and girls.

Each madrasa is divided into a lower section, which aims to simply educate children, and a higher section that is residential and aims to produce scholars versed in the Islamic arts and sciences.

Many new schools have opened in Madanpura in recent times that are not traditional madrasas, although they also teach Urdu and the Q'uran in Arabic. They are ostensibly quite modern, with uniforms for students, desks and chairs, and studies in English. While all this testifies to the awareness of weavers in terms of the future of their children, it seems to contrast the pre-modern feel of everything else in the mohalla and presents a 'tradition-modernity' conundrum for the observer.

MUHARRAM

Muharram marks the first month of the Islamic calendar. After Yazid I killed Husain on the tenth day of Muharram (a day called 'Ashura'), his family and followers were taken captive and held in Damascus.

Muharram is a period of mourning. There are a huge variety of Muharram celebrations in Banaras. Many Muslims incorporate rituals in remembrance of Hussain's suffering into their Muharram celebrations. These include fasting, self-flagellation with swords and chains and running over hot coals.

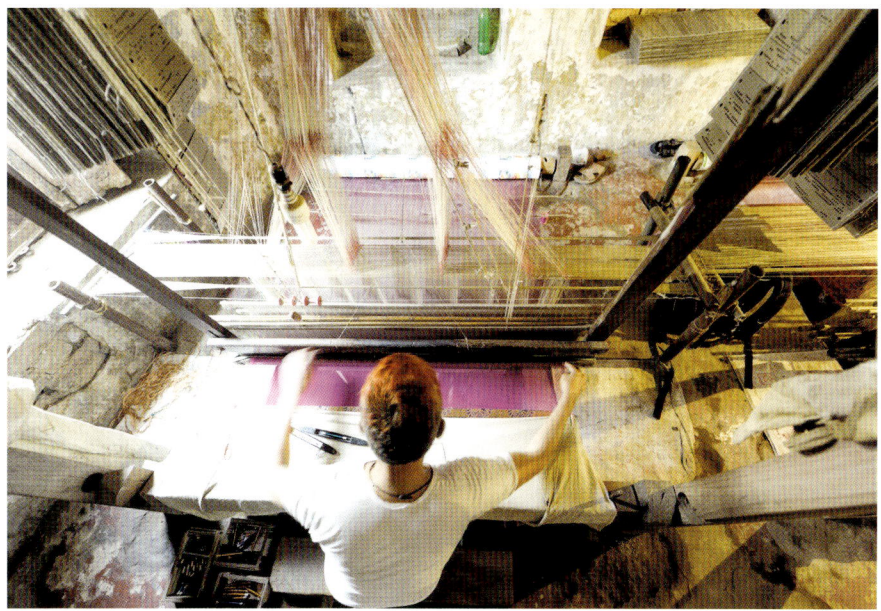

A weaver at work at a handloom.

Ⓒ BARHTALLA MOSQUE
In the memory of a Barh tree

➡ *Directions from Jamia Hameedia Rizvia Madrasa to Barhtalla Mosque: Turn left at the crossroads of Hatiya Mosque and the Jamia Hameedia Rizvia Madrasa. At the small T-junction turn right, then left again to continue straight down the lane until you come to another T-junction. The building you face is Barhtalla Mosque, named after a barh tree that no longer exists. On the left, the tall building is the renovated 1690 home of a prominent sari workshop and wholesale shop owner.*

What to Know Barhtalla means 'under the Barh tree'. Named after a Barh or Banyan tree (Ficus Bengalensis, famous for its roots) that no longer exists, the Barhtalla Mosque is one of the larger mosques of Madanpura. It also houses a mazar or Sufi shrine inside it.

Ⓓ SARI WEAVING WORKSHOPS
The nine-yard wonder

➡ *Directions from Barhtalla Mosque to Sari Weaving Workshops: Facing Barhtalla Mosque, turn left and follow the lane. On your left there is a sari polishing workshop, within which complete woven saris are coated with a fine*

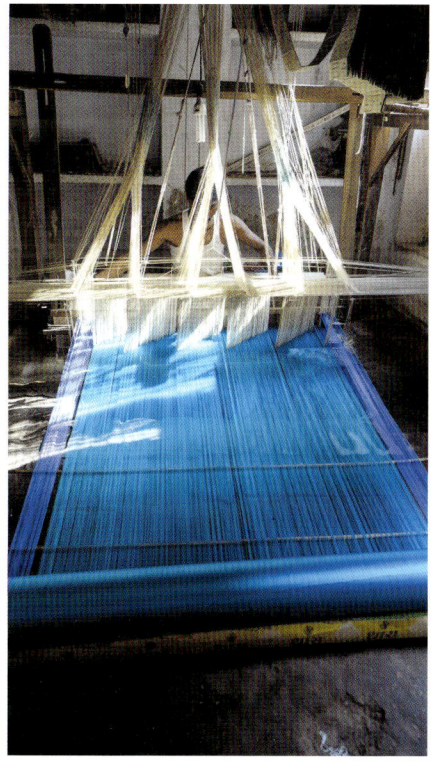

An artisan working on a loom, weaving a sari.

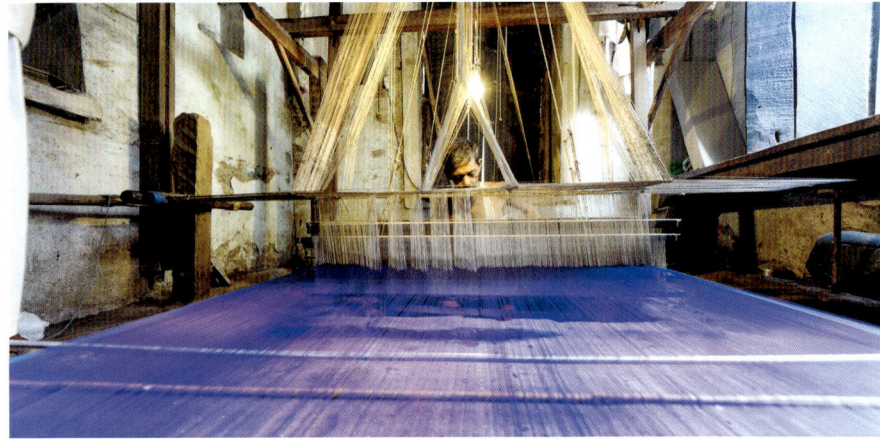

A sari in the making, with its warp threads stretched out on a loom.

polish, to add luster, and dried before being sent to the wholesale markets. The lane opens into a square bordered by tall buildings that house weaving workshops, recognizable by the handlooms within. Turn right and go straight, passing another small square on your right, until you come to a T-junction. The large mosque you will face is known as Bari Masjid. 'Bari' means 'big': this is Madanpura's biggest mosque. Five hundred men at a time can pray here. Continue straight (to the right of) Bari Masjid, past more workshops to your left. The small square with the elevated platform that you come to is known as Taziya Chauk. Turn right and then left. Pass the recently renovated Tayyab Shah Masjid and beautiful old buildings that house silk firms and homes. At the T-junction turn left and follow the lane out onto the main road. This last lane is lined with beautiful old mansions with intricately carved doorways and pillars. These house some of Madanpura's oldest and richest sari firms.

A firm is a registered body for trade or manufacture. The owner of the firm is called *kothidar*, *arhatriya*, or *mahajan*, and is usually not present in the weaving workshop.

What to Know Visiting a weaving workshop (*karkhana*) today is almost the same as visiting one or two centuries ago. The technology of the Banaras silk industry has not changed much.

What to See Workshops typically occupy the ground floor of a building. Their large windows

open out into the lane. They are most easily distinguishable by the sound of the looms. While the handloom produces a clacking, wooden noise, the power loom produces a mechanized drone. Power loom workshops tend to have closed windows or no windows at all.

In the past century, three workers operated an elaborate pit loom with a throw shuttle. The designs for the weave were made with a cotton thread design called *jala*. Today, the jacquard machine is used for designing and only one weaver operates the loom. The Hattersley domestic foot power loom, adopted in 1929, simplified the process further.

Looking inside the workshop, we see weavers sitting in rows, legs dangling into the hollowed pits beneath their looms, arms moving from side to side as they throw the shuttle. A radio plays and the artisans chat freely. A single workshop may have up to a dozen weavers. Some are brothers or cousins, others employees. Each unit is deliberately kept small so as to not fall within the purview of government legislations. The master weaver is indistinguishable from the other weavers because he works alongside them and dresses in the same way. He serves as a supervisor and mentor in the workshop. He is also the middleman between the weavers and the managing firm. He takes orders, supplies materials, and delivers finished products: on the way, he makes a small profit.

Ⓔ TAZIYA CHAUK
An open square for a special festival
What to Know The Taziya Chauk is a small open square between buildings. Each year, during the festival of Muharram, Muslims all over the city take out a procession from this open square with a *taziya* or replica of the tomb of Husain, the grandson of Mohammed, who was martyred on the battlefield.

What to See The *taziya* is made out of bamboo, kite-paper, and cloth, by locals or craftsmen. In Madanpura, on the fifth or sixth day the *taziya* is set up at Taziya Chauk and the people recite *nath*, a genre of singing in praise of the prophet.

Ⓕ OLD SARI FIRMS
Centuries of silk trade
What to Know The rest of the walk is marked by beautiful old mansions that house sari wholesale shops, workshops and

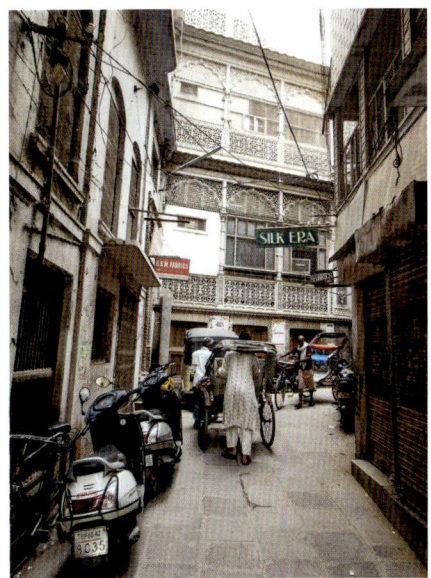

Silk shops in a typical Madanpura lane.

homes of weavers and businessmen. One of the largest firms is that of Swaleh Ansari, which has branched out from an original trunk into several shops, as is often the case with indigenous firms. As with other landmarks, the visitor has to ask passersby for Swaleh Ansari to be directed to the particular place, with many offers along the way to show better saris or fabrics at better prices. Some 20 years ago, Swaleh Ansari was elected the mayor of the city and did his community proud.

What to See Firms are stores, marked by their signboards, with shiny glass fronts or located within old buildings. All of them are the same inside. There is a *gaddi*, the place for buying and selling. *Gaddi* literally means 'mattress'. The master weaver or customer is ushered into a room with a white cushioned floor. Everyone sits comfortably on the cushioning and the saris are flung open one breathtaking piece at a time to be inspected. These sari firms are marked with signboards and anyone can visit them without an appointment.

In the main business district of Banaras called Chauk, north of Madanpura, the owners are Hindus usually from Punjabi Khatri, Gujarati, Sindhi, or Marwari communities. In Madanpura, the firm owners are Muslims who claim to belong to the Ansari community.

Ⓖ UCHI MASJID
A soaring structure
→ *At the main road, cross the road and enter the lane next to the small optical store called 'Chasma Fair'. Uchi Masjid is the high mosque facing you where the lane breaks into a T-junction.*

What to Know 'Uchi' means 'high'; and no one would disagree that this mosque is appropriately named. The mosques in this part of Madanpura are more recent than on the other side of the main road. About two centuries old, Uchi Masjid was built by a wealthy sari businessman.

Ⓗ KHANKA MAZAR SHRINE
For the elderly to unwind
→ *Facing Uchi Masjid at the T-junction, turn left down the lane and follow it until it forks.*

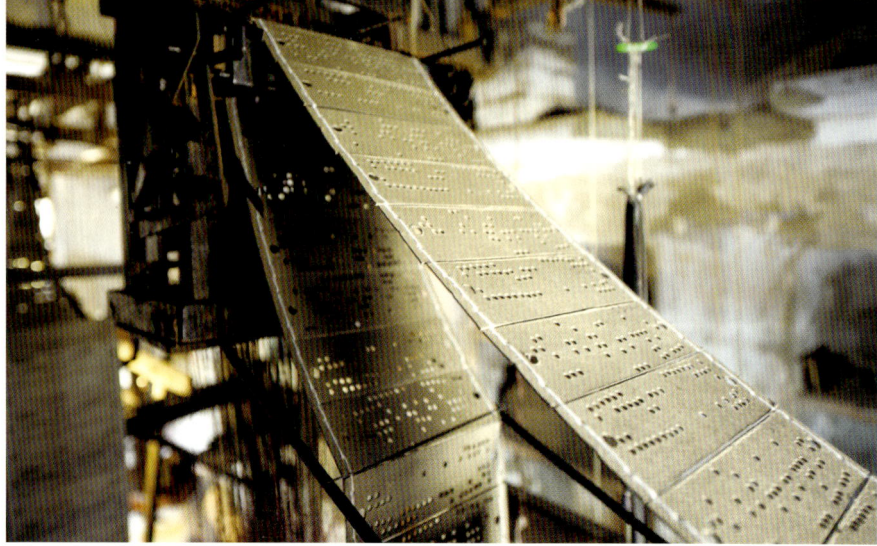
In a handloom, punched cards are used to weave threads into a design.

On the right is a brightly-painted shrine called Khanka Mazar, workshops that create sari designs, and the mosque called Phuti Masjid. The building at the fork is the shrine called Malang Baba Mazar.

What to Know 'Khanka' refers to a place where older people relax and eat together: the Khanka Mazar shrine is such a place. Around a century old, its specific origins are difficult to trace.

① SARI DESIGN WORKSHOPS
Traditional and innovative designs
→ *Directions from Khanka Mazar to sari design workshops: On the right after Khanka Mazar, there are three or four sari design workshops.*
What to See In these street-facing workshops, men sit on the floor punching holes into rectangular strips of cardboard. These punched cards are used to create designs in saris when they are being woven. The cards are punched according to patterns that are designed in other workshops, by hand or on the computer. Then the cards are hung high above the stretched sari on a handloom on a machine called the Jacquard. The warp and weft threads pass through the holes, creating specific patterns as they are woven together by the weaver.

① PHUTI MASJID
A mosque with modest decor
What to Know 'Phuti' means 'broken' and some say that Phuti Masjid was named after the stained glass in its windows. Others say its name comes from its extreme dilapidated state before it was renovated. Like the other mosques in this part of Madanpura, Phuti Masjid must not be more than a century or two old.

LOCAL SWEET TREATS
Not far from Phuti Masjid near the crossroad on the right are several street-side sweet shops. Above the sweet shops is a mosque known as Allu Ki Masjid, named after the sari businessman Allu who built the mosque. This small, but busy crossroad is special for its three or four sweet shops. The steaming woks here produce several types of popular, deep-fried, flour and sugar-based sweets known as **korma**. Most likely, these sweets first travelled from the Middle East to the Indian subcontinent many centuries ago, with the coming of the first Muslim rulers, and gradually evolved to their current form. It's a delight to try the **sticky nuggets**, **rolls** and **pancakes** of various kinds, as well as **chat** with the friendly sweet-makers.

Ⓚ MALANG BABA MAZAR
Dedicated to Sufi saint, Malang

What to Know A beautiful little neighbourhood Sufi shrine, Malang Baba Mazar houses the tomb of the Sufi saint, Malang. Step up into the verandah outside the inner shrine with your head covered, but do not enter the shrine itself.

The pir (saint) is believed to reside in spirit in his shrine. Worshippers of all religions visit the Sufi shrines of Banaras and so is the case at Malang Baba Mazar. People visit when they are suffering from any kind of physical or emotional discomfort, in order to get 'healed'. Even in good health, reading verses from the Q'uran is like giving a gift to the saint, and one can expect a 'gift' in return.

There is an urs ceremony annually, commemorating the death of the pir, with qawwali singing and worship. Urs literally means 'wedding', implying that at death, the soul unites with its maker.

Ⓛ AMBA SHAH KA TAQIYA COMMUNITY CENTRE
The resting place of Amba Shah

→ *Directions from Malang Baba Mazar shrine to Amba Shah ka Taqiya community centre: Outside Malang Baba Mazar, facing Phuti Masjid, turn left down the lane. At the next crossroad (marked by sweet shops), turn left. Pass another madrasa on the left, called Jamia Sulfia. On the right, pass a vegetable market to reach the Amba Shah ka Taqiya community centre. The lane goes under a cement gateway that was originally built by the Turkish emperor Sher Shah Suri (c.1472-1545), and ends at the main road.*

What to Know Amba Shah ka Taqiya means 'the resting place of Amba Shah'. Amba Shah was a Sufi saint, a popular local spiritual leader about whom little precise information can be found. His tomb, along with other prominent weavers and religious leaders, lies here.

The building is used as an office and community centre. Madanpura residents come here to enjoy wrestling matches, as the sign above the gate proclaims. The governing association of the weavers of Banaras, called the Bawani Panchayat, also meets here to settle disputes and take important decisions. The association consists of 52 of the city's most prominent weavers, headed by the leader called the 'Bawani Ka Sardar' (*bawan* means 52 in Hindi and *sardar* means leader). The sardar is elected by the sardars of smaller units, of 5, 14, 22 etc. The 'election' is partly a formality because the sardar title has been in the same house, and everyone knows that the son, occasionally younger brother or nephew, will inherit. He is given a turban (pagri) to signify his election. These leaders are never present in the weaving workshops. The sardar system is followed by all artisan castes in Banaras and is at least two centuries old.

BAWANI KA SARDAR

Babu Mehto, the current leader of 52 neighbourhoods and therefore the most powerful weaver in the city, has the authority to summon a panchayat or meeting of elders. The sardars of 1, 5, 14 and 22 neighbourhoods are required to attend this meeting. They jointly decide on professional moves, such as leading a delegation to the government to protest a rise in the cost of raw silk. More regularly, Babu Mehto gives decisions on inter-family and inter-personal conflicts, even husband-wife splits and property division between brothers. It is amazing to think of legal action such as this being taken by a popular leader rather than by the court. The courts thrive in Banaras, as they do elsewhere, and have an abundance of lawsuits to resolve. The sardar's authority runs parallel and is preferred, apparently, by average weavers as it is less expensive and long-winded and more compatible with their own ethos.

Given that prosperous master weavers have travelled abroad, have finely furnished homes and educated children (or at least sons), the persistence of this system is a fascinating example of the continuity of tradition in modernity.

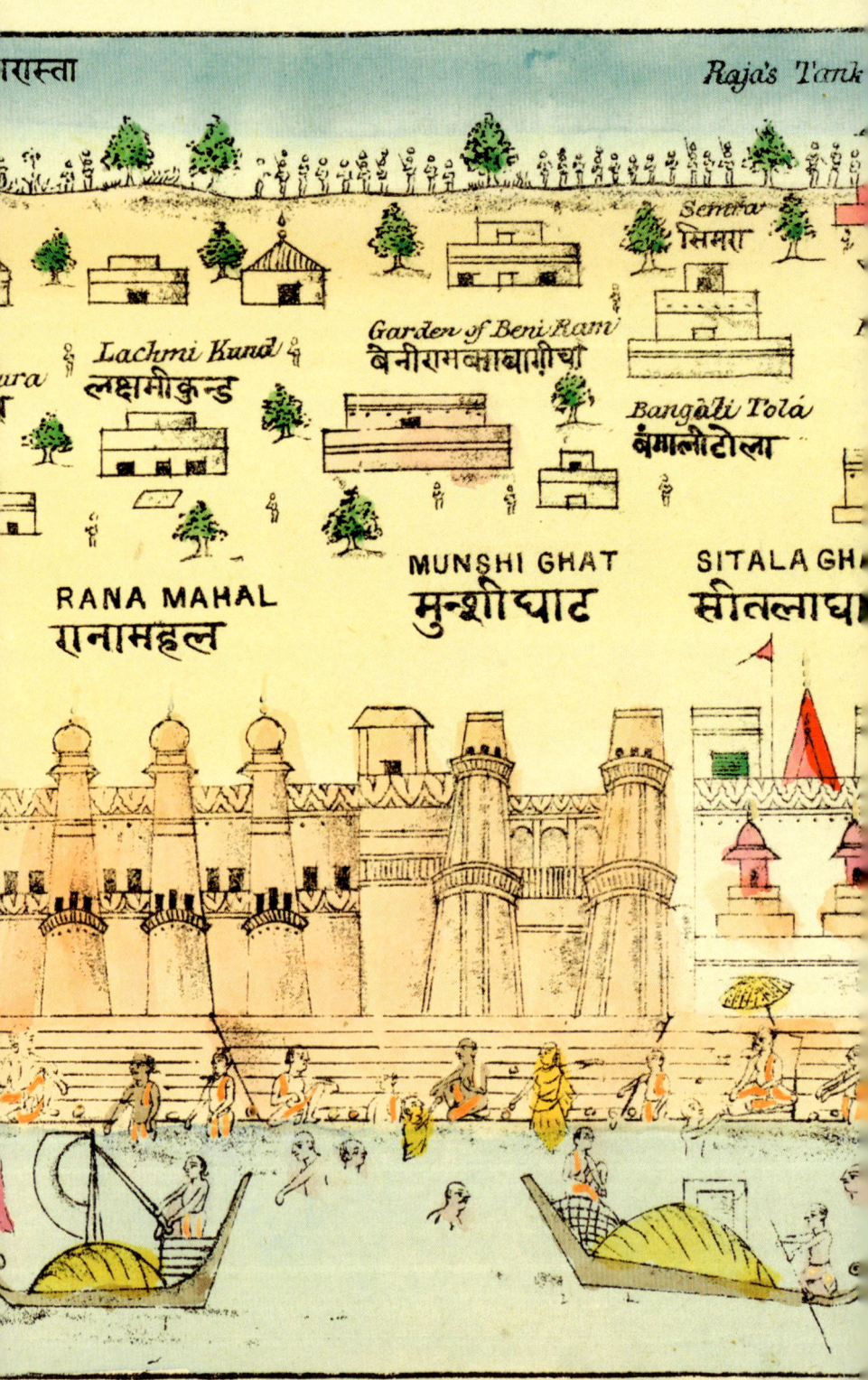

Semra
सिमरा

Lachmi Kund
लक्ष्मीकुन्ड

Garden of Beni Ram
बेनीरामबाबाबाग़ीचा

Bangali Tola
बंगालीटोला

ura

RANA MAHAL
रानामहल

MUNSHI GHAT
मुन्शीघाट

SITALA GH
सीतलाघा

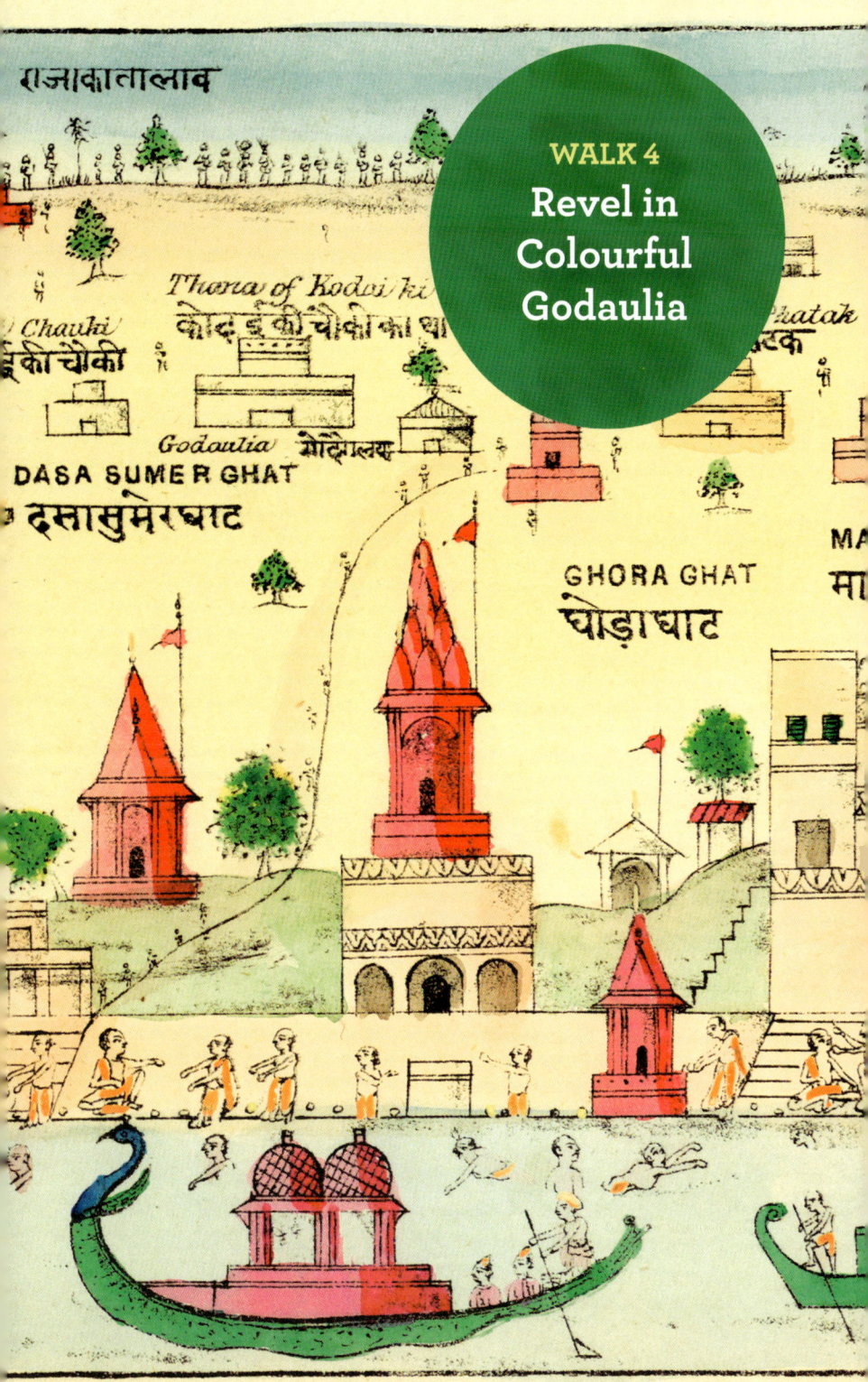

राजादातालाब

Thona of Kodai ki

कोदई की चौकी का थ

Chauki

ई की चौकी

Godaulia गोदौलिया

DASA SUMER GHAT

दसासुमेरघाट

GHORA GHAT

घोड़ाघाट

hatak

टक

MA

मा

Explore the city's busiest shopping street and ghat, stopping at temples and an astronomical observatory housed in an old palace. Walk through the main handicrafts market, a colourful lane with the city's most important Shiva temple and mosque, located at its end.

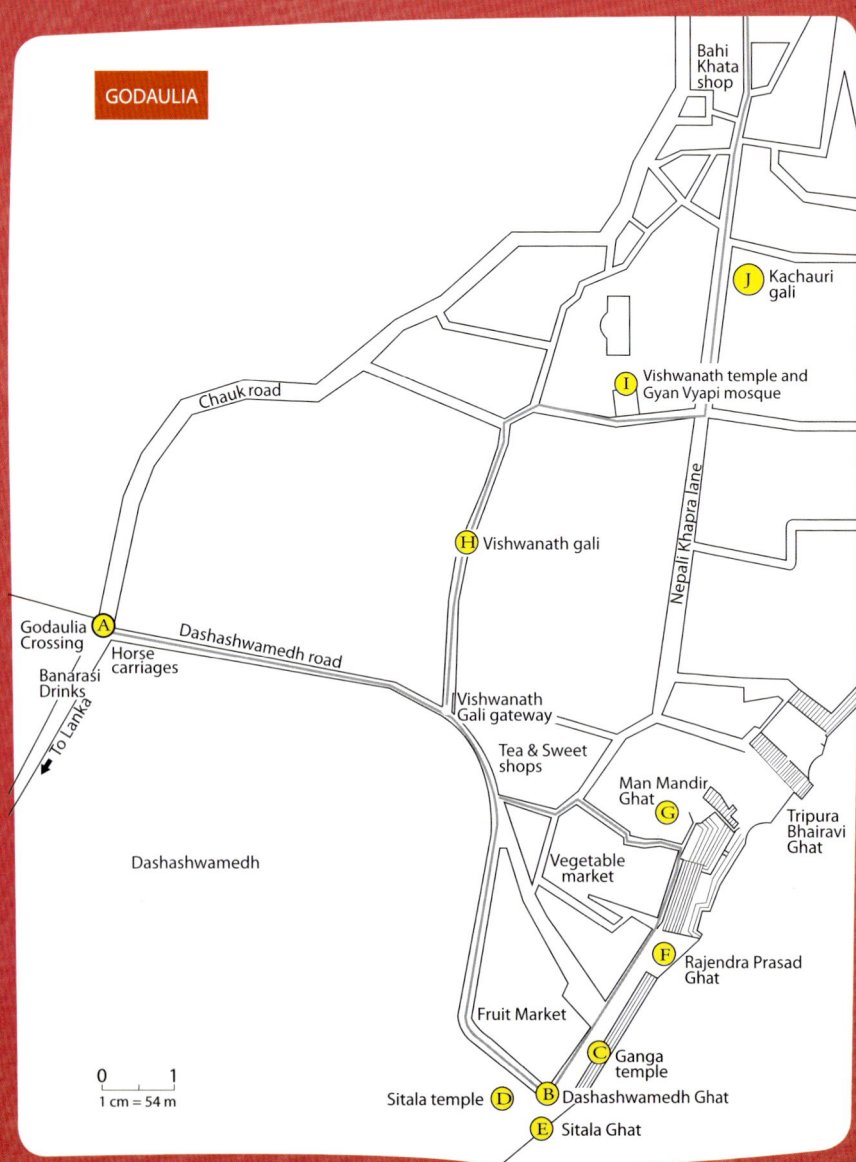

GODAULIA

Bahi Khata shop

J Kachauri gali

I Vishwanath temple and Gyan Vyapi mosque

Nepali Khapra lane

Chauk road

H Vishwanath gali

Godaulia Crossing

A Dashashwamedh road

Horse carriages

Banarasi Drinks

To Lanka

Vishwanath Gali gateway

Tea & Sweet shops

Man Mandir Ghat

G

Tripura Bhairavi Ghat

Dashashwamedh

Vegetable market

F Rajendra Prasad Ghat

Fruit Market

C Ganga temple

0   1
1 cm = 54 m

Sitala temple D   B Dashashwamedh Ghat

E Sitala Ghat

THINGS TO SEE

- Horse carriages
- Temples dedicated to Ganga and Sitala, goddess of smallpox
- Palace of the Rajput king, Man Singh, and his astronomical observatory
- Handicrafts market with silk fabrics, wood and stone work, jewellery and notebooks, favourite snacks and drinks
- Historic Vishwanath Temple and Gyan Vyapi Mosque

ALLOW

Four to five hours

WALK ITINERARY

Godaulia Crossing | Dashashwamedh Ghat | Ganga Temple | Sitala Temple & Ghat | Rajendra Prasad Ghat | Man Mandir Ghat and Observatory | Vishwanath Gali | Vishwanath Temple and Gyan Vyapi Mosque | Kachauri Gali and Khoya Gali

BEST TIME TO VISIT

Crowded, noisy and colourful, particularly on Mondays, weekends, summer evenings and festivals. Less chaotic between noon and 4 pm.

GETTING AROUND GODAULIA

Godaulia refers to the area between Madanpura, on the south, and Chauk on the north. It is bound on the west by the Assi-Godaulia road and on the east by the river, and the ghats Prayag, Sitala, Dashashwamedh, Rajendra Prasad, and Man Mandir.

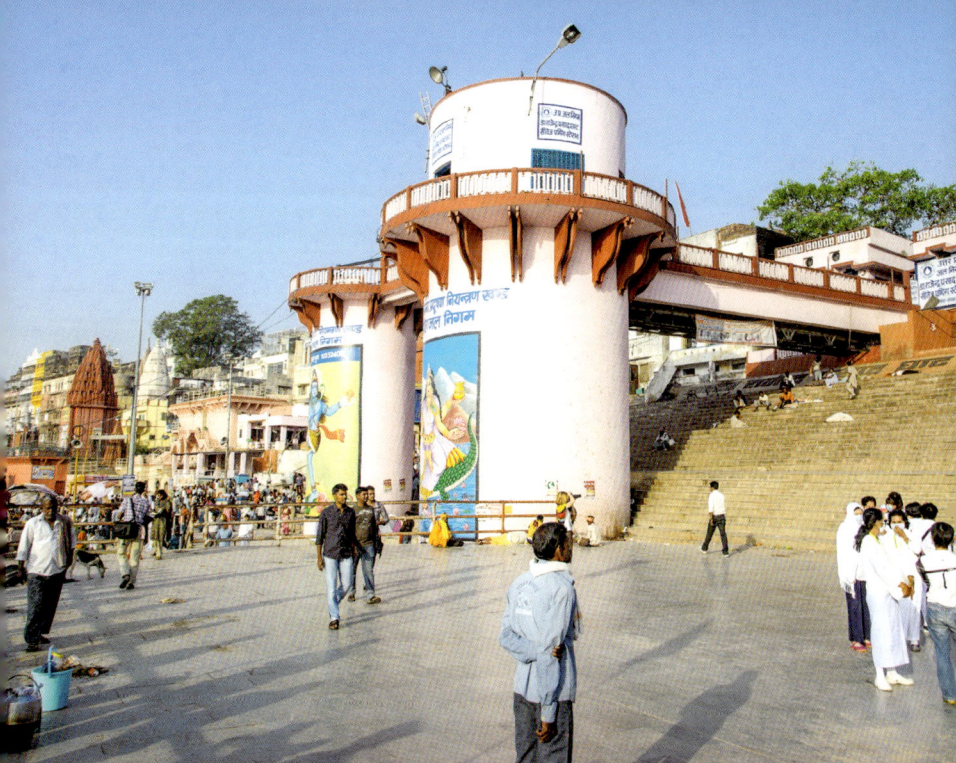

Rajendra Prasad Ghat, which hosts an elaborate ceremony to Ganga happens each evening and an annual music concert.

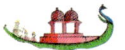

THE HISTORY OF GODAULIA

Until the end of the 19th century, 'Godaulia' was a stream, one of the many that crisscrossed Kashi's forests to empty into the Ganga. To the north of the Godaulia stream was the main city, a dense, built-up area stretched along the river. To its west and south were forests and streams, mansions, gardens, ponds and small houses of clay, thatch and tile.

At the end of the 19th century, the British converted Godaulia into a street. Today, this main street of Godaulia is an overwhelmingly busy shopping arcade. Walking to its end brings visitors to Dashashwamedh Ghat, the city's most important riverside tirtha or sacred place. Pilgrims who come to Dashashwamedh Ghat also visit the temple of Vishwanath, 'Lord of the World', the city's most important temple today, and anchor of that sector of the city that is believed to be situated on the middle prong of Shiva's trident.

To get to Vishwanath Temple, visitors must wind their way up the lane called Vishwanath gali, which showcases the city's handicrafts. Precariously narrow, the lane is typically packed with pilgrims hurrying to and from the temple and shoppers dawdling between the stores that glitter with wooden, stone, and silken products.

Above the shops and shrines are homes. The Banarasis who live here – artisans, businessmen, and priests – ensure that Godaulia thrives each day as a commercial and spiritual centre.

Ⓐ GODAULIA CROSSING

Horse carriages and shopping

What to Know The Godaulia crossing, or just 'Godaulia' in short, is nerve-wracking, as a result of its loudspeakers, crowds and mismanaged traffic.

What to See At the crossing, watch out for the horse carriages apart from the regular autos and rickshaws. These are called *ikkas* and were very popular in Banaras until the early 20th century. They were used by the elite of the city, who would race their *ikkas* down the streets. See examples of some of them, used by the former maharajas of

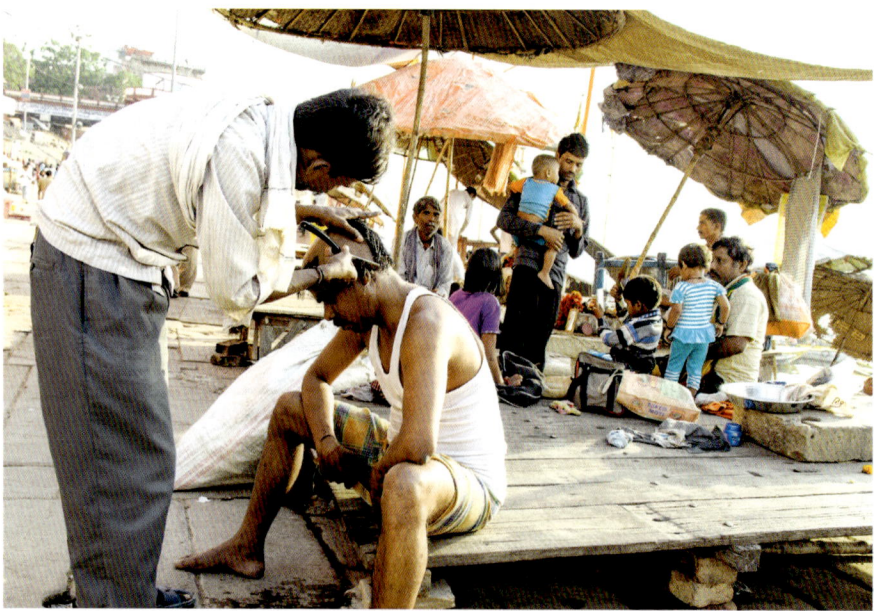

All sorts of businesses thrive in Godaulia. A man gets a haircut from a local barber.

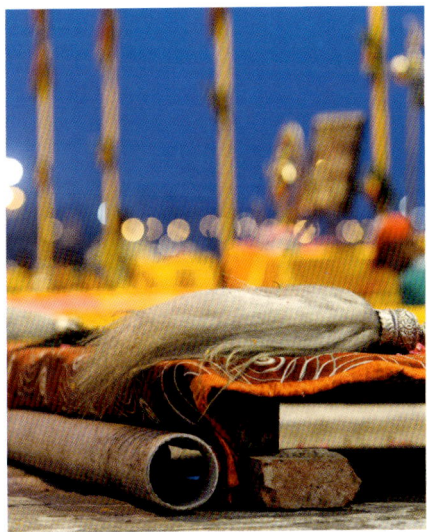
Flywhisk used to honour Ganga in the arti ceremony each evening at Dashashwamedh Ghat.

Banaras, in the Ramnagar Fort Museum, across the river.

Walking down the shopping street from Godaulia crossing, admire the many shops that sell apparel, accessories and snacks. Most middle-class Banarasis choose Godaulia for clothes and shoe-shopping.

Ⓑ DASHASHWAMEDH GHAT
Conches and devotional songs

→ *Directions from Godaulia to Dashashwamedh Ghat: From Godaulia, turn right. Walk down the entire length of the busy shopping street, passing a brown gateway on your left. When the road forks, take the right-hand fork, and go down the steps to the ghat.*

What to Know Today, the stone steps leading to the river here, is characterized by religious activity and shops selling flowers, incense and ritual items.

The ghat's vast open space makes it easy to imagine how ships docked here, loading and unloading people and cargo of all kinds, a millennium or more in the past, when Banaras was a hub for commerce and culture. The Peshwa or Maratha, prime minister of Pune in western India, Balaji Baji Rao, built the ghat in its present form in 1735.

What to See An elaborate arti (religious ceremony) takes place each evening. Saffron-clad Brahmin priests-in-training conduct the worship of the Ganga by blowing conches, ringing bells and rotating heavy fire torches. Professional musicians sing bhajans (devotional songs). Tourists in boats pull up to the ghat to

---

COOL DELIGHTS

At Godaulia crossing, there are shops with counters full of colourful bottles. They specialize in Banarasi drinks such as lassi and thandai. **Lassi** is whipped yoghurt, sweetened or salty and traditionally unflavoured. **Thandai**, which literally means 'coolness', is made of milk, spices and nuts. It is often taken with **bhang**, an intoxicant. The colourful liquids in bottles are flavourings and mixes for drinks. Enjoying lassi and thandai during a break from work, an evening stroll, or to combat the intense summer heat is an essential component of *mauj* and *masti*, the *joie de vivre* that all true Banarasis believe in. Refresh yourself with a glass if you are accustomed to street food, but remember to request one without ice.

TIPS FOR SHOPPING

Shopping in Godaulia can be over-whelming even for local Banarasis. The shopkeepers here have rightfully earned a reputation for being aggressive. It is true that many shopkeepers increase prices when dealing with tourists. Having a local friend makes shopping here easier. Also, keep in mind that the artisans who create the handicrafts sold here work painstakingly for months, using technology that has remained virtually unchanged for centuries. In the context of their labour and global prices, neither the artisans nor shopkeepers make high profits. A price that may initially sound too high may not actually be unreasonable when thought about from this perspective.

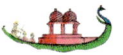

BRAHMA'S RITUAL

A long time ago, when there was a drought on Earth, Brahma the creator called on the sage-king Divodas to restore order. Divodas accepted on the condition that the gods wouldn't interfere in his rule. He sent them all from Kashi to their heavenly abode and set about establishing order.

But Lord Shiva, who had been banished to Mount Mandara, longed to return to Kashi. He appealed to the divine female *yoginis* for help. He wanted them to tempt Raja Divodas and disrupt his rule. But the *yoginis* were unable to do so. So Shiva turned to Surya, the sun god, for help. But Surya too failed. The *yoginis* and Surya, ashamed of their failure and enraptured by Kashi, settled down in the shining city instead.

Finally, Shiva turned to Brahma himself, who agreed to help him. Brahma disguised himself as a sage and went to the king with an appeal. He wanted to perform ten horse rituals called *ashwamedhs*, he said, for which he needed the good king's help. Brahma thought that one such ritual was complicated enough; surely the king would blunder while trying to perform ten! But Raja Divodas managed to perform the ten rituals without a single mistake. The spot where he did so came to be known as Dashashwamedh. Brahma was unable to help Shiva, so the story of how Shiva returned to Kashi continues…

watch the rituals while locals crowd the steps to enjoy the music and lights. Despite what some guidebooks claim, this arti is neither traditional nor authentic. The artis that took place along the ghats were traditionally humble and homely affairs.

TEA BREAK

Favoured among locals for unwinding, Dashashwamedh has several **tea shops** high above the steps that serve refreshing tea and allow one to enjoy the ghat activity from a distance.

Ⓒ GANGA TEMPLE
She who rides the crocodile

What to Know On the raised square pavilion is a temple dedicated to the river Ganga. For locals, the Ganga is not just a goddess or a river, but also a benevolent mother figure. They call her fondly 'Ganga *maiyya*' (*maiyya* meaning 'mother').

What to See The temple is single-spired and studded with interesting sculptures, including two of Ganga *maiyya* as she is often shown, riding a crocodile. There are many temples devoted to Ganga in the city, including another small shrine, high on the steps above Dashashwamedh Ghat.

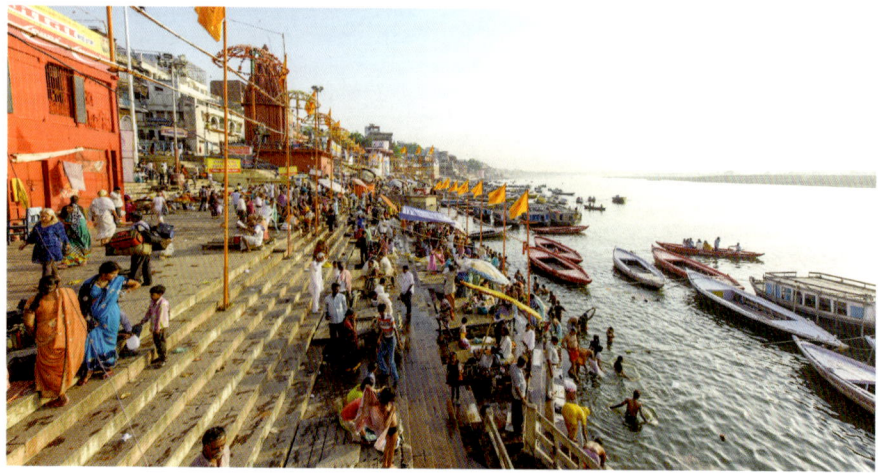

Temples overlooking Sitala Ghat.

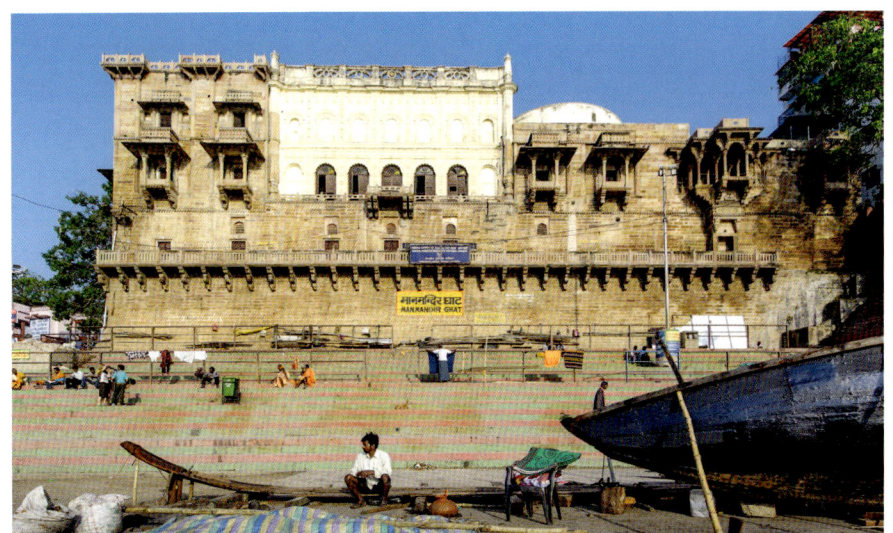

Man Mandir Ghat and palace, with one of the white astronomical instruments visible on the roof (top right).

Ⓓ SITALA TEMPLE
The Goddess of Protection
→ *Directions from Dashashwamedh Ghat to Sitala Temple: The elevated square temple is on the right-hand side of Dashashwamedh Ghat when facing the river.*

What to Know The goddess Sitala provides protection from smallpox, fevers and general illnesses. Her name means 'coolness'.

What to See Box-like on the exterior, the temple's interiors feature pleasant airy verandahs. Sitala sits on a throne in the central pavilion, wearing a red tinsel sari.

Surrounding her at the four corners are Dashashwamedheshwar or Shiva, Bhairav, and the goddesses Durga, Kali, Annapurna, Uma-Maheshwar (Shiva and his consort Parvati), and Santoshi Ma.

Ⓔ SITALA GHAT
Theatre and athletics
What to See A row of low pavilions line the steps of Sitala Ghat. These pavilions serve as staging areas for wrestling matches organized by local akharas, and for a few weeks in September or October, when the Ramlila takes place and scenes from Lord Ram's story are enacted.

THE STAGING OF THE RAMLILA
The Ramlila is the theatrical rendering of Ram's story, enacted over several nights in the season of Ashwin (September-October). It is a mobile performance, using multiple sites within a chosen neighbourhood, and spectacular, with flare lights, live music, glittering costumes, and towering effigies. Neighbourhoods across the city each put on their own Ramlila. Only pre-pubescent boys play the parts of the gods, who include the prince of Ayodhya, Ram, his wife Sita, his brothers Lakshman and Bharata, the monkey general Hanuman, the king of Ayodhya, Dashrath, and the demon of Lanka, Ravan. The boys are selected based on looks and declamation ability by a neighbourhood committee consisting of elder males, many of whom acted in the Ramlila as children and who now volunteer for various specialized jobs such as stage management and direction. The Ramlila is not a realistic production in the Western sense. It is understood as a symbolic representation of the gods' deeds. For more information on the history, philosophy and performance practice of the Ramlila, see page 125.

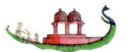

Ⓕ RAJENDRA PRASAD GHAT
Where horse rituals took place

→ *Directions from Sitala Ghat to Rajendra Prasad Ghat: Facing the river at Sitala Ghat, turn left and walk past Dashashwamedh Ghat, until you come to Rajendra Prasad Ghat, which is distinct for its large and smooth landing.*

What to Know In the past, Rajendra Prasad Ghat was called 'Ghora Ghat'. *Ghora* means 'horse', and they were brought from across the river in boats and traded at this spot. Also, in the second and third centuries A.D., horse sacrificial rituals took place here. In 1979, Ghora Ghat was named 'Rajendra Prasad Ghat' in memory of the first president of the Republic of India.

What to Do A classical music and dance festival called Ganga Mahotsav is held on Rajendra Prasad Ghat for three evenings during each season of Kartik (October or November), coinciding with the festival called *Kartik Purnima*. The paved landing serves as the stage, the audience sits on the steps above and the river forms the backdrop behind the performers. *Kartik Purnima* is the city's biggest river festival, held on the night of the full moon, when lamps are lit all along the riverfront and floated down the river.

Ⓖ MAN MANDIR GHAT AND OBSERVATORY
A futuristic palace

→ *Directions from Rajendra Prasad Ghat to Man Mandir Ghat & Observatory: The next ghat adjacent to Rajendra Prasad Ghat is Man Mandir, marked by the brown palace. The Observatory is on the roof of the palace. Reach the Observatory by going up the steps on Rajendra Prasad Ghat to the narrow lane lined by a vegetable market. Turn right into the small gate marked by an Archaeological Survey of India signboard.*

What to Know The Rajput king of Amber (present-day Rajasthan), Sawai Man Singh, built the imposing Man Mandir Palace in 1585. The palace's riverside façade boasts layer upon layer of carved stone windows.

The roof houses the futuristic astronomical instruments of the Hindu Observatory, built in 1710 by Man Singh's descendent, Sawai Jai Singh II.

What to See There are three halls, one through which you enter, the second with intricately carved walls and stained glass windows and a third that has been converted into a basic information centre with displays on the Amber dynasty and Jai Singh's interest in astronomy.

On the roof, monkeys are known to make the giant astronomical instruments their playground, so be extra careful, especially with your belongings, and do not hesitate to ask the palace staff to accompany you upstairs.

The impressive futuristic instruments on the roof include:

The *Dakshinobhitti Yantra* meant for measuring the altitude of astral bodies;

The *Samrat Yantra* used for measuring the time, declination and distance in time from the meridian (hour angle);

The *Narivalaya Dakshin Aur Uttar Gola* used for deducing whether an astronomical body is in the northern or southern hemisphere;

The *Chakr Yantra* meant for measuring the declination of the sun, moon, stars and their hour angle from the meridian;

The *Digansa Yantra* meant for measuring azimuth, or the angle telling the position of an astral body relative to a specific observation point.

Visitor Information: Open sunrise to sunset.

Ⓗ VISHWANATH GALI
Colourful crafts in a winding lane

→ *Directions from Man Mandir Palace to Vishwanath Gali: Turn right outside the palace and walk down the road away from the river. The brown gateway on the right, surrounded by tea and sweet shops with their large woks of steaming syrup, is the entrance to the Vishwanath Gali.*

What to Know Vishwanath Gali leads to Vishwanath Mandir, the city's most famous temple and a historically contested site. The original temple was built at the turn of the

Vishwanath Gali leads to Vishwanath Mandir, the city's most famous temple and a historically

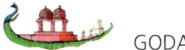
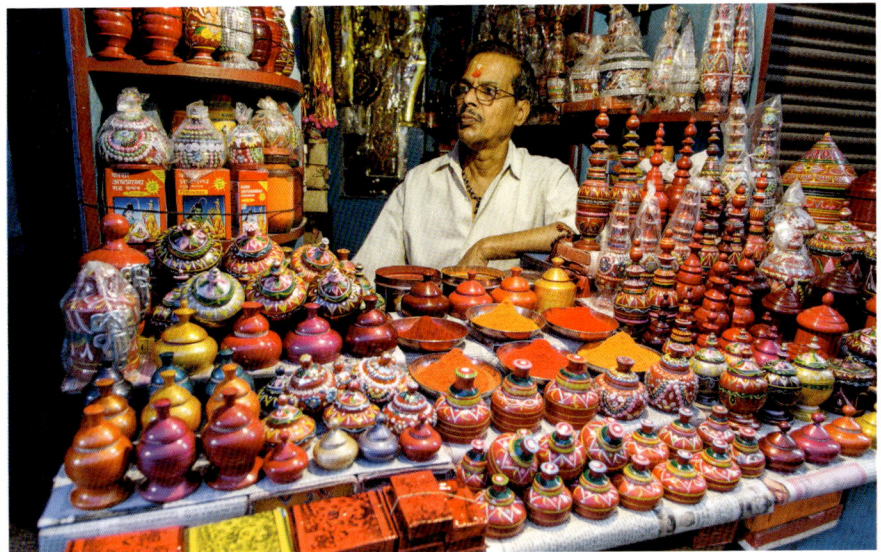

A woodwork shop in Vishwanath gali.

SHOPPING IN VISHWANATH GALI

Down the first part of Vishwanath Gali, there are shops that sell Indian and Western garments. The shops specialize in **silk**, but some sell cotton, woolen and synthetic fabrics as well. Many have tailors who can make garments to your size and design. Don't miss the spectacular silk saris and scarves in countless hues.

Wooden and stone handicrafts, including toys, figurines, god and goddesses, beads, carved boxes and chimes are also for sale here.

At the junction with the first lane leading left, there are four or five **supari shops**, marked by rows of colourful containers. Supari is an after-meal mouth freshener with digestive properties, which at times even acts as an intoxicant. Supari (areca nut of the palm areca catechu) is one of the ingredients that is used in pan or betel leaf. The other ingredients used in pan are *chuna* (slaked lime paste), *katha* (areca catechu heart-wood paste, an astringent and disinfectant, the main reason behind the redness in the mouth caused by pan), *gulkand* (rose-petal preserves), fruit preserves, and spices. Supari is added in pan, separately, or combined with fruit preserves, spices, nuts, and mint. The shops in Vishwanath gali make and sell their own combinations of supari, including the standard varieties. Walk past and shopkeepers are sure to call out to you, offering their latest exquisite creations. They are definitely worth a stop and a taste.

After the fabric and supari shops, stop by the **bangle shops**. Their interiors are lined with dazzling bangles of glass and metal of every size, colour and design, ranging in price from Rs. 10 to Rs. 500. Usually sold by the dozen, the bangles sold in Vishwanath Gali have immense appeal even to local Banarasis. The shopkeepers are experts at squeezing the joints of your hand together and easing on any set of bangles, no matter how small they seem.

At the lane's twist near the entrance of the Vishwanath Temple, there are several shops that sell prasad. Prasad consists of flowers – jasmine or marigold, loose or in garlands – sweets, and Ganga water to offer the deities within the temple.

Go straight past the first entrance to the temple to some **sculpture stores**. These feature sculptures of the gods in all sizes, mostly in marble, Chunar sandstone and brass.

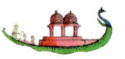

first millennium A.D. but thereafter it was repeatedly destroyed and rebuilt by various Hindu and Muslim rulers. Today, the site is shared by the Vishwanath Temple, built by Queen Ahilyabai of Indore in 1776 and the Gyan Vyapi Mosque, built by Aurangzeb in 1669. In 2004, there was a terrorist bombing at the Sankat Mochan Temple, in the south of the city. After this incident, the government stationed policemen at every entrance to the Vishwanath Temple, since it has become a potentially sensitive spot. It is interesting to talk to shopkeepers about how life here has changed since the terrorist attack and stricter vigilance has been enforced.

What to See Vishwanath Gali is a winding lane that features the handicrafts of Banaras such as gleaming silk and brocade, brightly painted wooden toys and figurines, glittering glass and metal bangles. The products are authentic and affordable.

When to Go Vishwanath Gali can be demanding, as colourful and tempting as it is. On special days such as Mondays (Shiva's day) it is packed with pilgrims visiting the Vishwanath Temple, who form a long queue near its entrance. On any evening, it is packed with shoppers. In the middle of a hot summer's day, however, the lane is sleepy and usually abandoned by shoppers. The shopkeepers sprawl quietly on the *gaddas* (cushions) inside their shops and leave shoppers undisturbed. The lane has radically different atmospheres at different times of the day and year. Afternoons are generally the least chaotic.

① VISHWANATH TEMPLE AND GYAN VYAPI MOSQUE
Sacred ground

→ *Directions to Vishwanath Temple and Gyan Vyapi Mosque: There are three public entrances into the temple-mosque complex. Gate 1 is a lane to the right where Vishwanath Gali twists and there are flowers and sweet shops. Also called 'Dhundi Raj', this is the most crowded entrance, so walk past it quickly. Follow the curve of the lane right, until you pass a small stairway and sculpture store on the left and come to Gate 4 on the right, also called 'Chhata Dwar'. Leave any electronics in a locker in one of the flower shops. Remember to take off your*

shoes here or further inside. After entering through the metal detectors, walk all the way around the high boundary wall of the Gyan Vyapi Mosque, to the temple.

What to Know It is an accepted fact that the Vishwanath Temple has been the most important Shiva shrine of Banaras for centuries. The first mention of it occurs in a text called *Kritya Kalpatru*, written by Lakshmidhar Bhatt circa 1110 A.D.

In fact, the present Vishwanath Temple is the fourth in a series that have been repeatedly destroyed and rebuilt. Qutb-ud-din Aibak destroyed Vishveshwara, as the temple was called, in 1194 A.D. Then Muhmud Shah Sharqi of Jaunpur moved the *linga* to the compound of another temple called Avimukteshwar in 1448 and built a mosque on its site. Sikandar Lodhi destroyed Avimukteshvar in 1490. In 1585 Narayanbhatta, a prominent scholar of Banaras, rebuilt the Vishwanath Temple with the help of his patron and one of Akbar's most trusted ministers, Todar Mal. In 1669,

SHOPPING

At the end of Kachauri gali is a row of shops that specialize in the **handmade *bahi khata***, a kind of notebook. These are traditionally used for bookkeeping. Many shopkeepers in modern stores still prefer to use a *bahi khata* for accounts, continuing the practice of their forefathers. The notebooks come in various sizes and thicknesses. They are bound with Japanese-style binding and covered with cardboard, pasted with red linen. The *bahi khata* originated in Rajasthan, where the covers are stitched slightly differently.

Across the street from the *bahi khatas* is the large 'Thakur Prasad' store. Thakur Prasad is an old Banarasi company that produces business diaries. The diaries are delightfully detailed, providing Hindu, Muslim and Gregorian dates for each day and extensive lists of the annual festivals. They are trilingual, using Hindi, Urdu and English. Armed with a *bahi khata* and a Thakur Prasad diary, you will be set for business in Banaras!

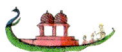

Aurangzeb destroyed the Todar Mal-built temple and constructed the Gyan Vyapi Mosque with minarets that were 71-metres high, leaving the back wall of the temple intact. Today, there are two mosques on the foundations of Todar Mal's Vishwanath Temple. Razia Sultana built the second during her reign between 1236 and 1240. The Gyan Vyapi Mosque gets its name from the Gyan Vyapi well in its compound, the 'well of wisdom', which was a part of the original temple, and in which, it is said, the original Vishwanath *linga* was hidden for some time. After Todar Mal's Vishwanath Temple was destroyed, its *linga* was probably sheltered in another temple, until the Maratha queen of Indore Ahilyabai Holkar built the Vishwanath Temple, that exists today, in 1776. She built it to mark the centre of Avimukteshwar, the holiest of the three pilgrimage routes.

A century later the Sikh ruler Maharaja Ranjit Singh had the spire gilded. Since then tourists have also referred to the temple as the 'Golden Temple'.

What to See There are several shrines in the temple complex. Vishwanath or Shiva occupies the central sanctum. The *linga* is typically covered with flowers, smeared with Shiva's favourite intoxicant bhang, and wet with Ganga water. Five ceremonies are performed daily, beginning with the *mangal arti* at 3am and ending with the *shringar arti* at 11pm. Though one of the most sacred temples, foreigners are not allowed inside the temple. The other shrines are of Gauri (a form of Shiva's consort Parvati), Vishnu, Kal Bhairav, Dandapani (a Yaksha diety), and Vigneshwara and Avimukta Vinayak (forms of Shiva's son Ganesh).

Ⓙ KACHAURI GALI AND KHOYA GALI
Milk specialities of Banaras

→ *Directions from Vishwanath gali to Kachauri gali: Beyond Vishwanath Temple, Vishwanath gali ends, emerging into two. Take the right lane to continue into Kachauri gali.*

What to Know You will know you have reached Kachauri gali when the air saturates with the rich smell of cooked milk. *Kachauris* are a kind of bread, a thicker version of the deep-fried *puri*. Kachauri gali is named after the fresh *kachauris* that are made and sold here. Khoya gali is another name for this lane because apart from *kachauris* there are shops that specialize in milk products such as lassi, *paneer* (a cheese made from splitting milk), *ghee* (clarified butter), and *khoya* (the oily residue left over after cooking milk).

Exiting Godaulia

Directions from Kachauri gali to Godaulia: Retrace your way back through Vishwanath gali and turn right down the main Godaulia shopping road to Godaulia crossing. Or continue down Kachauri gali past the Thakur Prasad store until you reach the Chauk road. Turn left on the Chauk road and walk back to Godaulia crossing (approximately fifteen minutes) or take a downhill rickshaw ride (approximately ten minutes).

A TYPICAL BANARASI BREAKFAST
Banarasis consider **kachauris** a specialty of their city. A Banarasi breakfast typically consists of *kachauris* with vegetables and **jalebis** (deep fried ringlets of flour dipped in sugar syrup). In the mornings before the streets fill up with traffic, every neighbourhood sweet shop and dhaba is filled with Banarasis eagerly consuming fresh *kachauris* and *jalebi*.

All along the length of Kachauri gali until its end where it meets the perpendicular lane called 'Rani Kua', the roadside shops serve *kachauri-jalebi*. They typically serve it only in the mornings, and before 8am, since Banarasis like to make an early start. It is a marvellous Banarasi experience to visit Kachauri gali in the early morning and breakfast with Banarasis on fresh, hot, fragrant *kachauri-jalebi*.

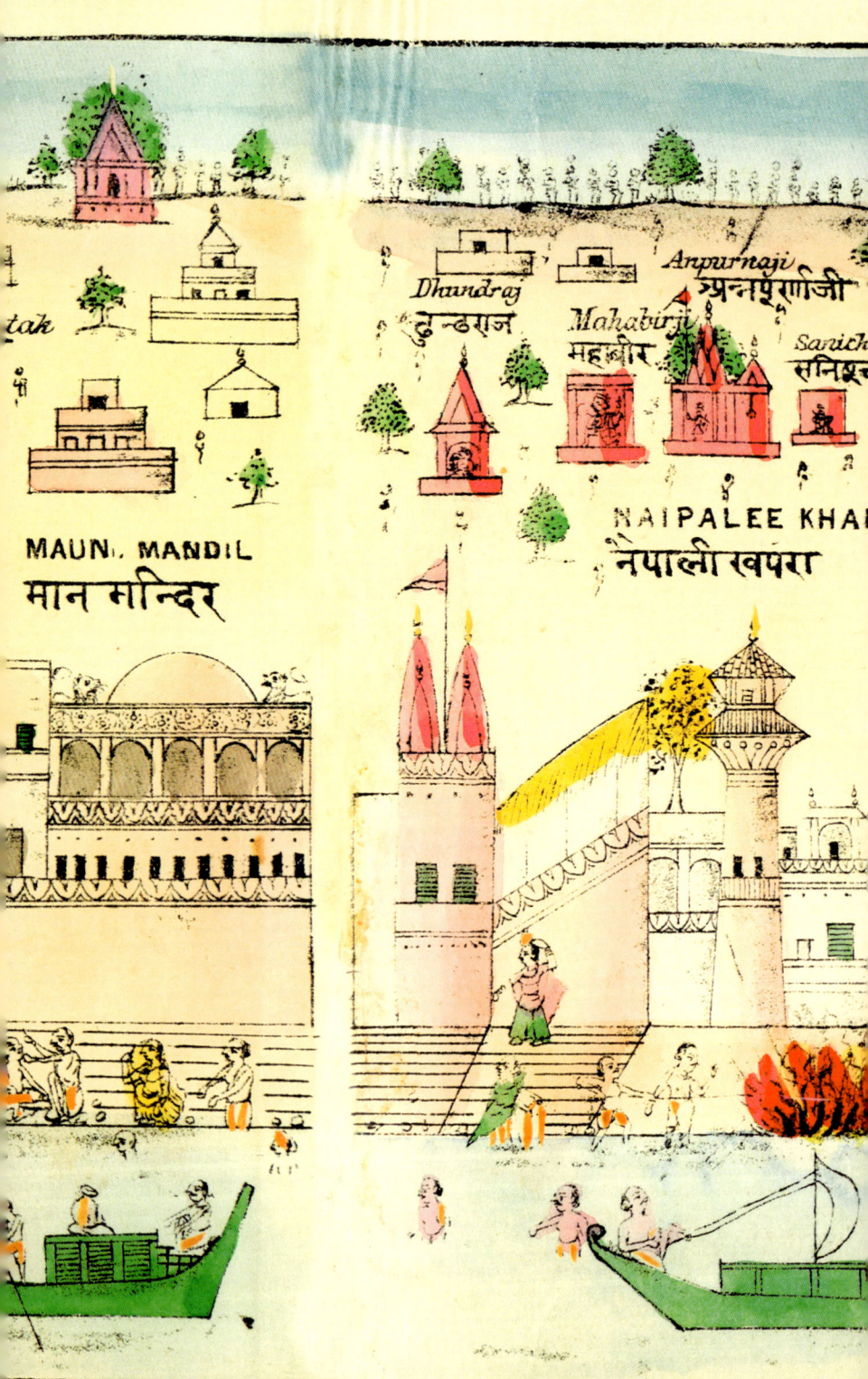

tak

Dhundraj
ढुन्ढराज

Mahabirji
महावीर

Anpurnaji
अन्नपूर्णाजी

Sanich
सनिश्च

MAUN. MANDIL
मान मन्दिर

NAIPALEE KHA
नेपाली खपरा

3

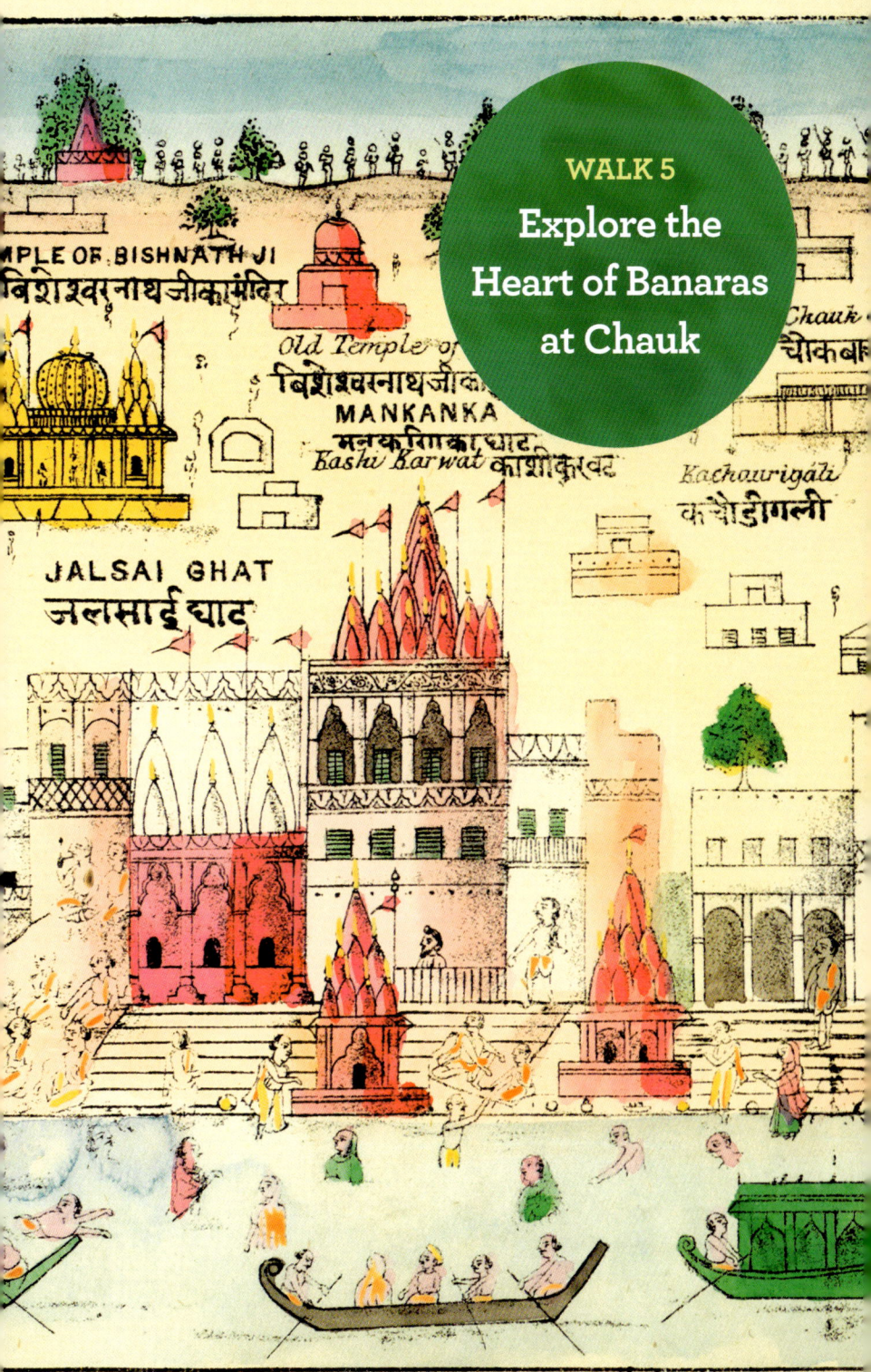

TEMPLE OF BISHNATH JI
बिशेश्वरनाथजीकामंदिर

Old Temple of
बिशेश्वरनाथजी

MANKANKA
मनकर्णिका घाट
Kashi Karwat काशीकरवत

Chauk
चौकब

Kachaurigali
कचौड़ीगली

JALSAI GHAT
जलसाई घाट

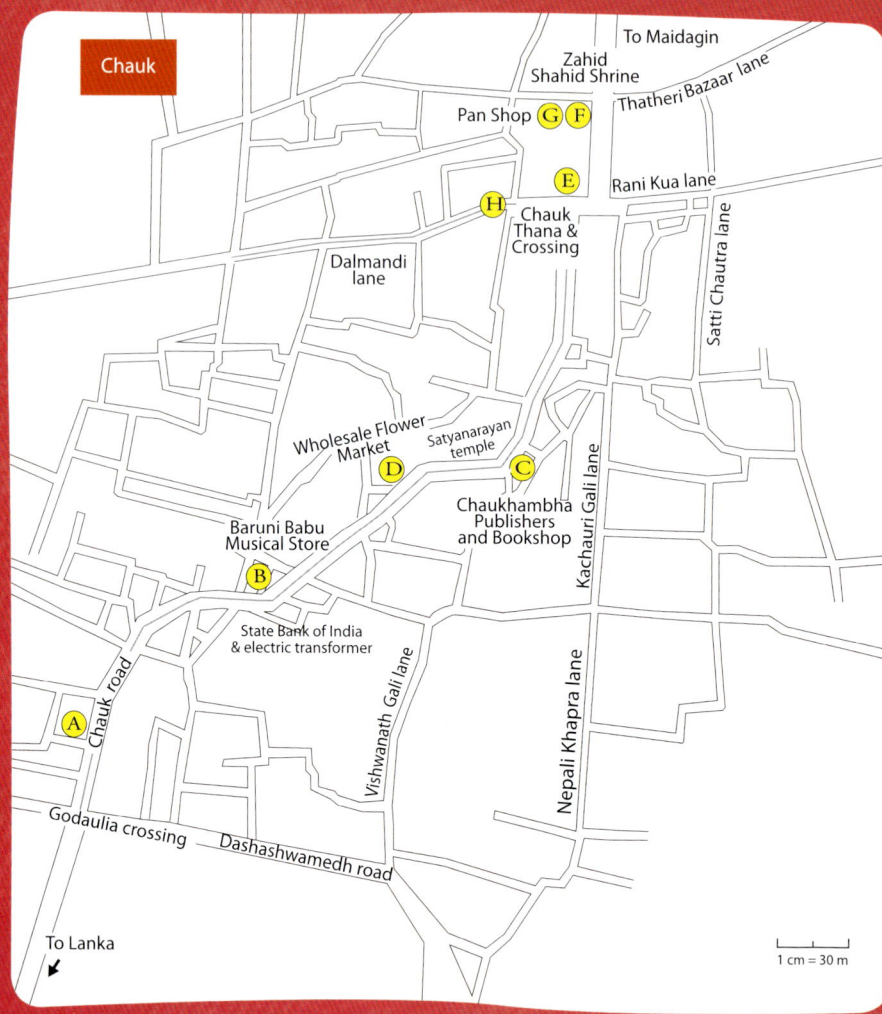

Chauk

To Maidagin

Zahid Shahid Shrine

Thatheri Bazaar lane

Pan Shop G F

E Rani Kua lane

H Chauk Thana & Crossing

Satti Chautra lane

Dalmandi lane

Wholesale Flower Market

Satyanarayan temple

D

C

Baruni Babu Musical Store

Chaukhambha Publishers and Bookshop

Kachauri Gali lane

B

State Bank of India & electric transformer

Vishwanath Gali lane

Nepali Khapra lane

A

Chauk road

Godaulia crossing

Dashashwamedh road

To Lanka

1 cm = 30 m

Walk the main square of the business district with its distinct market place, from a famous musical store to an ancient pan shop, from a wholesale flower market to the busy Dalmandi lane.

THINGS TO SEE
- Old shops with intruments and books
- Wholesale flower market
- Lanes representing four goals of life
- Popular Sufi shrine
- Historic pan shop
- Busy Dalmandi lane

ALLOW
Two to three hours

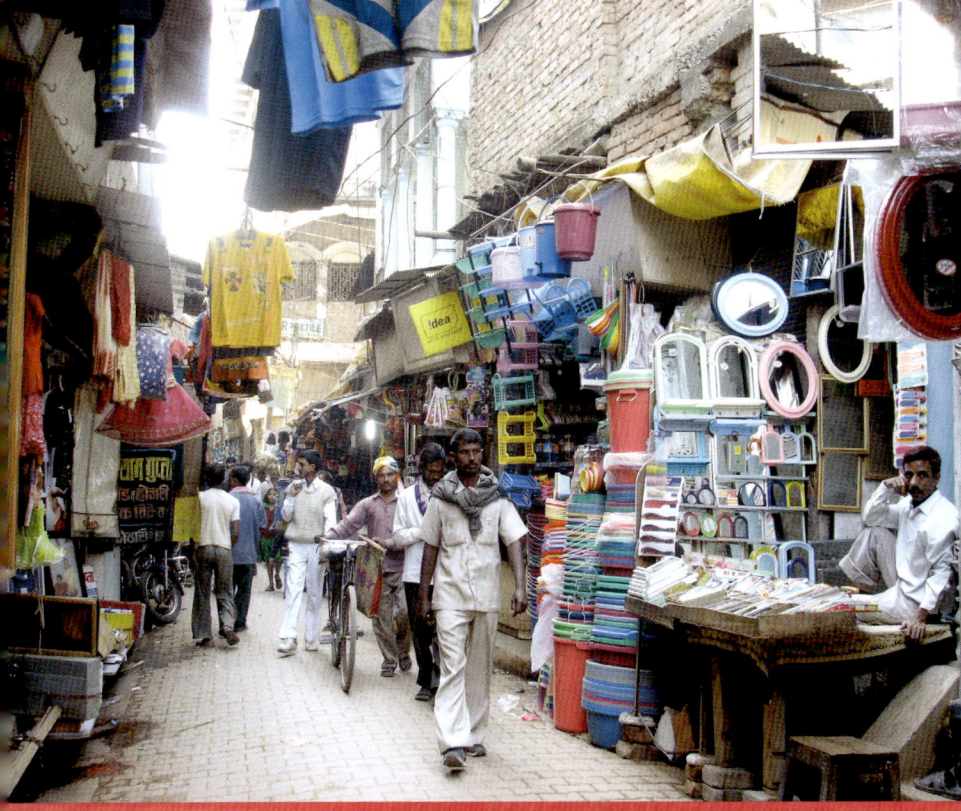

Dalmandi lane with its variety of shops.

WALK ITINERARY
Chauk Road l Baruni Babu Musical Store l Chaukhambha Publishers and Bookshop l Wholesale Flower Market l Chauk Thana and Crossing l Zahid Shahid Shrine l Pan Shop of Prahlad Prasad Chaurasiya l Dalmandi

GETTING AROUND CHAUK
From Godaulia crossing, the Assi-Godaulia road continues northwards. This road goes up the Chauk hill to the summit and the central crossroads of Chauk, which is marked by the Chauk police station (Chauk *thana*). The road links on the east to the riverfront ghats of Dashashwamedh, Rajendra Prasad, Man Mandir, Mir, Lalita, Manikarnika and Scindhia ghats through a maze of lanes, the main ones being Brahmanal, Rani Kua, and Thatheri galis. To the west of the north-south Chauk Road are the main lanes of Dalmandi and Raja Darwaza.

It is best either to walk or take a rickshaw. Note that since the Chauk Road goes over a hill, rickshaw pullers usually dismount at the incline and pull their rickshaws for a short while. Many Banarasis also typically dismount at this point and walk alongside the rickshaw, in order to make the pulling easier.

THE HISTORY OF CHAUK

All old Indian cities have a 'chauk' (literally, a square) or a downtown business district, a nucleus of sorts. The Chauk of Banaras is a marketplace with a wide range of products. Within the lanes, there are shops of sweets, spices, dried fruits and nuts, perfumes, medicines, silk, jute and plastic, metal objects and everything else imaginable. The Chauk of Banaras is unique because it is also the location of the city's main cremation ground and what earlier used to be its courtesans' district.

The Chauk came into being when the ancient fort at Rajghat was destroyed in 1194 AD and the city shifted southwards over the following centuries. Forests were razed to make way for habitation. Then, wealthy individuals – merchant-bankers and royalty from other parts of India – constructed mansions and temples around which smaller houses were built, the entire block protected by gates at night. And so we find mention of the names Rani Kua, 'the well of the queen', Phatak Sukh Lal Shah, 'Sukh Lal Shah's gateway' and Raja Darwaza, 'the gates of the king'. The names of the neighbourhoods and lanes in Chauk record their own history.

In popular terminology, Chauk is called pakka. Pakka means 'solid' or 'constructed' and is in contrast to kachcha, which means made of mud, thatch or tile. In the past, Banarasis used pakka to refer to the central area of Chauk and kachcha for the rest of the city, which was forested and then cleared for agriculture. They considered pakka to be significant and sacred and kachcha peripheral and non-sacred. The terminology is still used today, particularly by those concerned with the pakka mahal (built quarters) of Chauk, but no longer holds practical significance.

In the pakka mahal, buildings are two to three-storeys high and stand wall-to-wall. Wind your way through the busy sandstone-paved lanes, under rows of latticed balconies, some preserved, others on the verge of disintegration. Glance through elaborately carved doorways into the old 'inward-facing' Banaras houses: they all have courtyards encircled by rooms. Courtyards and ground-floor rooms of residences are often used for conducting business-related activities. The upper floors serve as private spaces for women and domestic activities. There are interesting connections between the geography and activities of the place, understood intimately by those who live here and do business, who visit for religious purposes, or come to bathe, stroll and relax. As a visitor, one can see glimpses of these connections.

Ⓐ CHAUK ROAD
Old shops and unique treasures

→ *Directions from Godaulia crossing to the Chauk Road: The Chauk Road is the road leading north from the Godaulia crossing, continuing in the same direction as the Assi-Godaulia road.*

What to See The road that leads over the Chauk hill was built towards the end of the 19th century along with the other main streets of Banaras. It is an amazingly busy road, crowded with bullock carts and SUVs, flashy new showrooms and tiny shops that are decades old, stocking silk, ayurvedic medicines, musical instruments and books. These occupy the ground-level floors of lofty and exquisite old buildings.

As you walk down the road, you realize that there is something magical about the rhythm of people and their commerce, in the close, uninterrupted row of shops. You could set up a household from shopping here or find anything you might need for any occasion. There are the everyday things for sale, like cotton clothes and footwear, and there are things that seem extraordinary, like silks, framed pictures of the gods, and savoury snacks piled high on carts all along the road.

In the middle of the intense activity you can find an uncanny sense of relaxation. Maybe this is because this is an old-fashioned market, and the people running it seem determined not to change even while they produce change through the goods they sell.

B BARUNI BABU MUSICAL STORE
Intricate instruments
→ *Directions from Chauk Road to Baruni Babu Musical Store: The tiny shop, difficult to spot, is on the left-hand side after the road's first major curve. On the opposite side of the road is a huge electric transformer and the State Bank of India.*

What to See Musical stores include the famous old Baruni Babu. Step inside, perch on the wooden bench kept for customers, and find yourself surrounded by shelves of tablas, harmoniums, violins, sitars, sarangis, and guitars, new and shining, or rickety and loose-hinged, waiting to be repaired. The shop doubles as a workshop, so if you are lucky, you may get to watch a sitar being created out of wood and wire.

C CHAUKHAMBHA PUBLISHERS AND BOOKSHOP
Original publishers of Banaras
→ *Directions from Baruni Babu Musical Store to Chaukhamba Publishers and Bookshop: Continuing northwards on the Chauk Road, Chaukhamba is on the right, across the street, after the Baruni Babu Musical Store.*

What to See There have been several major publishers in Banaras in the past including Chaukhambha, Motilal Banarasidas and Vishwavidyalay Prakashan, which brought out a special series of books in Sanskrit and Hindi. Many publishers still have their outlets on Chauk Road. The majority stock textbooks for schools and colleges, but retain a charming old-world atmosphere replete with dust, paper, polished wood and cotton cushions. Chaukhambha, Motilal Banarasidas and Vishwavidyalaya publishers, however, have extensive lists in stock, and you can spend a happy hour browsing through their Sanskrit literary and Indology collections, including topics such as astrology, music, Vedic grammar, and Vedic mathematics.

D WHOLESALE FLOWER MARKET
→ *Directions from Chaukhambha Bookshop to the flower market: Continue northwards down the Chauk Road. The entrance to the flower market is on your left just before the climb levels off, through a covered tunnel-like entrance.*

What to See The largest courtyard is the site for one of Banaras' busiest wholesale flower market, where dozens of flower vendors offer their wares: elegant white stalks of tuberose (Rajnigandha or 'fragrance of the night'), pink and blue lotuses (Kamal), marigolds galore (Genda), and fragrant bunches of jasmine (Rat Ki Rani or 'queen of the night'). Retailers buy loose flowers and garlands from this market to sell outside temples all over the city.

E CHAUK THANA AND CROSSING
The four goals of life
→ *Directions from Chaukhambha Publishers and Bookshop to Chauk Thana and Crossing: Outside the bookshop, facing the road, turn right and continue north up the Chauk Road until you reach the busy Chauk crossing. The red, fort-style building within the compound is the Chauk police station.*

What to See The colonial fort-style Chauk Thana was the most important police centre in the past, after the Kotwali police station in Maidagin. It looks like a medieval fort, together with a drawbridge.

From the Chauk crossing you will notice four lanes going in different directions. According to Banarasis, Vishwanath Gali, winding south to Godaulia, represents dharma or religious duty because it leads to temples. Thatheri Bazaar, going east to the river, represents artha or business, as in the sari business and the sale of other products. Dalmandi, heading west away from the river, represents kama or pleasure, as in courtesans, food and drinks, and perfumes. Finally Brahmanal, leading to Manikarnika, the shamshan or cremation ghat, represents moksha or release from the cycle of birth and death. In this sense, the Chauk crossing is considered to be the confluence of dharma, artha, kama and moksha, which are the four goals of life in Hindu thought.

F ZAHID SHAHID SHRINE
Blessings for all

→ *Directions from Chauk Thana to Zahid Shahid shrine: Standing outside the police station facing the road, the Zahid Shahid shrine is on the left. It is a single, small room with steps leading up to it and an open front.*

What to Know Worshippers of all religions come here every Thursday. There is an urs ceremony annually, commemorating the death of the pir, with qawwali singing and worship.

Visitors' information: Enter the shrine only with your shoes off and placed below the steps (not on them or touching any part of the shrine), and with your head covered.

G PAN SHOP OF PRAHLAD PRASAD CHAURASIYA
Betel leaves with a history

→ *Directions from Zahid Shahid shrine to Prahlad Prasad Chaurasiya's pan shop: Facing the crossing outside the shrine, the pan shop is on the right.*

What to Know Between the Zahid Shahid shrine and the wall of the Chauk Thana is a picturesque old pan shop. The signboard above it reads, in Hindi: 'Ancient pan shop of Banaras: pan for all auspicious occasions; pan of all designs; pan of gold and silver leaf. Prahlad Prasad Chaurasiya (awardee of the President of India).' The 'Special Pan' available here is delectable, covered with silver leaf, fastened with a clove (laung), and offered graciously on a toothpick. Inside this famous old shop, the panwala (seller of pan) sits in the typical fashion, cross-legged before a low table with a metal surface. His ingredients are stored in a special casket called a pandan. Others are spread out on his table or stacked on a shelf next to him. He uses a red cloth to wipe each pan leaf carefully.

What to See On the walls of Prahlad Prasad Chaurasiya's shop are black-and-white photographs of Rameshwar Prasad Chaurasiya, his father and the original owner of the shop, meeting important politicians, including Lal Bahadur Shastri, the second prime minister of India and an important figure in India's Independence Movement.

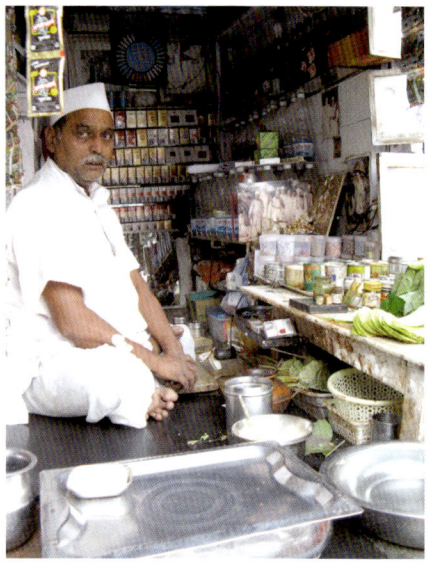

Prahlad Prasad Chaurasiya in his pan shop.

Next to his shop is a stone bathtub-like vessel that he has protected from being misused, broken or thrown out. The date etched on the side is 1928. There are very few of these vessels left in Banaras. They were used to hold drinking water for passing cows or horses that belonged to the city's milkmen and elite.

PAN

Pan is betel leaf wrapped around several ingredients. It acts as a breath freshener, digestive and mild stimulant. Banarasis enjoy chewing it at odd hours of the day and with extra enthusiasm on special occasions such as concerts and festivals. If you meet a Banarasi who is finding it difficult to speak, it is because his mouth is filled with pan. It produces a red juice when chewed. The ingredients in pan include supari (areca nut), which is also eaten separately, chuna (slaked lime paste), katha (areca catechu heart-wood paste, an astringent and disinfectant, the main reason behind the redness in the mouth), gulkand (rose petal preserves), fruit preserves, and spices. There are special wholesale markets in the city for pan leaves and ingredients.

What to Do If you are lucky, you will get to catch Prahlad ji, wearing a white kurta-pajama and cap, sitting at his shop (his son also runs the shop today). Chat with him and he will expound on the shop's key role in the Indian freedom struggle. In the decades before India's independence in 1947, Congress leaders who lived in Banaras or visited the city would exchange news by sending each other notes hidden in the pan made by Prahlad ji's father.

Ⓗ **DALMANDI**
The old courtesans' lane
→ *Directions from Prahlad Prasad Chaurasiya's pan shop to Dalmandi: Walk past the Chauk Thana, keeping it to your right. The first lane to your right, leading west, is Dalmandi.*
What to See Dalmandi, leading west from the Chauk crossing, is a retail market where a whole range of factory-made products are sold, from shoes to kitchen utensils. Particularly interesting are the shops that

sell Islam-related books, pamphlets, caps for worship and images of the Ka'ba in Mecca. There is a mosque further down the street.

Just as you enter Dalmandi, the first lane on your right is a market called Nariyal Bazaar or 'coconut market'. Here you can find paper and tinsel garlands and ornaments that are used in weddings.

What to See Dalmandi used to be the street of courtesans. They would sit at windows high above the street, suggestively obscured. Inside the ornate interiors, they would dance, wearing the finest silks woven in the lanes of Madanpura. The high society of Banaras would saunter in, savoring the most delectable Banarasi pan at the shops below. The lane would be scented with subtle and sweet perfumes and strains of music would float in and out of the windows.

Exiting Dalmandi: The simplest way back to the Chauk Thana is to turn around and retrace your steps down the Dalmandi lane.

The Shia Muslims of Dalmandi

Over 90 per cent of the Muslims in Banaras belong to the Sunni sect. Historically, there have been only a couple of neighbourhoods in the city where Shia Muslims live, and Dalmandi is one of these. The sign of this is the fact that the Shia Muslims of Dalmandi celebrate Muharram differently from the Sunni Muslims of other neighbourhoods. Muharram is the first month of the Islamic calendar. It is a period of mourning that commemorates the martyrdom of Hussain, the grandson of Mohammed, on the battlefield. After Hussain was killed by Yazid I on the tenth day of Muharram (a day called 'Ashura'), his family and followers were taken captive and held in Damascus.

The Shias of Banaras incorporate rituals into their Muharram celebrations in remembrance of Hussain's suffering. These include fasting, self-flagellation with swords and chains and running over hot coals. They also take out a winding procession of a white horse meant to represent Hussain's horse Duldul, who survived his master's martyrdom. Sunni celebrations do not incorporate such rituals to the same degree, or they do not incorporate them at all. Shias also sing in a beautiful genre called 'Marsiyah' during Muharram. A marsiyah is an elegy, originally in Arabic, in Banaras composed in Urdu or Hindustani and even in the local language Bhojpuri. Marsiyah is full of imagery of mourning and death. Banarasi Muslims cannot resist poetry and performance and marsiyah is very popular in Banaras. There have been Hindu poets in Banaras who composed marsiyahs as well.

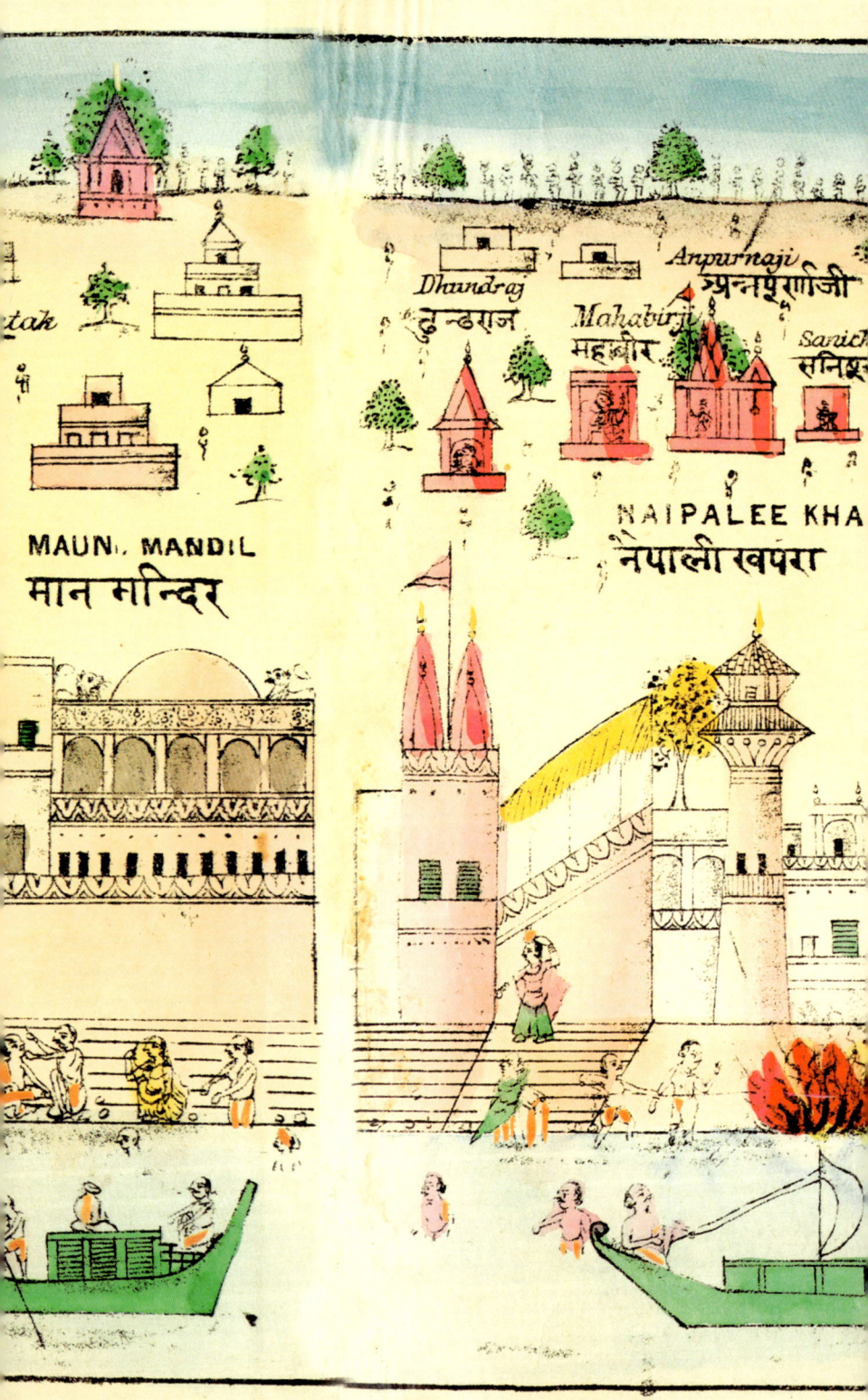

Dhundraj
ढुन्ढराज

Mahabirji
महाबीर

Anpurnaji
अन्नपूर्णाजी

Sanich
सनिश्च

MAUN. MANDIL
मान मन्दिर

NAIPALEE KHA
नेपाली खपरा

tak

3

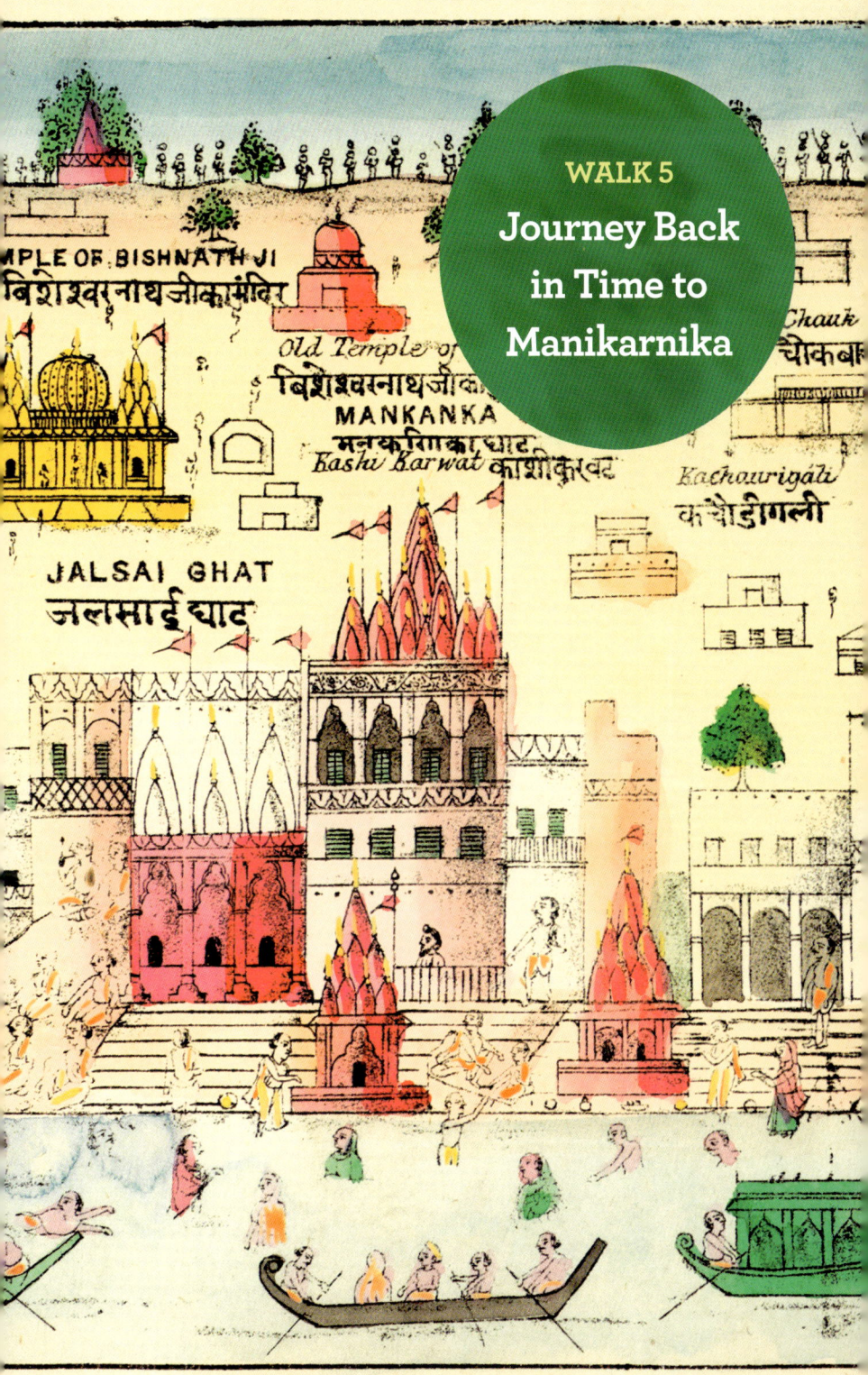

WALK 5

Journey Back in Time to Manikarnika

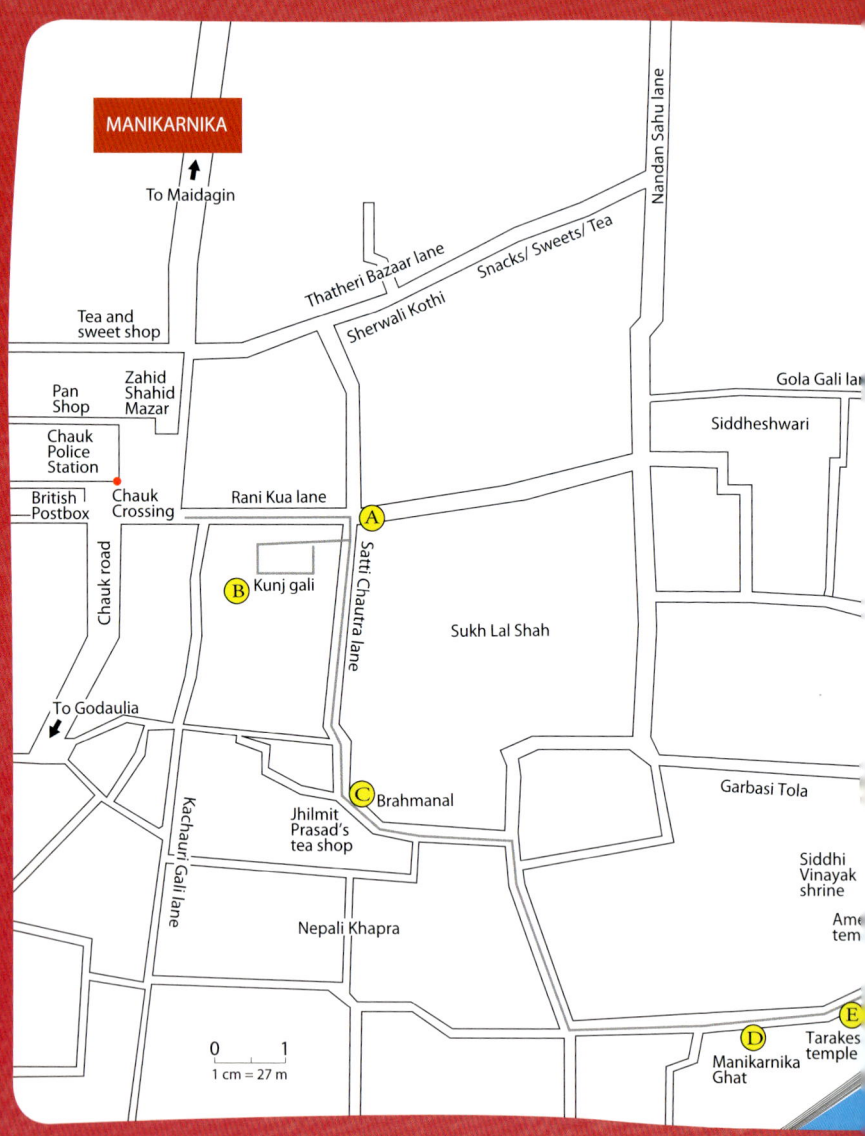

MANIKARNIKA

To Maidagin

Thatheri Bazaar lane

Snacks/ Sweets/ Tea

Nandan Sahu lane

Sherwali Kothi

Tea and
sweet shop

Gola Gali lan

Pan
Shop

Zahid
Shahid
Mazar

Siddheshwari

Chauk
Police
Station

British
Postbox

Chauk
Crossing

Rani Kua lane

Chauk road

Satti Chautra lane

A

B Kunj gali

Sukh Lal Shah

To Godaulia

Kachauri Gali lane

C Brahmanal

Garbasi Tola

Jhilmit
Prasad's
tea shop

Siddhi
Vinayak
shrine

Nepali Khapra

Ame
tem

E

0   1

D Tarakes
temple

1 cm = 27 m

Manikarnika
Ghat

From the summit of the old business district, walk
through busy lanes to the city's main silk market
and cremation ground, visiting a water reservoir, Lord Vishnu's
riverside meditation spot, and temples, all mentioned in
ancient texts.

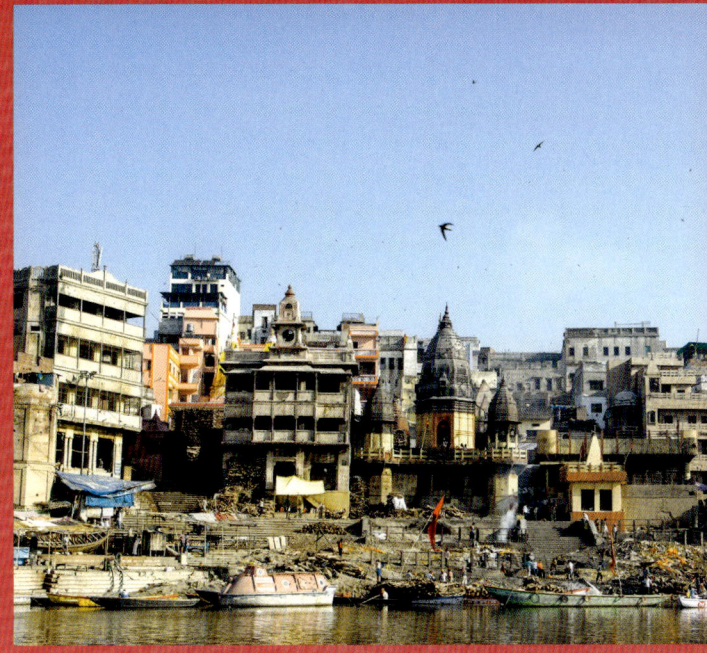

Manikarnika Ghat is the most important cremation ghat of Banaras.

THINGS TO SEE
- Markets for betel nut and silk
- Famous cremation ghat
- Palace of Doms
- Legendary reservoir carved by Lord Vishnu
- Mughal balcony for musicians

ALLOW
Three to four hours

WALK ITINERARY
Satti Chautra lane I Kunj Gali I Brahmanal I Manikarnika Ghat I Tarakeshvar Temple I 'Kashi Karvat' Temple I Manikarnika Kund & Vishnu Charanpaduka I Amethi Temple I Siddhi Vinayak I Alwar Temple I Manikarnikeshvar Temple

GETTING AROUND MANIKARNIKA
South of the Chauk Thana, the first lane leading east to the river branches further into the lanes called Kachauri Gali, Satti Chautra and Brahmanal. Brahmanal winds eastward to the city's main cremation ghat, Manikarnika. To the north of this area are the lanes Rani Kua and Thatheri Bazaar. To the south is Vishwanath Gali.

arnikeshvar
e

r temple

Manikarnika
Kund & Vishnu
Charanpaduka

Kashi Karvat
temple

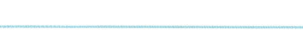

THE HISTORY OF MANIKARNIKA

Manikarnika is the name of the city's most important cremation ghat, located on a northern section of the riverbank. As the Sanskrit saying goes, *kashyam marnam mukti*, or 'Death in Kashi means liberation'. This liberation, or moksha, is liberation from samsara, the material world, with its endless cycles of death and re-birth.

But how does Banaras provide moksha?

In religious thought, Kashi represents the cosmos. Kashi's geography is divided into a series of concentric pilgrimage routes. In traversing this sacred geography, the pilgrim traverses the universe.

Just as it represents the cosmos, Kashi also represents the body. Kashi is *purush* or the primordial man, whose feet lie at Assi, head at Rajghat and loins at Manikarnika. And so Kashi represents an overlapping of micro-cosmos (the body) and macro-cosmos (the cosmos).

Death is central to this religious symbolism. Because Kashi lies outside ordinary time and space, it also lies outside the laws of karma that dictate the causal effects, positive and negative, of one's actions in a lifetime. Anyone who dies in Kashi, saint or sinner, will be forgiven of his or her sins. The whole of Kashi is considered *mahashamshan* or 'great cremation ground'. The cremation pyres at Manikarnika burn continuously. This symbolizes perpetual destruction and creation.

Kashi contains all of space and time. Likewise, it contains the four goals of human existence – *kama* (pleasure), *artha* (profit), *dharma* (duty) and *moksha* (liberation). Manikarnika Ghat and the surrounding lanes embody this quality of Kashi. Alongside somber funeral pyres, life continues. This juxtaposition of life and death might unnerve you on your first visit to Manikarnika. But it is characteristic of Shiva himself and of the ethos his city believes in, which is openness and freedom. The supreme virtue in Banaras is not singly pleasure, profit, duty, or liberation but a balance of all.

Death is also big business in Banaras. In the dense lanes that surround Manikarnika Ghat, live and work the funeral priests, called pandits, pandas and purohits. We must remember that they are professionals doing a job. Pandits are learned people (as defined in English dictionaries) and pandas are ritual specialists. Purohits are worship specialists. They spend years in training and do not earn that much, given their specialized training. All their work is in Sanskrit and esoteric for everyone else even in their own society. Banaras is the place with the greatest concentration of such specialists, and has been for millennia a centre of Sanskrit learning in ritual manuals and procedures.

(A) SATTI CHAUTRA LANE
Goddess Satti's neighbourhood

→ *Directions from Chauk police station to Satti Chautra: Walk down the lane directly opposite the Chauk Thana leading east, called Rani Kua ('well of the queen,' named after a well that existed along the lane). Take the second right down a lane called Satti Chautra.*

What to Know The long lane, Satti Chautra, is named after a small, old temple referred to locally as 'Satti Ma ka mandir' (the temple of the goddess Satti). At the start of Satti Chautra, notice the silk shops with 'porches' lined with white cushions, called *gaddis*. These shops are points of negotiation for sari weavers and sari wholesalers. They spill over from an old sari bazaar called Kunj Gali tucked between Rani Kua and Satti Chautra.

SHOPPING

Along the busy lane opposite the Chauk Thana, called Rani Kua, there are fascinating shops. At its sprawling entrance, there are elaborately arranged stalls of fresh **juice**, stores of **namkeen** (savoury snacks) and shops displaying saffron and golden **stoles for cremations**. At the corner where Rani Kua begins are shops of **dried fruit**, fragrances called *itr* (exquisite concentrated **perfumes** made from flowers and sandalwood) and shops of **supari** (betel nut) and **churan** (an after-meal digestive made of fruit and spices). The shopkeepers, dressed in the old-fashioned Banarasi style of crisp white dhoti-kurta, crack betel nuts into bite-size pieces as they wait for customers.

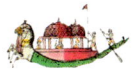
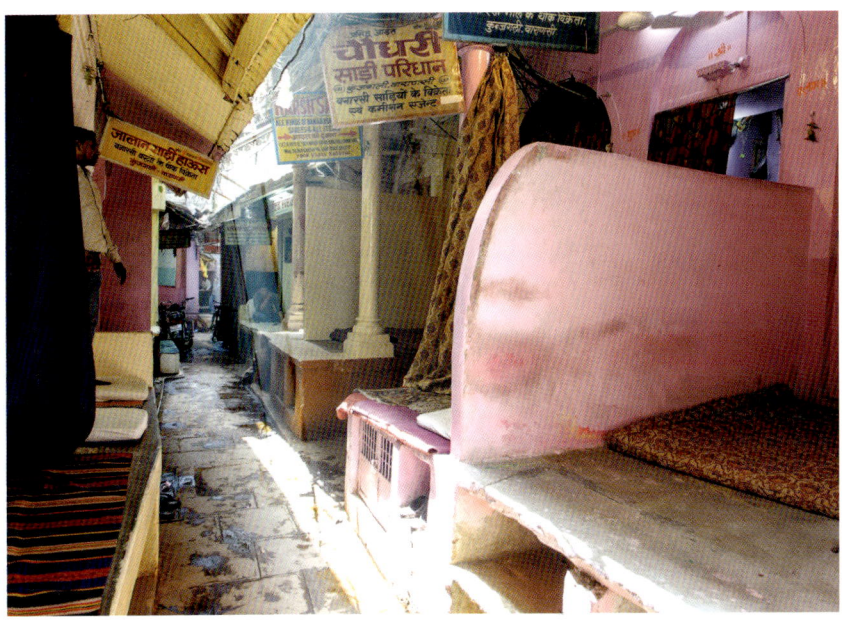

Silk shops in Kunj Gali.

Ⓑ KUNJ GALI
The city's old silk market

→ *Directions from Satti Chautra to Kunj Gali: Step through the first doorway-cum-stairway on the right along Satti Chautra lane, leading west. Once inside Kunj Gali, there are exits in all directions. To return to Satti Chautra, circle or retrace your way back.*

What to Know Kunj Gali, bordered on three sides by other streets, is arranged in a tight grid built exclusively for the trade of silk. The shops are also called *gaddis* after the white padding on which weavers and shopkeepers negotiate. The most distinctive and intriguing feature of these silk shops is the cushion facing the street. As you walk through, you may feel you are walking through the hallway of a house. The shops have spaces for several phases of deal-making. The outer *gaddi* serves as the preliminary place for interaction and the inner *gaddi* for final negotiations.

The naming of a street or neighbourhood after a temple or important personage is typical of old Banaras.

How interesting that during these careful processes, the artisans, shopkeepers and customers are supposed to sit comfortably on cushions and feel as relaxed as possible.

Weavers from the neighbourhoods of Madanpura, Adampura, Jaitpura, Lallapura and Khojwa walk through Kunj Gali with bundles of silk wrapped in white linen on their heads to sell. All entrances to the market are marked by tunnelled doorways, as all Banarasi neighbourhoods were protected in the past by gates that were closed at night.

The shops in Kunj Gali are both retailers and wholesalers. You may see a group of tourists being led through the lanes and welcomed into a shop. A network of middlemen work to bring tourists to shops here, for a small payment made to them by the shopkeeper. The wholesalers sell to local, national, and international outlets, with the main *gaddi* owner often travelling to far off destinations with bundles of

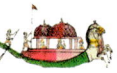

samples to convince new customers and keep old ones happy.

Talk to any of the businessmen within the market and they will tell you that the market of Kunj Gali is special because the business transactions are conducted largely on the basis of *vishwas* (trust), although each transaction is also written down carefully in the businessman's *bahi khata*. Several stages of negotiation take place between the wholesaler, the customer, the head weaver and the middleman. Each depends on the other for the entire transaction to take place successfully. Products are usually ordered in bulk in advance. The payments, which often exceed lakhs of rupees, are made against IOU's or credit notes, all in the old indigenous system. Historians have noted that Indian capitalism and trade has worked for centuries through this system of trust and an individual's word. In such a system, *vishwas* is vital for success.

Most of the shops have a history of at least half a century. The ownership of each shop passes from father to son. Older shopkeepers here readily reminisce about the evolution of the sari business in their lifetimes. Before the turn of the 20th century, silk products were made exclusively for the elite and royalty. Real gold and silver thread (*zari*) was woven into silk and gems often used to decorate each piece of fabric. The sari was longer and wider. Around the turn of the century, the middle class began to demand Banarasi silk products. Gold and silver *zari* gave way to metal thread with gold or silver plating, and plastic beads replaced gems.

Ⓒ BRAHMANAL

The winding way to the cremation ghat
→ *Directions from Satti Chautra to Brahmanal: Continue in the same direction as before (south) down Satti Chautra until the lane passes under a tunnelled doorway and ends at a tea shop and vegetable market. The perpendicular lane facing you, running east-west, is Brahmanal. Turn left (east) down Brahmanal to reach Manikarnika Ghat.*

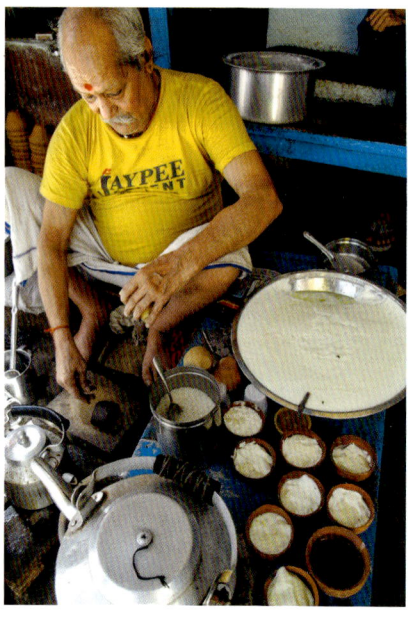

Tea and fresh yoghurt at Jhilmit Prasad's tea shop in Brahmanal.

What to Know Brahmanal is the lane representing *moksha* or liberation and leads to Manikarnika Ghat, the city's main cremation ground. Through this winding lane, lined with shops, residences, and a vegetable market, funeral processions pass

JHILMIT PRASAD'S TEA SHOP
At the junction of Satti Chautra and Brahmanal sits a delightful **tea shop** (see map on page 84). Jhilmit Prasad, the original owner, was a wrestler who worked out in the akharas of Banaras and won prizes for his wrestling. His son Bablu runs the shop today. Photographs of the city's most popular wrestlers, including Jhilmit Prasad himself, line the back wall. The shop serves tea and yoghurt (with or without sugar), which make excellent snacks for a tired walker. Its location and cosy benches make it the perfect spot for catching your breath, eavesdropping on conversations and observing neighbourhood goings-on.

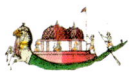

frequently, accompanied by chants of *Ram nam satya hai* ('the name of Ram is the Truth'). The body of the deceased, swathed in yellow cloth and laid on a bamboo stretcher, is held on the shoulders of male members of the family and friends.

Ⓓ MANIKARNIKA GHAT
The world-famous cremation ground
→ *Directions from Brahmanal to Manikarnika Ghat: At the end of Brahmanal, turn right (this lane remains Brahmanal). Then take the next left to Manikarnika Ghat.*

What to Know Unlike anywhere else in India, Banaras' main cremation ground is located in Chauk, in the heart of the city. The whole area within the Panchakroshi pilgrimage route that encircles Banaras is pure, so even the cremation grounds Manikarnika and Harishchandra are considered pure and non-polluting. Some Banarasis say that in the past, the whole of Kashi was *mahashamshan,* the great cremation ground, and that

> The location of the main cremation site is unique as it allows for cremations in the heart of Banaras. It is famous world over for multiple cremations.

Manikarnika and Harishchandra emerged as distinct ghats later. When pilgrimage routes were demarcated, Manikarnika was included as a stop on the innermost and most important routes.

Manikarnika was the first ghat to be constructed with stone, in 1302. The Maratha Peshwa Bajirao rebuilt it in 1735 and the Maratha Queen of Indore Ahilyabai Holkar in 1791.

On the ghat, multiple pyres burn simultaneously. Thousands of corpses are cremated here annually. During monsoon the river is easily 50 feet higher than in winter, and so cremations are carried out on a higher platform, built in 1912 by Raja Moti Chand, a landowner and patron of the arts in Banaras.

What to See Apart from the pyres, there are shops selling pyre wood, incense, cloth and other funerary materials. The people present on the ghat include shopkeepers, family and friends of the deceased, various religious specialists and cremation specialists

CREMATIONS IN BANARAS

It is difficult for those who do not cremate to understand the rituals of cremation and the experience of being in a culture where this is the accepted procedure. But it is also difficult for those from a cremation culture to understand the Banaras cremations, because Banaras is unique even in India. It is deliberately continuous with the past, and the past extends to almost three millennia of recorded history. It is rough and crude and even harsh, deliberately following the model of Shiva as an uncouth and uncivilized god. It is masculine and ordinarily no female or child attends a cremation. If you, the tourist, do, you will of course be turned off. It is strictly for insiders who are there because there was a death in their family. Cremations are finally about the loss of a loved person. So they are full of intense emotion. These emotions are also culture-specific so it is not easy to explain why people do what they do or say what they say about what they do. In other words, don't linger or make your presence felt. Avoid taking photographs and if you absolutely must, do so from a discreet distance, and do not be surprised if you are stopped.

You may have seen unsavoury pictures of half-burnt corpses, even before coming to Banaras. But the phenomenon of half-burnt corpses is not related to Hinduism or death in Banaras. It occurs because of poor municipal conditions, individual people's carelessness and the desire for spectacle on the part of the photographers.

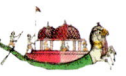

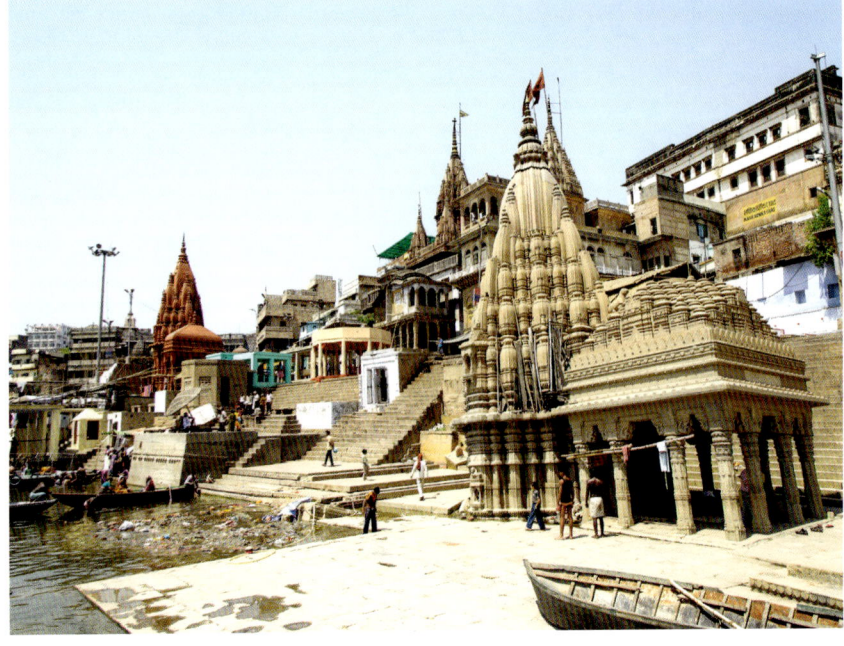

Kashi Karvat Temple.

called Doms. The Doms belong to a caste of funeral attendants, considered untouchable in the past. They construct the pyre and charge a tax (*kar*) for providing the fire to ignite the pyre. The head of the Doms, whose position is hereditary, is known as Dom Raja. His palace on Manikarnika Ghat has a terrace that overlooks the river. On the two riverfront sides of the terrace are two garishly painted lions.

KASHI KARVAT

Over the years Banarasis have created many stories to explain why the temple leans to one side. One story describes that a wealthy merchant's son built the temple in honour of his mother. As the sculptors completed the last carving on the temple, the son was filled with self-pride. Shiva was angered at the son's arrogance and in an instant, caused the temple to sink into the ground.

Ⓔ TARAKESHVAR TEMPLE
Lord of the crossing

What to Know Further south, past the cremation pyres stands the single-spired temple of Tarakeshvar. Tarakeshvara means 'lord of the crossing', as *tarak* is 'crossing' and *ishwara* is 'lord'. Shiva in this form, wearing a five-headed mask of bronze, is believed to whisper the *tarak mantra*, the prayer of crossing, into the ear of the deceased to liberate his or her soul. Mourners decorate Tarakeshvar after cremation rites.

Ⓕ 'KASHI KARVAT' TEMPLE
The twist of birth and death

What to Know North of the Tarakeshvar Temple, an elaborately-carved temple leans into the river. This temple is popularly called Kashi Karvat because *karvat* means 'turned over'. The real Kashi Karvat Temple is actually further south in a neighbourhood called Nepali Khapra, where, as local Banarasis explain, its name refers to the turning over of birth and death.

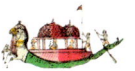

G MANIKARNIKA KUND & VISHNU CHARANPADUKA

Where Vishnu meditated

What to Know Further north on the ghat, nestled among tall buildings, is Manikarnika Kund, one of the original kunds or water tanks of the Forest of Bliss.

What to See The Vishnu Charanpaduka, below the steps and slightly south of Manikarnika Kund, is a pavilion with a slab of marble on its floor. The marble slab represents the footprints (*charan*) of Vishnu as he meditated. Only a select few have been cremated at this spot, such as the maharajas of Banaras, who are considered the earthly manifestation of Shiva.

In Hinduism, heat is considered to be a source of generative power. Vishnu created Manikarnika Kund out of the heat of his limbs and the energy of his yogic meditation. The myth that describes how he did so also tells us that Manikarnika is where Shiva and Parvati created the entire cosmos. Therefore, Manikarnika is the site of both physical death and cosmic creation. This illustrates the connection drawn between the body and the cosmos in Hindu thought, and in Kashi.

H AMETHI TEMPLE

Dedicated to Lord Shiva and Goddess Durga

→ *Directions from Manikarnika Ghat to Amethi Temple: Above Vishnu Charanpaduka, a few feet south of Manikarnika Kund, a staircase of uneven width goes up and westwards. This crooked staircase is filled with shrines, Shiva lingas and Hanuman figures. A double doorway and steep staircase on the left leads up to the Amethi Temple.*

VISHNU, SHIVA, AND MANIKARNIKA KUND

"During the period of cosmic dissolution (*mahapralaya*) all creation was destroyed and everything was plunged into darkness. There was neither sun nor moon nor stars, no sense of perception and no cardinal points. All that existed was Brahman which cannot be apprehended by the mind or described by speech, and which is without shape, name or colour or any physical attribute. The undivided one (*advaita*) desired to become two and accomplished this by his own divine play *(lila)*. 'I (Shiva) am the material form of that immaterial Brahman. Oh, Parvati, together we created the sacred area of Kashi.' 'Wandering in this forest of bliss, Shiva and Parvati desired to create another being to whom they could hand over the burden of the whole of creation, which would leave them free to bestow 'liberation' on all who die in Kashi. Shiva turned his gaze full of nectar on his left side (at Parvati) and a beautiful being was instantly created. This was Vishnu, whose breath was the Vedas, through which he was omniscient, and according to which he was instructed to perform his task.' Vishnu dug a tank with his discus and filled it with the sweat of the terrible austerities he performed by its side for 50,000 years in order to construct the universe. At the end of this time, Shiva and Parvati came there and saw Vishnu burning with the fire of his asceticism. Shiva was entranced, and with a violent trembling of delight, his earring dropped into Vishnu's tank, which Shiva decreed should henceforth be known as Manikarnika. Aroused with difficulty from his austerities Vishnu was told to demand a boon. He requested that he should always behold the divine couple as at that moment; that he should take the form of a black bee perpetually drinking the nectar of Shiva's lotus-like feet, and that since Shiva's ear-ring had been studded with *mukta* (pearl), this sacred place (*tirtha*) should confer mukti (liberation). 'Shiva agreed and added that for those who reside in Kashi, it will always be the Satyuga (the age of truth), always the auspicious time of the summer solstice (*uttarayan*), and a festival day; and that pious deeds performed here will result in immortality."
– From *Death in Banaras* by Jonathan P. Parry (pp 13-14)

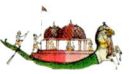

VISHNU'S TALE

At the time Brahma called on Raja Divodas to establish order in Kashi, Divodas banished all the gods from Kashi, so that he could perform his duties undisturbed. Shiva, who was sent to Mount Mandara, was so besotted with his lovely Kashi that he spent all his time plotting his return. He asked all the gods for help, sending them to Kashi one by one to disrupt Divodas' perfect rule. First he sent the goddesses called *yoginis*, then Surya the sun, then Brahma, and then his guardian deities, the ganas. But they were all unsuccessful at creating trouble for Divodas. Not only this, content at having returned to luminous Kashi, they settled down there one by one.

Finally, Shiva turned to Vishnu, who agreed to help him. Vishnu disguised himself as a Buddhist monk and moved through Kashi, spreading Buddhist messages. Quite soon the city was in chaos, for what the monk taught contradicted Hindu doctrines. Divodas looked on in dismay and with a strange new fatigue.

Then one day a sage came to Divodas' court. Seizing the opportunity, Divodas confessed to the wise sage his apathy for his kingly duties and asked how he could find release from the material world. The sage, who was actually Vishnu in disguise, told Divodas that if he established a Shiva *linga* in the city, he would be transported to heaven in a chariot. Divodas had sinned in banishing Shiva, the sage told the king, but he had proved himself a just ruler and was in Shiva's heart.

And so Vishnu welcomed Shiva back to Kashi. But Vishnu wanted to live in Kashi as well. He and Shiva decided that henceforth the city would be divided into two to prevent conflict. The section south of Manikarnika would be Shiva's and north would belong to Vishnu.

What to Know This Shiva-Durga Temple was built in the mid-19th century by the king of Amethi in Awadh (the central part of modern-day Uttar Pradesh). Its pillars are elegant and its stonework is fine, in contrast to many other temples in Banaras. The temple has crimson spires and golden pinnacles. Towards the right of the entrance is Durga's lion in bronze and towards the left is Shiva's bull.

Naubatkhana
The tunnelled entrance and shuttered windows above the temple's doorway constitutes a *naubatkhana*. Developed in the Mughal era, the *naubatkhana* was used for musicians to perform and to announce important events and personages. They were usually built above the entrances of forts, palaces, temples, mansions, gardens, or even neighbourhoods, by kings, wealthy merchants, and temple patrons. They were quickly adapted into Hindu architecture.

The Amethi Temple *naubatkhana* is an example of this adoption and there are several other such examples in Banaras. In fact, there are few Mughal *naubatkhanas* in Banaras.

① SIDDHI VINAYAK
Lord Ganesh's shrine
→ *Directions to Siddhi Vinayak Temple: Adjoining the staircase of the Amethi Temple, built as a large niche in the wall, is the temple of Siddhi Vinayak.*

What to Know Although just a niche in the wall, this Ganesh shrine is important, being one of the 56 Vinayaks, or special forms of Ganesh, that are organized in an intricate pattern linked by pilgrimage routes throughout the city. Ganesh is the elephant-headed son of Shiva and Parvati, Lord of obstacles, a figure of auspiciousness and bestower of bliss. He is worshipped at rituals of birth and death and at the start of new ventures.

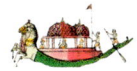
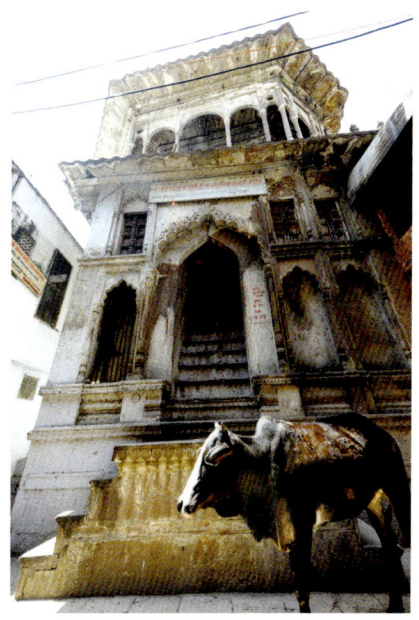

The *naubatkhana* entrance of Amethi Temple.

of the gods and goddesses. And some even say that Kashi was once the city of Vishnu. Versions of the myth of Raja Divodas explain how Shiva came to be the great lord of Kashi, how Vishnu came to call Kashi home and how Shiva and Vishnu share the city (see box story Vishnu's Tale on facing page).

The priest of the Alwar Temple believes that the temple's location may explain why it houses both Shiva and Vishnu. It was built on the border of the old Vishnu city to the north and the newer Shiva city to the north, when Shaivism, or the devotion of Shiva, was becoming popular at the turn of the millennium.

Ⓙ **ALWAR TEMPLE**
Dedicated to Lord Shiva and Lord Vishnu
→ *Directions from Siddhi Vinayak Temple to Alwar Temple: Across the stairway of the Amethi Temple, a short and narrow flight of stairs leads, through a courtyard, to the Alwar Temple.*
What to Know The comparatively lesser known Alwar Temple was built by the king of Alwar state (present-day Rajasthan). The quiet, dark interiors open into a floral balcony, overlooking the Manikarnika reservoir and ghat. The temple is unusual in its lack of the raised inner pavilion typical of Shiva temples.

The temple is also unique because it houses both Vishnu and Shiva. Today, there is a sectarian divide between devotees of Vishnu and devotees of Shiva. But there is room for Vishnu as well as Shiva in Kashi, just as there is room for every one

Ⓚ **MANIKARNIKESHVAR TEMPLE**
The first of 108 shrines
→ *Directions from the Alwar Temple to the Manikarnikeshvar Temple: Climb a few steps up, away from the river, (west) from the Amethi Temple. Turn right into the first lane (going north), which might appear to be a dead-end but in fact twists (east). The largest open doorway on the left at the end of this lane leads into the Manikarnikeshvar Temple.*
What to Know Dark and damp like the city's oldest and most popular temples, the Manikarnikeshvar Temple is important because it is the first of 108 shrines on the Panchakroshi pilgrimage. The actual *linga* of Shiva is positioned about 20 feet underground. Originally, a tunnel connected the *linga* to the ghat. Today, visitors are meant to have *darshan* (sacred sight) of the image by looking down from the railing at the *linga*.

Exiting Manikarnika
Directions from Manikarnikeshvara Temple to the Chauk road: From the Manikarnikeshvara Temple, the simplest route to the Chauk road is to retrace one's steps back to Manikarnika Ghat and westwards through Brahmanal.

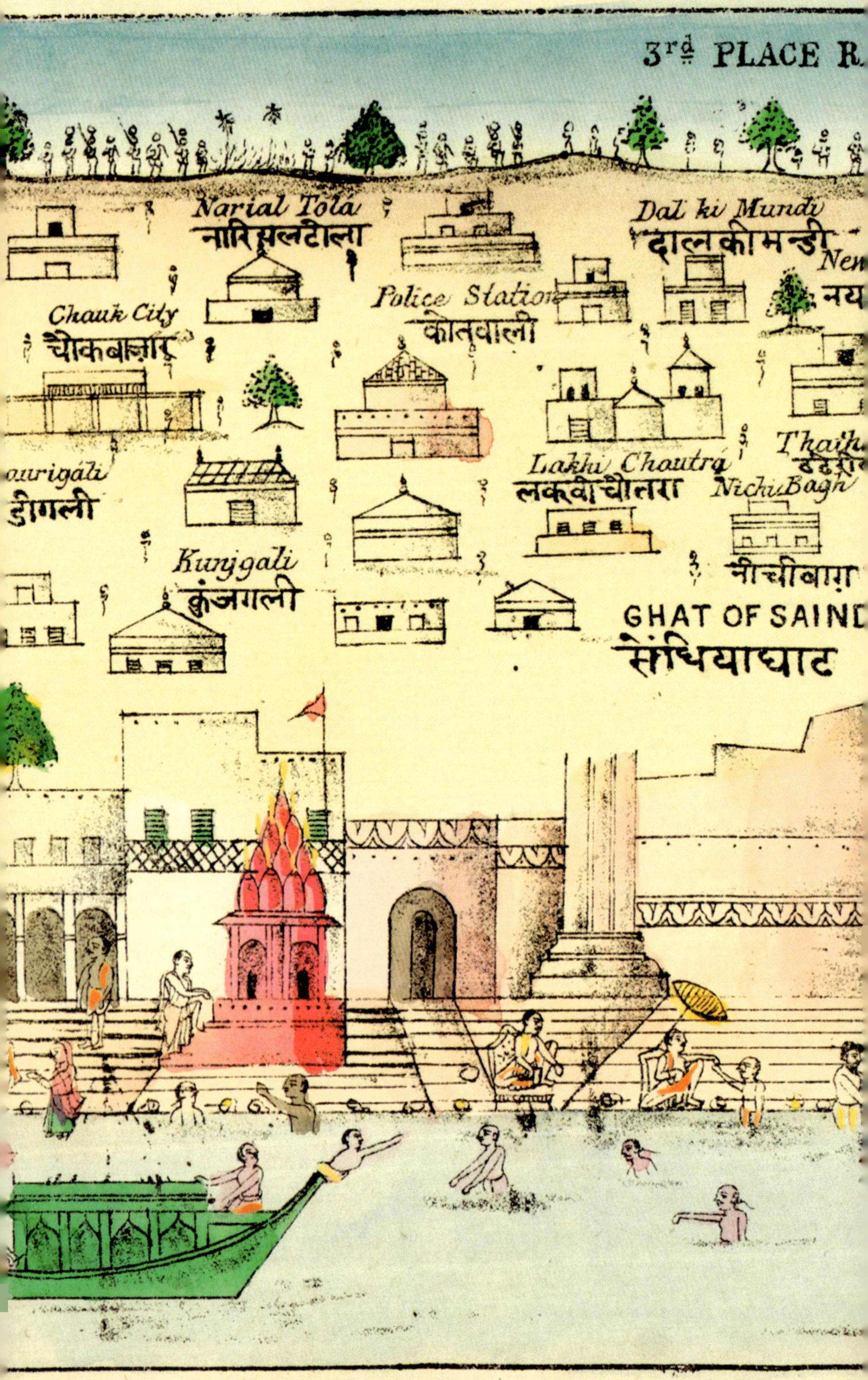

Narial Tola
नारिसलटीला

Dal ki Mundi
दालकीमन्डी
New
नय

Chauk City
चौकबज़ार

Police Station
कोतुवाली

Thaih
ठठरी

ourigáli
डीगली

Lakhi Choutra
लक्वीचौतरा

Nichu Bagh
नीचीबाग

Kunjgali
कुंजगली

GHAT OF SAIND
संधियाघाट

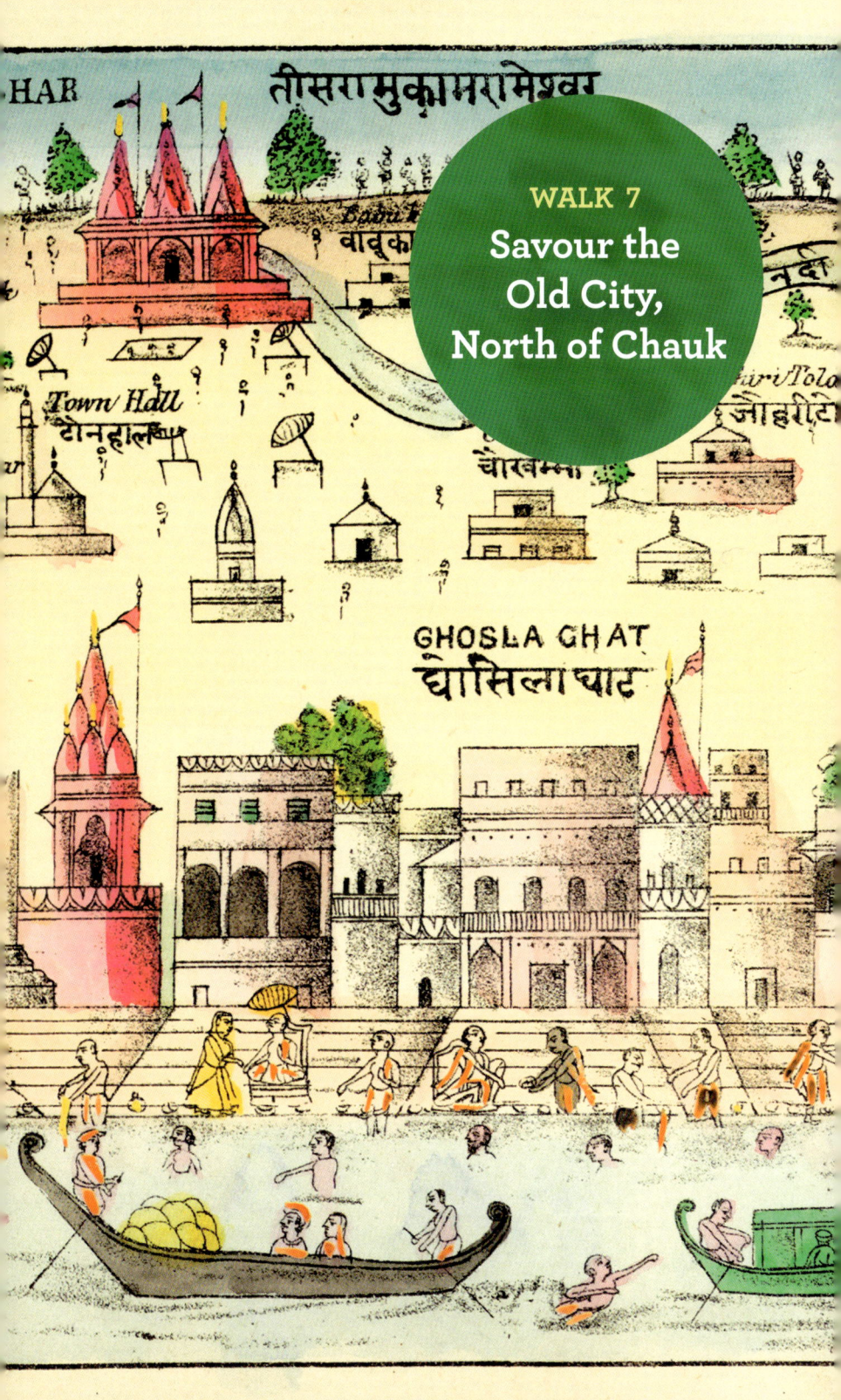

HAB

तीसरामुकामरामेश्वर

वावूक

नद

Babu K

WALK 7

Savour the
Old City,
North of Chauk

Town Hall
टोन्हाल्ख

चोरबम्भा

ri Tola

जोहरीटे

GHOSLA GHAT
घोसिलाघाट

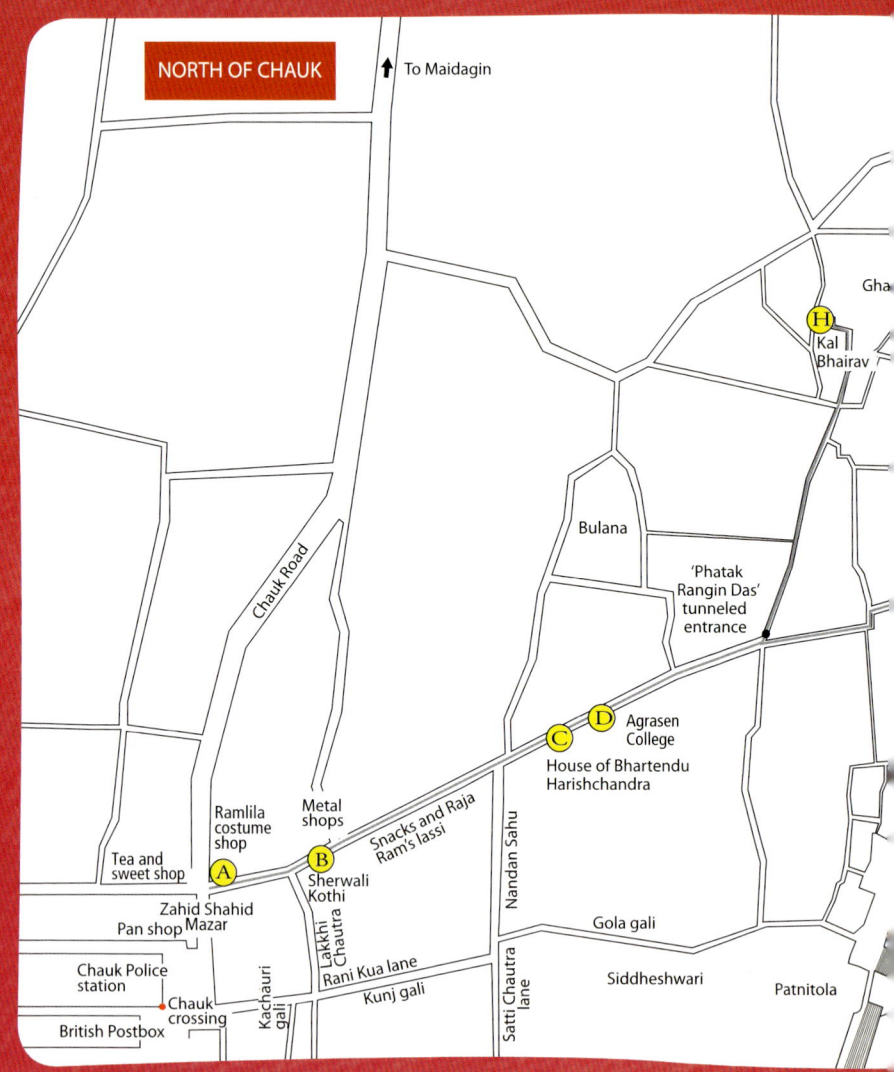

To Maidagin

Gha

Kal Bhairav

H

Chauk Road

Bulana

'Phatak Rangin Das' tunneled entrance

Agrasen College

D

C

House of Bhartendu Harishchandra

Snacks and Raja Ram's lassi

Metal shops

Ramlila costume shop

Nandan Sahu

Tea and sweet shop

B

Sherwali Kothi

A

Zahid Shahid Mazar

Pan shop

Lakkhi Chautra

Rani Kua lane

Gola gali

Chauk Police station

Kachauri gali

Kunj gali

Satti Chautra lane

Siddheshwari

Patnitola

Chauk crossing

British Postbox

Follow the lanes from the metal market Thatheri Bazaar to Alamgiri Mosque and Bindu Madhav Temple at Panchganga Ghat. Then walk north through the quiet lanes to the Kal Bhairav Temple.

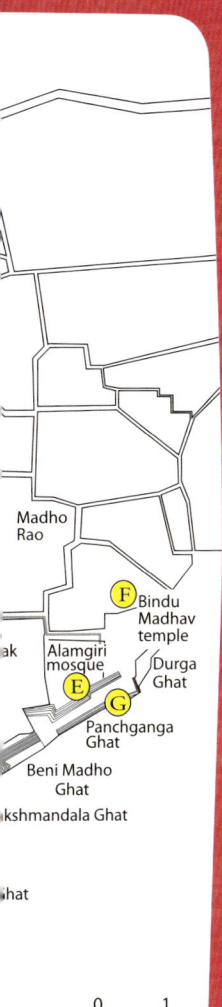

Madho
Rao

F Bindu
Madhav
temple

k Alamgiri
mosque

Durga
Ghat

E

G

Panchganga
Ghat

Beni Madho
Ghat

kshmandala Ghat

hat

0   1
1 cm = 30 m

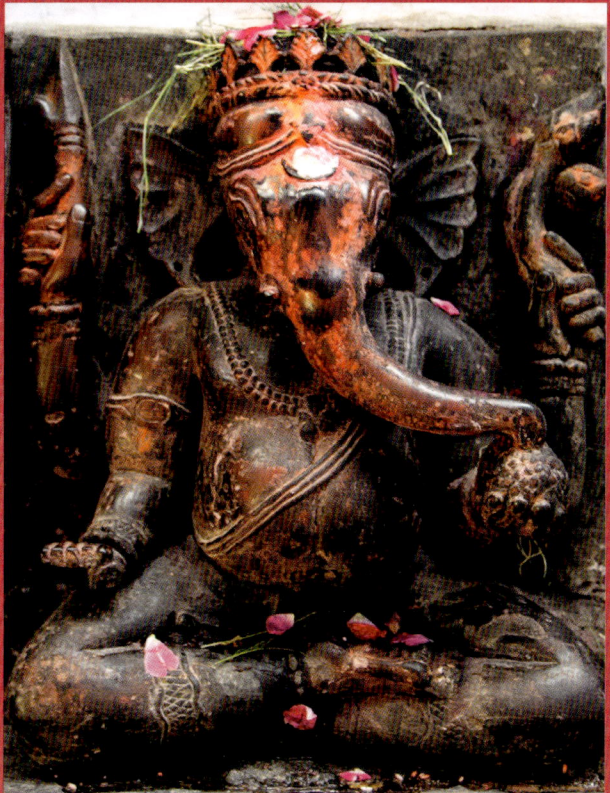

A Ganesh idol, worshipped with vermillion and rose petals.

THINGS TO SEE

- Market of traditional carved metal work
- Costume shops for Ramlila actors
- Mosque built by Mughal emperor, Aurangzeb
- Temple dedicated to Vishnu
- Riverside lamps to celebrate the festival of lights
- Temple devoted to Shiva's wrathful form

ALLOW

Three to four hours

WALK ITINERARY

Thatheri Bazaar I Sherwali Kothi I House of Bhartendu Harishchandra I Agrasen College I Alamgiri Mosque I Bindu Madhav Temple I Panchganga Ghat I Kal Bhairav

GETTING AROUND NORTH OF CHAUK

The galis north of Chauk extend from Thatheri Bazaar through Bansphatak, to the main road of Maidagin and the Visheshwarganj market in the north. To the east of these lanes are the riverside ghats Bhonsale, Ram, Panchganga, Lal, Gai, Trilochan, Gola, Telia, Naya, Prahlad, and Rajghat.

THE HISTORY OF NORTH OF CHAUK

Until the 12th century AD, the heart of the city was not at Godaulia and Chauk as it is today but was further north, extending from Gai Ghat to the Rajghat Fort. In the lanes above Gai Ghat stood Patan Darwaza, the city's southernmost gate. To the west and south was Anandavan, the Forest of Bliss.

Ferries crowded with passengers anchored here. Families would troop to the river to greet their guests, bringing bullock carts to take their luggage home. Cargo would be loaded and unloaded from ships, and would include bundles of silk and brocade, pale slabs of Chunar stone, baskets of spices, horses with gleaming coats, and later, textiles from England.

Above the riverbank were hermitages, monasteries, and schools for learning the Vedas, ayurveda, mathematics, and philosophy. Ascetics and gurus continued traditions of renunciation and pursuit of *gyan* (deep knowledge). At Panchganga Ghat, Kabir, an immensely popular poet, studied with the sage Ramanand in his ashram.

Quiet and slow-paced compared to the rest of the city, the northern lanes and ghats retain some of the flavour of old Banaras. Old mansions are interspersed with cottage-like homes, ancient trees and shrines. Few tourists venture this far north.

Ⓐ THATHERI BAZAAR
The Metalwork Market

→ *Directions from the Chauk Thana to Thatheri Bazaar: Walk up the Chauk road, passing the Chauk police station on your left. Go down the first lane on the right after the police station and Chandan Shahid Sufi shrine, opposite a milk and tea shop. Thatheri Bazaar is down this lane. A small shop of glitzy costumes marks the mouth of Thatheri Bazaar. Sherwali Kothi, the house of Bhartendu Harishchandra and Agrasen College are all located on the right-hand side along the lane.*

What to See Thatheri Bazaar is the city's metalwork market. Not too long ago, the making of brass and copper vessels and *naqqashi* (carving on metal) was a major cottage industry in Banaras. The metal workers were called *thathera*s or *kasera*s. They continue to work in workshops, hidden behind the street-facing shops that sell their products. If you visit a shop, the shopkeeper will carefully weigh the item you select on a pair of delicate scales, since prices depend on weight. The metal products, which include items for religious and domestic use, hang picturesquely in bunches.

The metal workers of Banaras

*Thathera*s work in workshops under one master metal worker, who works alongside them and dresses in the same way. *Thathera*s usually wear a light cotton vest, with lungi, a single piece of cloth, wrapped from the waist to below the knee, which is an informal dress popular among men in

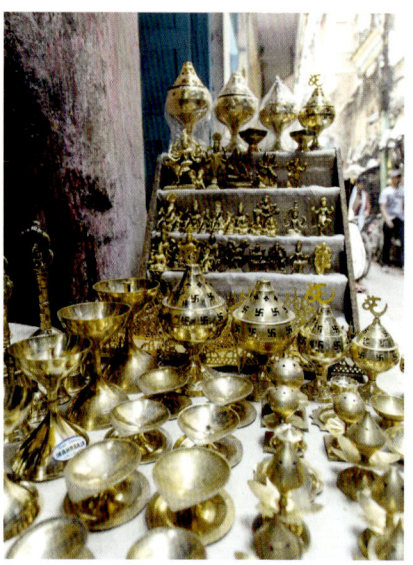

A metalwork shop.

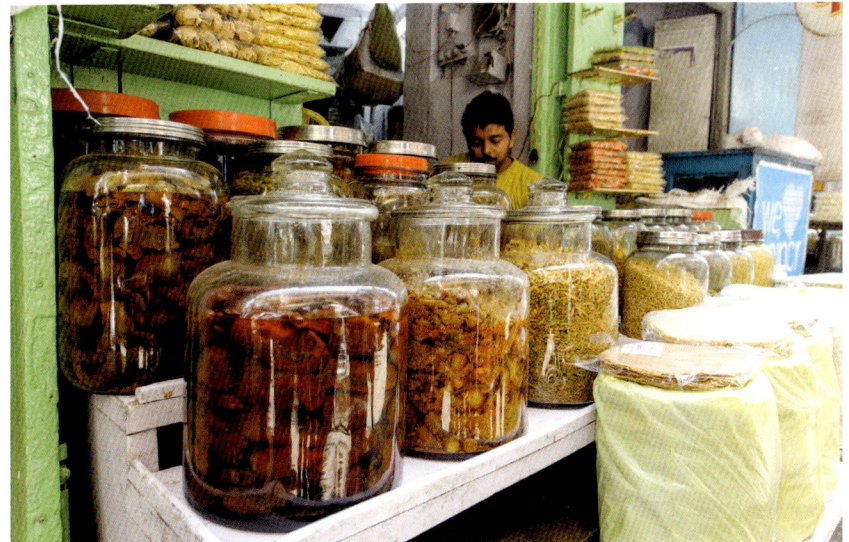

A shop of pickles and savoury snacks.

HOUSE OF SAVOURY SNACKS & PICKLES

Near the first cross street, there are shops specializing in **sweet-and-sour pickles** (achar) and **savoury snacks** (namkeen and papad). The makers of achar, namkeen and papad are forever experimenting with new recipes and the shopkeepers always have new varieties to tempt you with. The shops in Thatheri Bazaar are arranged in typical fashion, with neat rows of glass and plastic jars. There are hundreds of achar and namkeen shops in Banaras, but the ones in Thatheri Bazaar are among the best. Continuing their legacy, they offer a wide range of mouth-watering products made of excellent ingredients. Achar and papad must be eaten with a meal, but *namkeen* is an excellent on-the-go snack!

The most common achars are *aam* (mango), *neebu* (lemon), *mircha* (green or red chillies), *karaunda* (a grape-sized, sour fruit) and *murabba* (a round, sugary fruit). Papad consists of paper-thin circles of lentils or potatoes crushed with spices, to be deep-fried or baked at home and eaten with a meal.

Dalmoth, a kind of namkeen, is a crunchy mixture of peanuts, raisins, fried strips and balls made of gram flour and chickpea flour, lentils and spices. *Dalmoth* also comes in various varieties, each with its own name and subtle flavour. There is even one modern mixture called 'Cornflakes Mix'. *Khastas*, another variety of namkeen, are deep-fried, flaky patties of processed wheat flour stuffed with spices.

Sweets, snacks, and milk products in Thatheri Bazaar

Past the metal stores, you will pass some famous **old sweet shops** of Banaras, such as Shri Ram Bhandar, marked by their glass cases. These shops specialize in sweets prepared in pure ghee. Shop for a traditional set of sweets here, such as the one called *panch mel* ('mix of five').

Continuing down Thatheri Bazaar, after Agrasen College, watch out for a shop displaying vats of **fresh yoghurt**. Refresh yourself with a cup of creamy, chilled **lassi** churned by the owner Raja Ram or his son. It will be one of the best you will taste in the city.

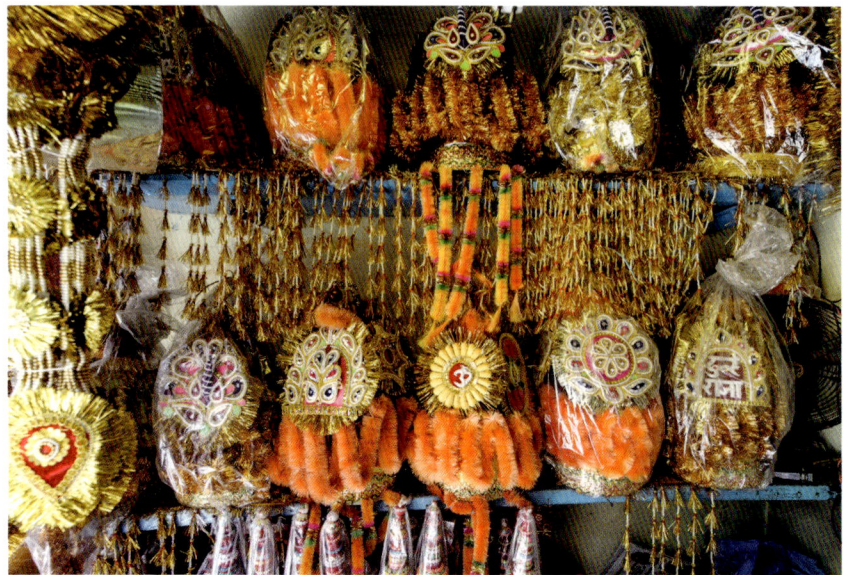

A display in a Ramlila costume shop.

Banaras. Their work is specialized, divided into tasks such as moulding, joining and polishing.

One possible cause for this is the fact that no artisan is involved in the trading of his product.

Thatheras do not have any direct influence or stake in their industry's progress. So, a shop that sells traditional brass items one day could easily switch to factory-made stainless steel products the next.

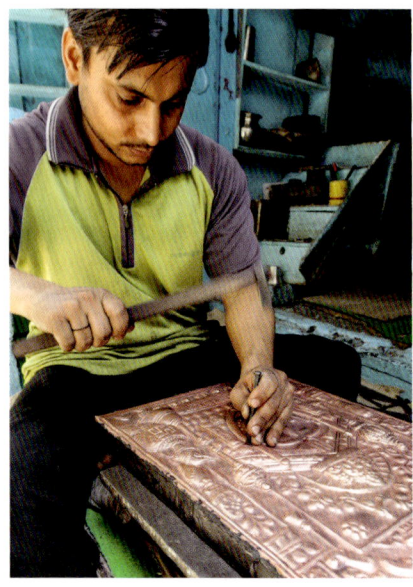

A metalworker working in his shop.

RAMLILA COSTUME SHOPS

All the way down Thatheri Bazaar, starting from its entrance, there are shops displaying glitzy costumes and crowns. These shops specialize in Ramlila paraphernalia and provide the Ramlila organizing committees all over the city with costumes, crowns, beards, clubs and jewellery they need to transform the actors into the Ramlila characters. The making of the Ramlila costumes and jewellery is a minor cottage industry in Banaras with sometimes entire families working by hand on their rooftops or courtyards, sewing fabric and setting plastic jewels. The shops also sell clothes, crowns, and jewellery for idols in temples and homes.

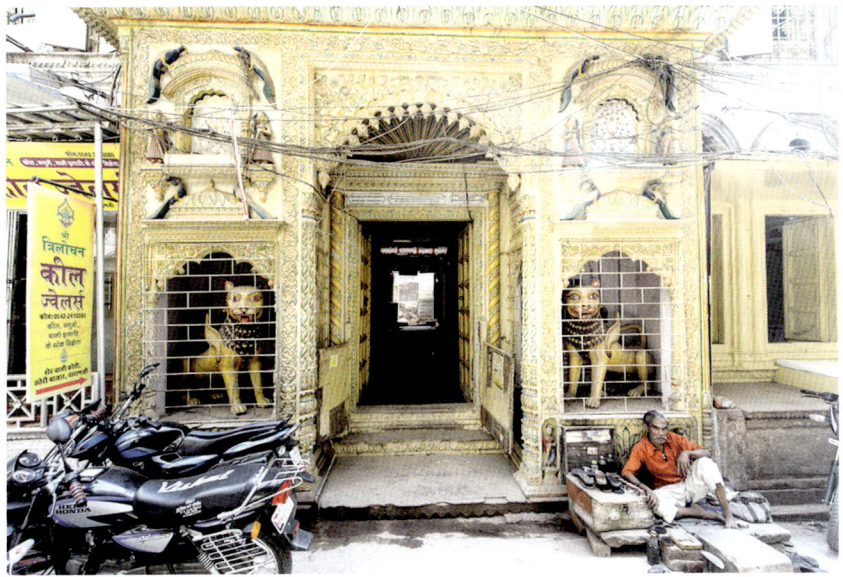

Sherwali Kothi, an old mansion owned by the Shahs, one of the main business families of Banaras.

*Thathera*s do not call themselves *thathera* or *kasera,* but Haihayavamshi Chhatri, which is a lineage of the Chhatri or Kshatriya caste. This is a recent title and not established. They claim to be descendants of the armourers of Kshatriya warriors, who spread out from the west all over north India. However, they continue to be referred to as *thathera, kasera* or Vishwakarma by older members of their group and outsiders. Vishwakarma is the name of their patron diety, the divine architect of the entire universe and the gods' heavenly palaces.

*Thathera*s, like all artisans, possess a strong sense of identity and community in their work and home culture. But they are different from other artisan groups in that they prevent their women from doing any work apart from domestic work.

Ⓑ SHERWALI KOTHI
Mansion of Lions
What to See The old mansions that line Thatheri Bazaar typically belong to sari businessmen and are used as both residence and business outlets. Many of them now prefer to live in one of the modern neighbourhoods and conduct their business from a posh outlet.

One of the most impressive mansions in the area, is Sherwali Kothi. Two roaring marble tigers guard the gate. There are elephants and peacocks fanning their feathers, also in marble. 'Sherwali Kothi' means 'mansion of lions'. The house belongs to the Shahs, one of the old business families of Banaras.

Soon after Sherwali Kothi comes the house of the famous 19th century Hindi writer Bhartendu Harishchandra. These mansions are off-limits to visitors, but one can still admire them from outside.

Ⓒ HOUSE OF BHARTENDU HARISHCHANDRA
Remembering 'the father of modern Hindi literature'
What to Know Bhartendu Harishchandra is popularly remembered as the 'father of modern Hindi literature'. He was born in 1850 into a wealthy and prominent family of bankers who worked closely at different times with the British and the Maharaja of Banaras. His family's house in Thatheri Bazaar, owned by his descendants, is a typical pakka mahal mansion.

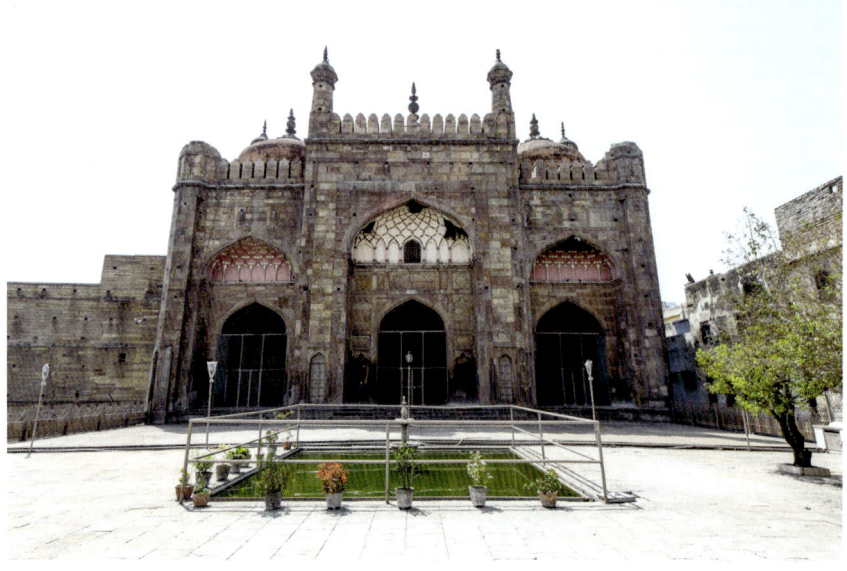

Alamgiri Mosque.

Bhartendu passed away when he was only 34 years old, but he wrote more than a 100 books ranging from plays, poems and criticism. He began journals and magazines, translated from Sanskrit, Bengali, Prakrit and English into Hindi and developed a new style of Hindi literature and theatre that became the new, 'modern' standard.

In the 19th century, a wide variety of theatrical forms were popular in Banaras and north India, such as the Ramlila and a genre called *svang*. These were both religious and secular. They were characterized by their oral, improvisational, open-ended, elaborate and erotic nature. Bhartendu's dramas, in contrast, were scripted, structured and realistic. They incorporated the rules of classical Sanskrit and Aristotelian dramatic theory.

Bhartendu was familiar with his city's traditions, but saw them as crude entertainment. His ideas of social upliftment and of drama as a means for this reflected the elite, reformist impulses

Many smaller mosques were built in Banaras using the design of the Alamgiri Mosque as a model.

of the 19th century, of reclaiming the past, reforming the present and progressing into a modern future.

Ⓓ AGRASEN COLLEGE
A historic school

What to Know Up until the time of Independence, most schools in India were set up by organizations of a particular caste, religion, or community. Prominent communities built schools in addition to palaces, places of worship and ghats in order to further establish their presence in Banaras. The Agrawals were one of the main merchant-banker castes of 19th-century Banaras. They formed the Agrawal Samaj (Society) in 1896 and set up a school in 1918. In 1967, the name was changed to 'Agrasen' because the abolition of caste discrimination after Independence made it illegal to even publicly refer to a caste name. Two separate schools were set up for boys and girls. Interestingly, the girls' school is the more renowned today.

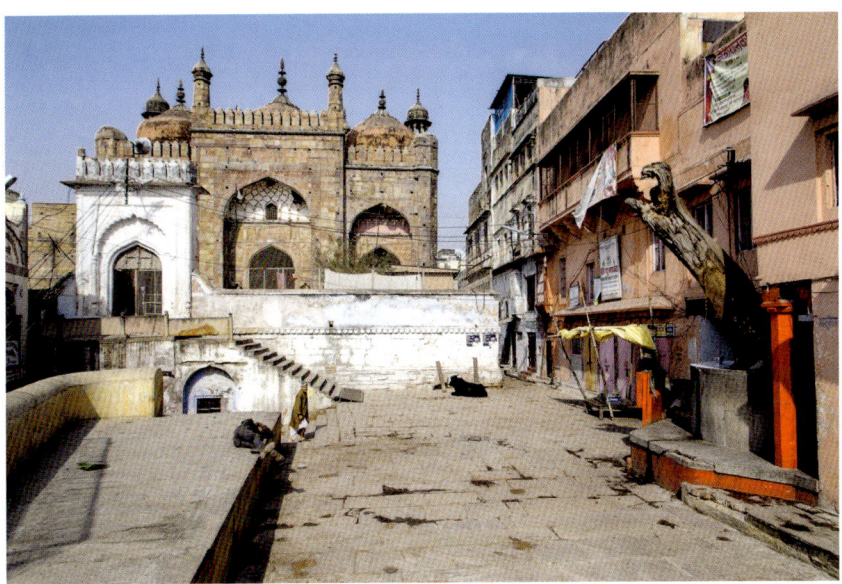

Alamgiri Mosque (centre) and Bindu Madhav Temple (right).

E ALAMGIRI MOSQUE
The highest minarets

→ *Directions from Thatheri Bazaar to Panchganga Ghat: Thatheri Bazaar ends at a small crossroad. Continue straight under the tunnelled doorway. Turn right and then right again, which will lead you briefly along the wall of the Alamgiri Mosque and then into the temple-mosque complex.*

What to Know In the 11th century, during the reign of the tolerant Mughal emperor Akbar, the Rajput king of Jaipur, Man Singh built a Vishnu Temple in Banaras called Bindu Madhav. In 1673, Aurangzeb razed the temple and built Alamgiri Mosque on its foundations. Its minarets were the highest and slenderest in Mughal architecture, a popular subject for 19th-century Company School painters. At that time, they were also the most prominent landmark in the city's skyline. In the 20th century, one of the minarets collapsed and the other was pulled down to maintain symmetry.

As a whole, in terms of design, the Alamgiri Mosque is one of the two most elaborate mosques in Banaras (the other being the Gyan Vyapi Mosque in Godaulia). It was built using Mughal architectural techniques that were the most modern at their time.

What to See The Alamgiri Mosque is constructed of red sandstone with brick and limestone mortar. There are trios of domes and pairs of slender minarets topped with miniature domes. The prayer hall inside, open to visitors, is spread over three sections. One section faces Mecca and the other opens out into the paved court. The court outside has a central fountain.

F BINDU MADHAV TEMPLE
Dedicated to Vishnu

What to Know The present Bindu Madhav Temple is housed inconspicuously in a modest building across from the Alamgiri Mosque. Aurangzeb razed the original temple and built the mosque on its foundations. The Maratha ruler Bhawan Rao rebuilt Bindu Madhav in its present form in the 19th century. Bindu Madhav was the city's most important Vishnu temple. According to legend, Bindu Madhav was the second temple Vishnu established in Kashi, after Adi Keshav further north.

Across the terrace from the temple is the ashram of Ramanand, a 15th-century saint and reformer. Ramanand was a follower of the south Indian Vaishnav tradition, but was most unconventional as a guru. He took under his tutelage not saffron-clad Brahmin boys but untouchables and even a woman. Ramanand taught during a period of Bhakti devotion and counter-cultural asceticism, which arose during the 15th century to challenge the ritualized system of Brahmanical religion. The Bhakti movement was characterized by a blossoming of devotional poetry in the vernacular. Kabirdas, Raidas and Tulsidas were major Bhakti poets, who studied at different times under Ramanand at his ashram in Panchganga. The three together were largely responsible for making Banaras a centre of the Bhakti movement.

What to See The temple doors are flanked by the mythical bird Garuda, Vishnu's vehicle, and by the monkey-god Hanuman, Ram's helper. Garuda and Hanuman play central roles in the Mahabharata. Inside stands the famous black marble statue of Vishnu. Ten incarnations of him are painted on the interior wall. There are 72 Shiva *linga*s and other images of Ganesh and Shiva.

The sculptures of Garuda, Hanuman, and Vishnu are from the original Bindu Madhav Temple. Jean Baptiste Tavernier, who came to India in the mid-17th century to deal in jewels, described the original Bindu Madhav as a cross-shaped 'pagoda' with towers on each of the four arms and a spire rising from the central sanctum. The image within was six feet tall and garlanded with rubies, pearls and emeralds. During this time of grandeur, the poet Tulsidas sat before Vishnu and wrote in praise of the temple. A century before him, the poet Kabir is believed to have received his initiatory mantra from his guru, Ramanand, here.

Kabir

There are many stories about Kabir's birth and early life. According to one story, Kabir was adopted as a baby into the home of low-caste

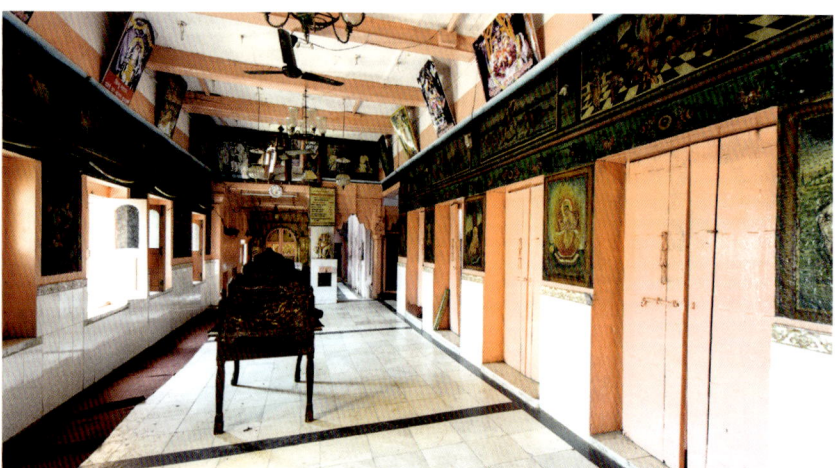

Interior hall of Bindu Madhav Temple.

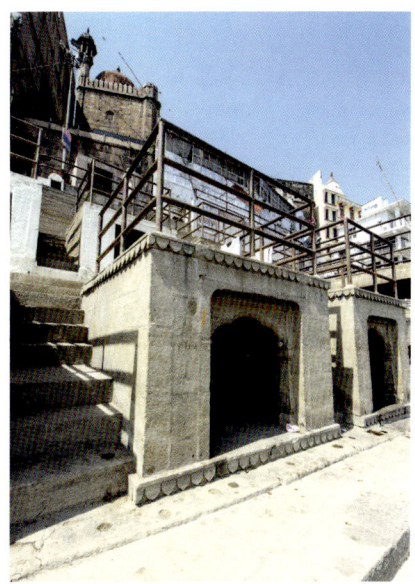

The shrines to the five rivers on Panchganga Ghat, with Alamgiri Mosque visible high above.

Muslim weavers named Niru and Nima. He grew up as a Muslim *julaha* (low-caste weaver).

Kabir's poetry was characterized by its terse criticism of all religious doctrine, its colloquial tone and its wit and irony. Despite his unwillingness to be a part of religion, his followers began a sectarian movement to continue his teachings after his death called the Kabir Panth. Members of Kabir Panth called themselves Kabir Panthis. They established a centre in the north of the city that came to be called Kabir Chaura after their ashram. Kabir Panth today has spread all over north India.

G PANCHGANGA GHAT
Todar Mal's architectural legacy

→ *Directions from Bindu Madhav Temple to Panchganga Ghat: Outside the temple, cross the paved court with Alamgiri Mosque to your right. Step under the arched walkway and go down the long, steep flight of steps to the river.*

What to Know *Panch* means 'five': Panchganga Ghat is named after the confluence of these five rivers. Bathing here is particularly auspicious, and the ghat is the second-last stop on the river-based Panchatirth pilgrimage.

Akbar's minister Todar Mal built Panchganga Ghat in 1580. It remains one of the most magnificent sections of the riverfront, with staircases of breathtaking height and steepness. Emperor Aurangzeb designed the Alamgiri Mosque's dimensions to match its particularly high position on Panchganga Ghat.

Panchganga is the place in Banaras that Vishnu chose as his home. He bathed here and established the Bindu Madhav Temple. In the popular myth of Raja Divodas, it was Vishnu who reclaimed Kashi for Shiva and helped him return to his beloved city. Some say that Panchganga Ghat marks the end of Shiva's half of the city to the south and the beginning of the old northern city of Vishnu (see Vishnu's Tale on page 92). The mythology and geography of Kashi are interwoven.

High on the steps, the poet and scholar Jagannath composed his famous poem in praise of the river, the *Ganga Lahiri*. He was a

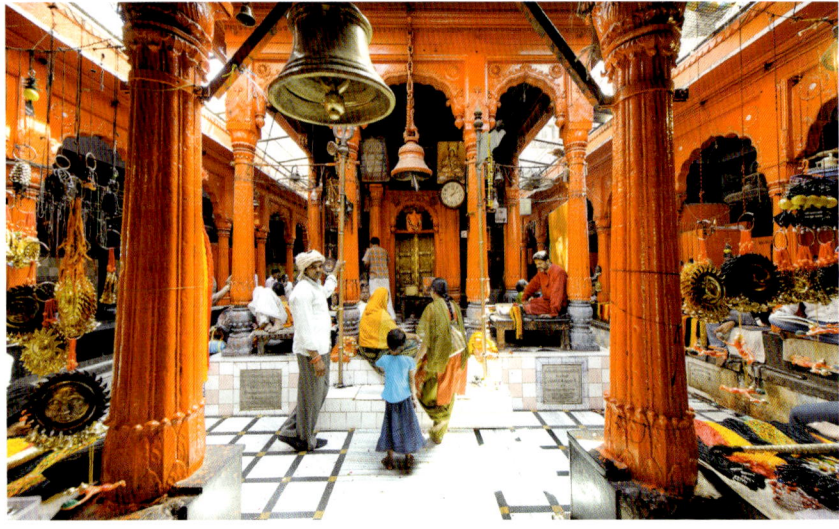

Kal Bhairav Temple.

Brahmin who became an outcaste for having a Muslim lover. According to legend, they sat together on the ghat, and with each verse he wrote, the river swelled a step higher.

What to See Unique to this ghat are the rows of cubicles built almost at the water's edge. Some of these cubicles house a *linga* or a shrine. Others are used for yoga, meditation, or relaxation.

One cubicle contains five shrines dedicated to the five mythical rivers said to flow into the Ganga at Panchganga Ghat. The five rivers are Kirna ('sunrays'), Dhutpap ('cleansed of sin'), Saraswati, Yamuna, and Ganga. Dhutpap and Kirna have small side shrines and are shown in their physical form. Yamuna is depicted riding her tortoise, Saraswati her peacock, and Ganga her crocodile.

Above the cubicles, a little to the north, are two ten-foot-tall, conical, carved structures. Ahilyabai Holkar, queen of the Malwa kingdom (present-day Maharashtra) built these pillars during her reign in the latter half of the 18th century. They are called Deep Hazari

> The *bhairavs* were terrifying deities depicted with wild hair and long moustaches, sharp teeth and lolling tongues and with raging eyes and grimacing faces.

Stambh, which means 'holder of a thousand lamps'. Ahilyabai Holkar, who ascended the throne after her husband and father-in-law were killed in battle, was famous for her military prowess and sense of justice.

Ⓗ KAL BHAIRAV
God of Death

→ *Directions from Panchganga Ghat to Kal Bhairav Temple: Follow the lane along the wall of the Alamgiri Mosque. Take the next left, then turn right, and continue straight at the crossroads. Turn left at the fork and then take an immediate right to the crossroads of Thatheri Bazaar and Satti Chautra. The lane to the right (going north, parallel to the river) leads to the Kal Bhairav Temple. Follow this lane as it curves and twists through the neighbourhoods of Bulanala and Golghar. At the second crossroads, small but busy, turn right and then right again. The lane narrows and winds around Kal Bhairav Temple.*

What to Know *Bhairav* is a form of Shiva, evolved from the ancient families of deities called *yakshas, ganas, nagas,* and *bhairavs.*

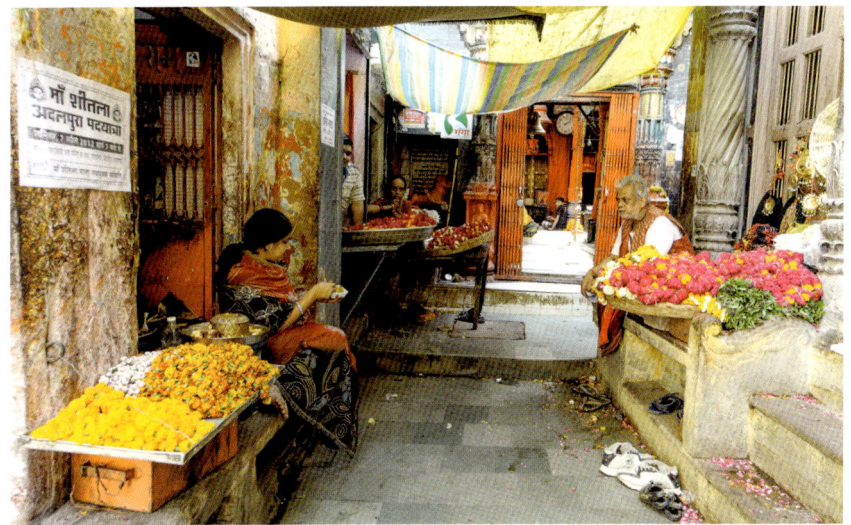

Flower sellers outside Kal Bhairav Temple.

Over time, *bhairavs* came to be regarded as the *ganas* or guardians of Lord Shiva, and were said to chase away evil spirits and demons. They were also adopted as Shiva's sons, and in this form were called *Batuk Bhairav* (*batuk* means 'son'). Out of the 64 original *bhairavs*, eight became more important, and a ninth, Kal Bhairav, the most important of all.

Kal means, variously, time, death, darkness or fate. It is believed that one look at Kal Bhairav expunges the sins of a lifetime. Even Yama, the God of Death, is afraid of Kal Bhairav. It is said that Yama is not allowed to enter Kashi to fetch souls. Here, Kal Bhairav, the Dark One, has assumed the duties of the God of Death. Kal Bhairav also takes on the duties of Chitragupta, the mythical scribe who watches people on earth and keeps a record of their deeds. Thus, Kal Bhairav is in charge of both life and death in Kashi.

Kal Bhairav is the physical form of Shiva's wrath. When Vishnu and Brahma argued about who was supreme, Shiva split the earth with his fiery *linga* of light and revealed himself as Bhairav. Bhairav sliced off Brahma's fifth head, which stuck to his hand. Shiva then sent Bhairav to wander the earth in order to expunge his sin of killing a Brahmin. When the skull dropped out of Bhairav's hand and Bhairav had conquered death, Shiva appointed him to be the chief officer of justice in Kashi.

At one time, Kal Bhairav was popular among Shiva ascetics, such as those of the Kapalika, Gorakhnathi and Kanpatha sects. For them, Kal Bhairav best represented that form of Shiva who defies all convention and definitions. Today, the temple's visitors consist primarily of regular Banarasis, many of whom live close by and come for daily worship. Unlike the Vishwanath and Kedar temples, Kal Bhairav is not a stop on the main pilgrimages. As a result, it has a friendly and relaxed atmosphere.

What to See Kal Bhairav is one of the most loved temples in Kashi and is popularly called 'Bhaironath'. Intimate and enclosed, its small sanctum and narrow verandahs are usually crowded with worshippers. Shiva's dog-mount guards the entrance into the courtyard. Kal Bhairav, occupying the inner sanctum, is golden-faced and wears a garland of silver skulls. Here there are also subsidiary shrines to Hanuman, Radha-Krishna, Parvati-Ganesh and Devi.

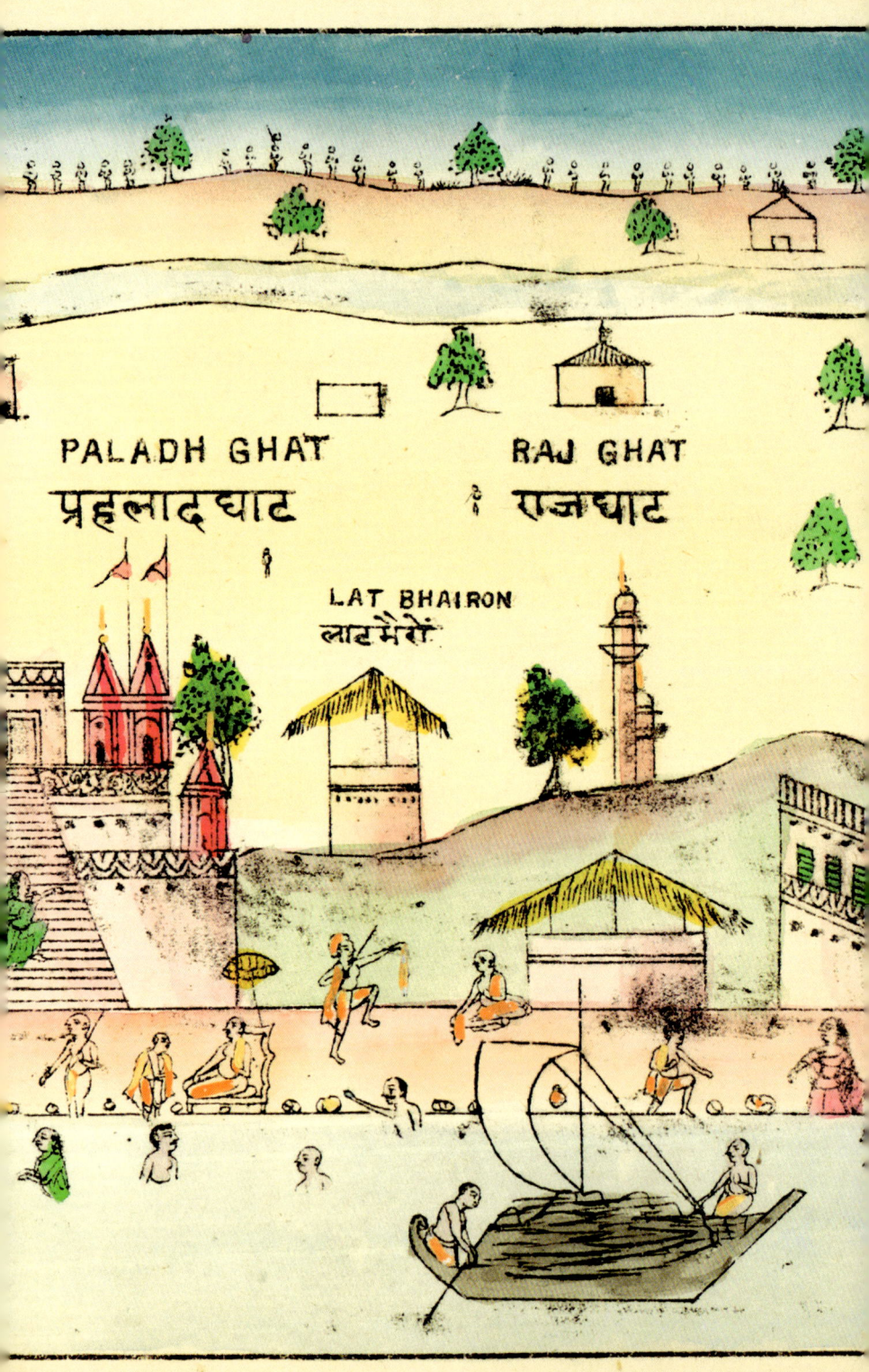

PALADH GHAT
प्रह्लाद घाट

RAJ GHAT
राजघाट

LAT BHAIRON
लाटभैरो

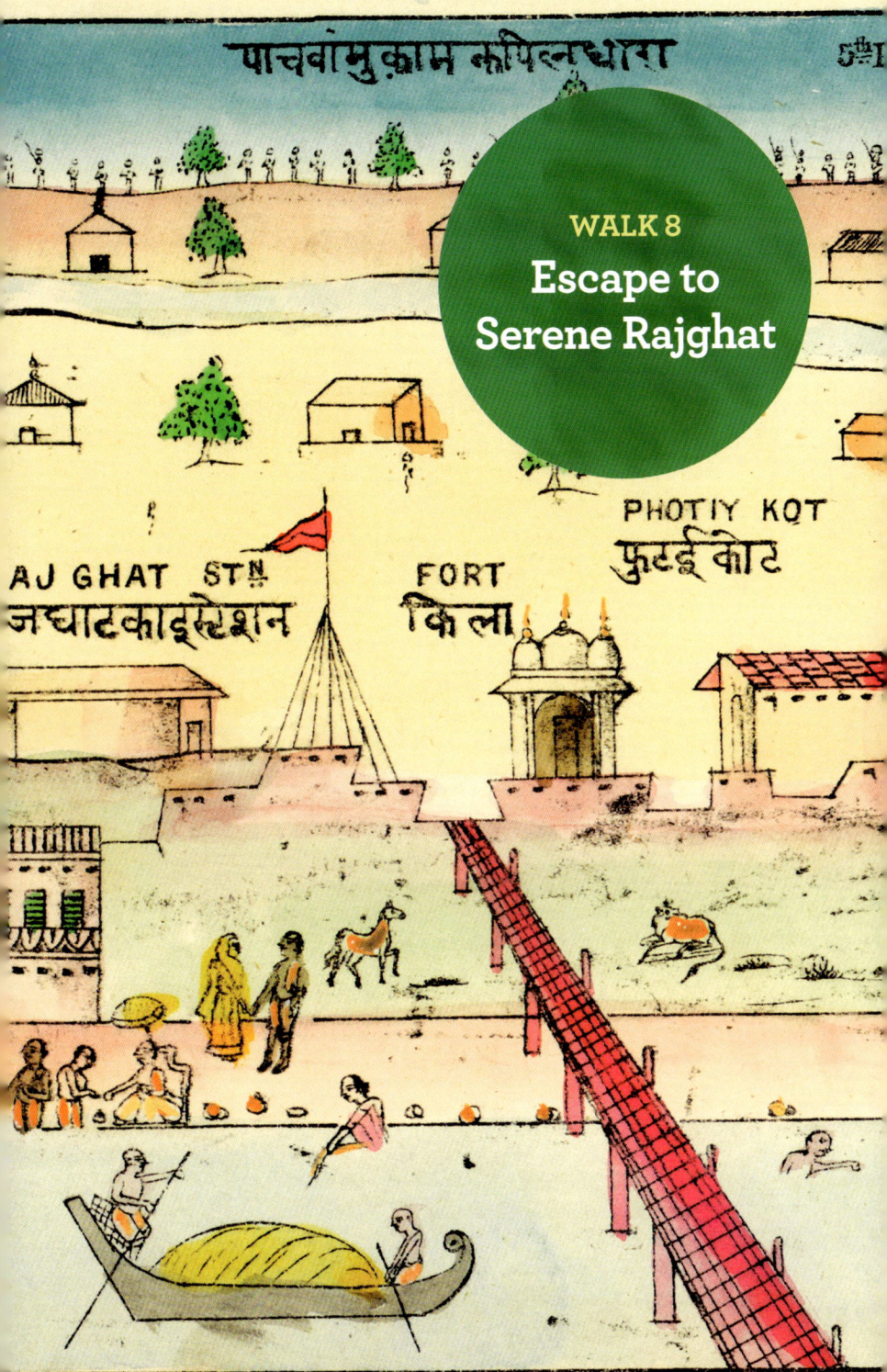

पाचवाँमुक़ाम कपिलधारा

5th

AJ GHAT ST<u>N</u>
जघाटकादूरेश्चन

FORT
किला

PHOTIY KOT
फुटई कोट

WALK 8

Escape to Serene Rajghat

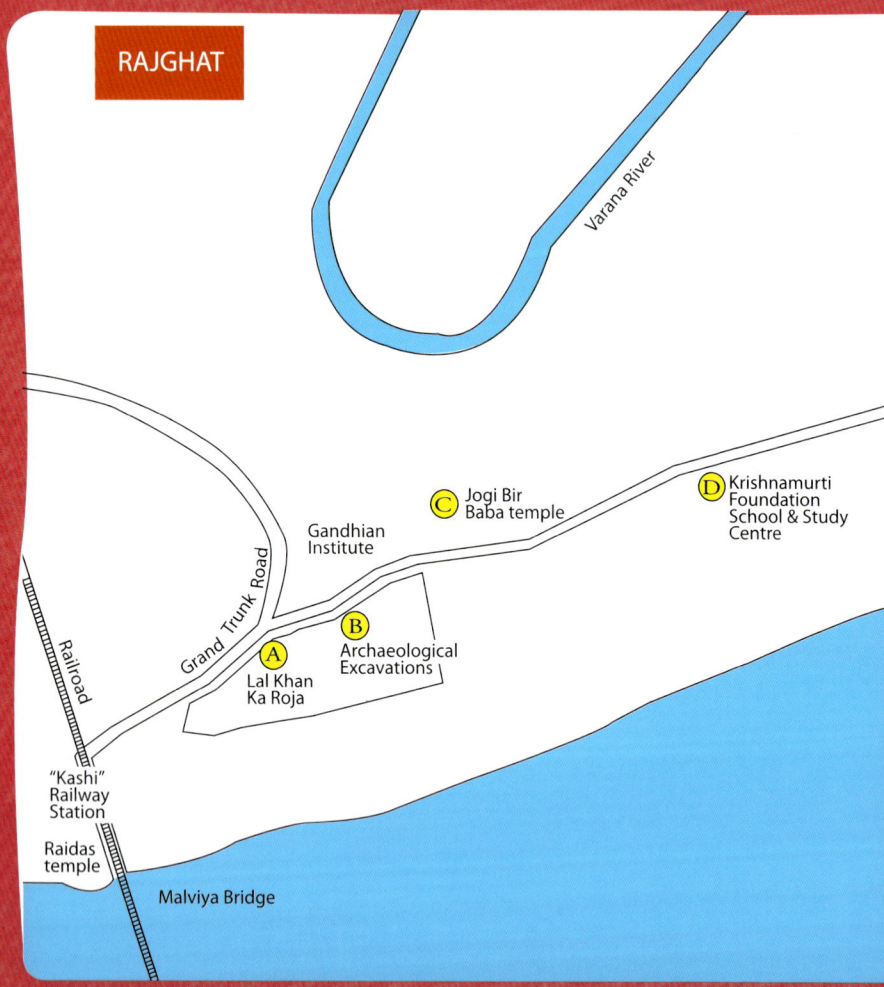

RAJGHAT

Varana River

Krishnamurti Foundation School & Study Centre D

Jogi Bir Baba temple C

Gandhian Institute

Grand Trunk Road

Archaeological Excavations B

Railroad

A
Lal Khan Ka Roja

"Kashi" Railway Station

Raidas temple

Malviya Bridge

Visit the tomb of Mughal minister, Lal Khan. Walk through the landscaped Krishnamurti Foundation campus, stopping at the local deity Jogi Bir's shrine, to Adi Keshav Temple and an adjoining akhara. End by exploring the tomb of Muslim saint, Chandan Shahid nearby.

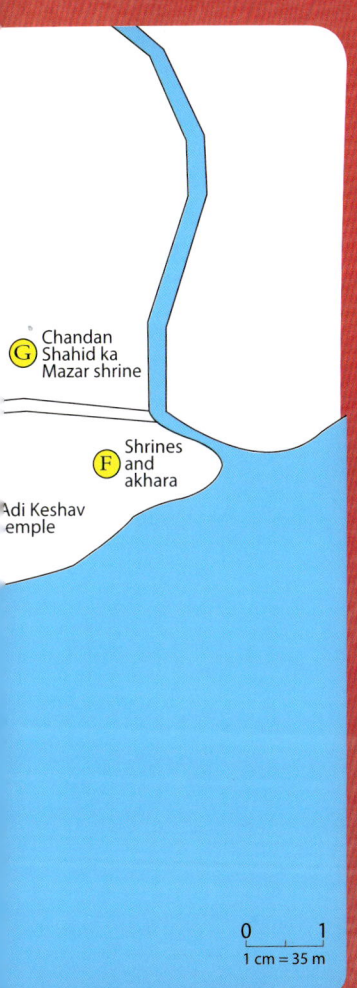

Chandan
Shahid ka
Mazar shrine

Shrines
and
akhara

Adi Keshav
Temple

0   1
1 cm = 35 m

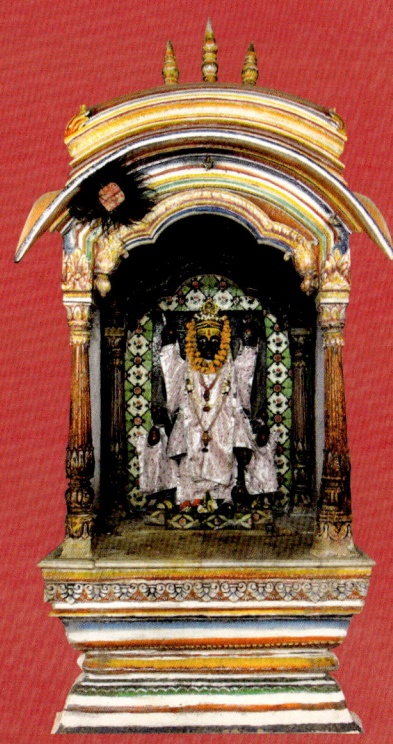

The black four-armed image of Vishnu at
Adi Keshav Temple.

THINGS TO SEE

- Colonial era bridge
- Tomb of Lal Khan, Mughal minister
- Shrine of the local deity, Jogi Bir
- Campus of Krishnamurti Foundation
- Adi Keshav Temple or the 'original Vishnu' temple
- Tomb of popular Sufi saint, Chandan Shahid

ALLOW: Two to three hours

WALK ITINERARY

Lal Khan ka Roja I Archaeological Excavations I Jogi Bir Baba Temple I Krishnamurti
Foundation School & Study Centre I Adi Keshav Temple I Shrines and akhara I Chandan
Shahid ka Mazar

GETTING AROUND RAJGHAT

'Rajghat' refers to the elevated plateau along the Ganga, north of Maidagin. It
stretches from the ghat of Rajghat, near the railway station called 'Kashi', and past the
Malviya Bridge, to the Adi Keshav Ghat on the river Varana, where the far northern
neighbourhoods of Adampura and Jaitpura begin.

THE HISTORY OF RAJGHAT

In the 1960s, archaeologists excavated an ancient city at the northern edge of present-day Banaras. The elevated plateau along this bend of the Ganga was undoubtedly an excellent spot for a city. High and sturdy, it was protected on the east by the Ganga and on the north and west by the river Varuna. We can only wonder if ancient Kashi was the base of an Aryan tribe called Kashi or perhaps the capital of the Kashi kings who fought in the famous war described in the Sanskrit epic, Mahabharata.

We do know, from the Mahabharata, the Puranas, and the Buddhist Jataka tales, that between the 8th and 6th centuries BC, Kashi was one of the sixteen great kingdoms of the Aryans, along with Koshala to its north and Magadha to its east. Through these centuries, these three powerful neighbours vied for supremacy. In the 20th century, Kashi became the capital of the Gahadvala kings, who developed it as an important centre for both Buddhism and Hinduism. Then, around the end of the first millennium AD the Muslim general, Qutb-ud-din Aibak destroyed the ancient fort at Rajghat, and from this point in time on, Banaras spread southwards into the neighbourhoods we know today.

Today, Rajghat is considered one of the city's outlying neighbourhoods. With its woods, small homes and clay riverbanks, it has a pastoral atmosphere. But it is not in the least an unimportant part of the city. Skirted by Grand Trunk Road and Malviya Bridge, busy thoroughfares for trucks and trains, it is home to a variety of historic sites and institutions of religious and cultural importance.

Ⓐ LAL KHAN KA ROJA
Timurid-style turquoise tiles

What to Know The tomb appears as a splendid turquoise and cobalt mirage beside the dusty, busy road leading to the Malviya Bridge. It was built in 1773 for Lal Khan, a Muslim minister in the court of Maharaja Balwant Singh, the first king of Banaras. After Aurangzeb's death, the Mughal Empire grew progressively weaker. Provincial viceroys became practically independent. Banaras was under the control of Mir Rustam Ali, who was known for his patronage of cultural events, both Hindu and Muslim. He entrusted his property to a Brahmin named Mansaram, who was the founder of the Banaras ruling family. Balwant Singh was Mansaram's son. While Mir Rustam was known for his patronage of cultural events, Lal Khan was known for strict law enforcement, although he too left his mark on the city's cultural life.

What to See The tomb stands in the middle of a walled Persian-style paradise-garden. Four modest, but elegant minarets adorn the corners of the garden. When the Rajghat

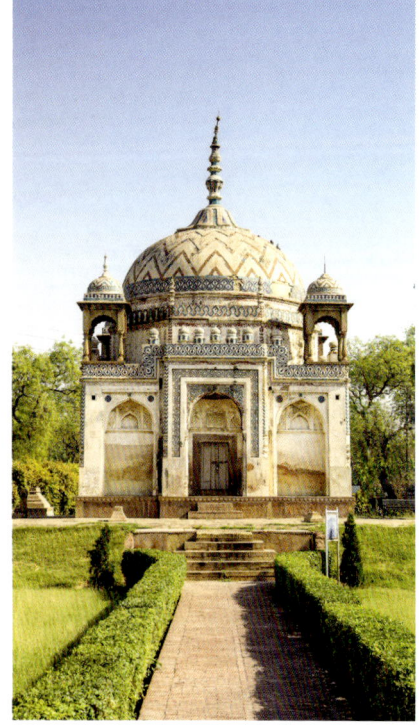

Lal Khan's tomb surrounded by Persian-style gardens.

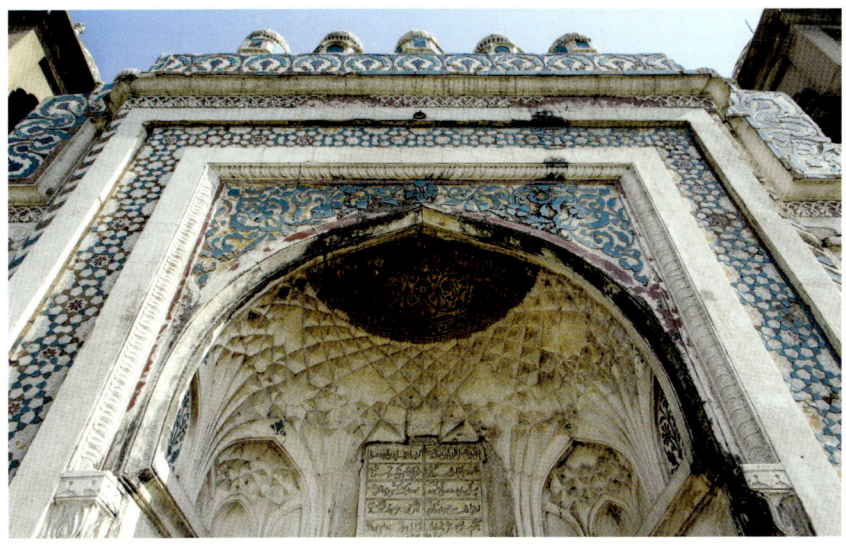

Cobalt and turquoise-coloured tiles adorn the arched doorways of Lal Khan's tomb.

road was built, the northwestern section of the original garden was cut off, along with one of the towers.

The main doors of the tomb are made of pink sandstone. The cobalt and turquoise-coloured tiles that geometrically crowd the arches are Timurid-inspired and held together with yellow and red plaster. This serves as a reminder of the syncretistic nature of the culture of Islamic dynasties in India. The Mughals were Timurid and Mongol in lineage, Turkish and Persian in their cultural ancestry.

The busy Malviya Bridge, built in 1887 as Lord Dufferin Bridge, dominates the view of the river and Banaras from the tomb. The road that leads east is the famous Grand Trunk Road (G.T. Road), today a national highway called 'NH 2'. The G.T. Road is a successor of the road that the Mauryan emperor Chandra Gupta Maurya built in the 3rd century B.C. to facilitate trade between Taxila (in present-day Pakistan) and Pataliputra (in present-day Bihar). After

The Rajghat plateau is one of the oldest settlement sites in the world with remains dating to 800 BCE.

Chandra Gupta Maurya, the Mughals and then the British continued to maintain and extend the road.

Beyond the bridge, see the spire of a massive marble temple dedicated to Raidas, the 14th-century saint. Raidas (1418-1547) was an 'untouchable' cobbler by profession. Like his contemporary poet, Kabir, Raidas wrote catchy, nuanced poetry in the vernacular that was a critique of Brahmanical Hindusim. His temple at Rajghat was built in 1983. He would have been bemused, and perhaps annoyed, to see a temple built and dedicated to him. Like the rest of the devotional Bhakti poet-saints of the 15th-16th centuries (of whom at least three, Raidas or Ravidas, Tulsi and Kabir, spent part of their lives in Banaras) he preached against image and temple worship and other practices of orthodox religion. He wanted a devotee to approach his or her god personally without the mediation of a priest, rituals, or the elite Sanskrit language.

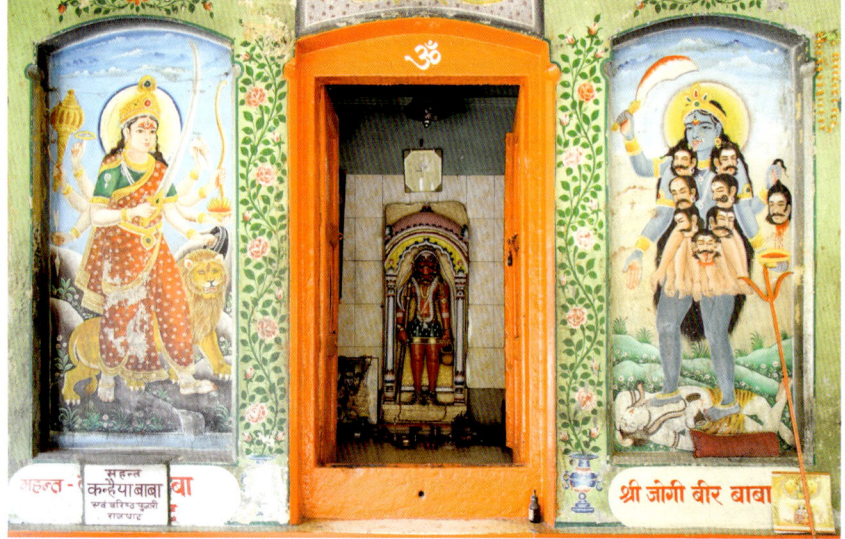

Jogi Bir Baba in his sanctum, with Banarasi-style paintings of Durga (left) and Kali (right) adorning his doorway.

B ARCHEOLOGICAL EXCAVATIONS
One of the world's oldest cities

What to Know The brick remains of the ancient city were unearthed accidentally by a group of construction workers who were extending a railroad track. Soon after, in the 1960s, the Banaras Hindu University began excavations and dated the terracotta pottery, iron implements and seals to 800 BCE, making the Rajghat plateau one of the oldest settlement sites in the world.

C JOGI BIR BABA TEMPLE
Powerful pre-Aryan heroes

→ *Directions from the Rajghat excavation site to the Krishnamurti Foundation and Jogi Bir shrine: Outside Lal Khan's tomb, turn left down the road that follows the river northeast. On the left, pass the Gandhian Institute, which researches Gandhi and the Gandhian movement. Immediately after the Gandhian Institute, a gateway marks the entrance to the Krishnamurti Foundation School. The road, used by the public, leads past the Foundation buildings to a cluster of homes, Adi Keshav Temple, the riverbank, and Chandan Shahid's tomb. Then it continues across the Varuna on a little bridge to the village of Sarai Mohan, a village of fisher people who have gradually turned to other jobs. One could walk across the villages northwest to Sarnath, which is only*

WHO ARE THE BIRS?

Birs are pre-Aryan folk heroes, somewhat akin to Muslim *pirs* in that many of them are spiritual leaders. *Bir* comes from the Hindi word *vir* or 'brave'. They were perhaps *gundas* (local gangsters), when gundas were Robin Hood-like brave leaders, and they may have been martyred while fighting.

JOGI BIR BABA'S MIGHT

Two-hundred years ago Rajghat was just a forest, with only a few huts scattered far apart. Each day at sunset, the forest would grow dark and quiet and the animals would come out. The people of Rajghat, feeling afraid, would shut their doors. But Jogi Bir Baba would walk boldly through the forest with his brass pot to collect water from the river. His wooden clogs would clap and echo between the trees, and the people would no longer feel afraid.

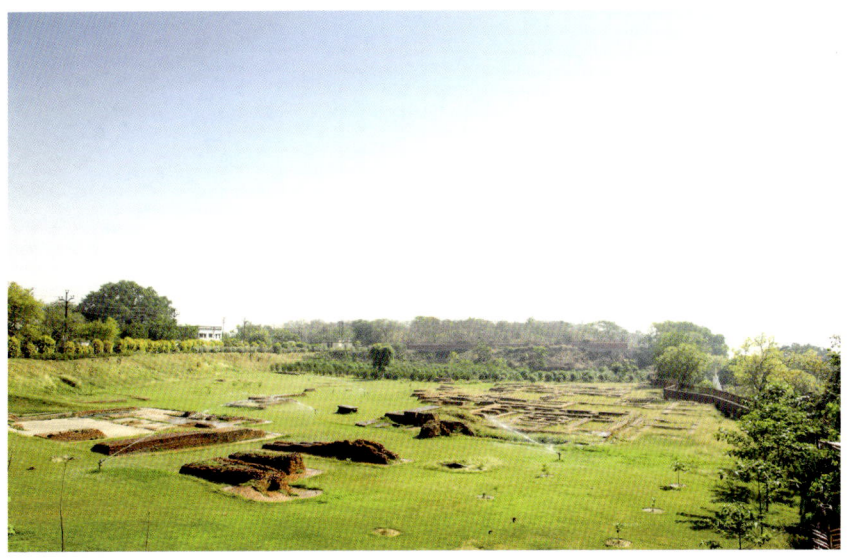

The archaeological remains of ancient Banaras.

some 5 km away. Krishnamurti's followers used to do that on full-moon nights.

What to See The squat, colourful Jogi Bir Baba holds a cane and *kamandal* (brass pot for Ganga water). Over his right shoulder hangs a sickle. Bright paintings done in natural dyes adorn both sides of Jogi Bir's doorway. To the right of him stands Durga with her lion and to the left is Kali on a slain demon, wearing a garland of bloody heads. This style of 'Banarasi' painting originates from Rajasthan. Banarasi practices are a synthesis of cultural habits from all over India since people from north, south, east and west India have settled in the city over the centuries.

> Banarasi practices are a synthesis of cultural habits from all over India since people from north, south, east and west India came to reside in the city over the centuries.

Ⓓ KRISHNAMURTI FOUNDATION SCHOOL & STUDY CENTRE
An education along the Ganga

→ *Directions from Jogi Bir Temple to Krishnamurti Foundation: Outside the temple, turn left and continue down the road. You will find yourself in the Krishnamurti Foundation campus.*

What to Know The Krishnamurti Foundation School in Banaras is an old and reputed institution. It covers a wooded area spread over 300 acres along the Ganga, interspersed with secluded cottages, winding paths and school buildings that are designed in the old Maratha architectural style.

What to See The school buildings are off-limits to visitors, but the Krishnamurti Study Centre remains open to all between 9am and 5pm. Housed in a cool, quiet cottage, it provides books, audio-video resources, lectures and workshops for learning about and reflecting on Krishnamurti's teachings.

Jiddu Krishnamurti
Jiddu Krishnamurti (1895-1986) was a religious teacher and philosopher who wrote and spoke on a wide range of subjects including the human mind, meditation and education.

He was born to a pious family in Madanapalle, a small town in Andhra Pradesh. He was raised under the tutelage of Annie Besant, President

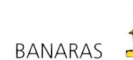

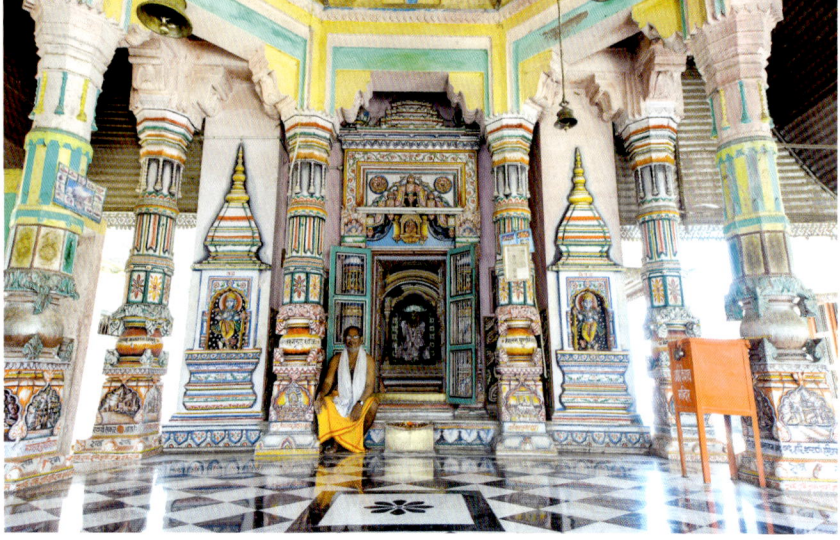

Central sanctum of Adi Keshav Temple.

of the Theosophical Society (see Annie Besant: President of the Theosophical Society on page 141). Besant proclaimed that he would be the World Teacher, come to bring salvation to mankind. The Theosophists established an organization called Order of the Star in the East, of which he was the head, to prepare the world for his coming.

When he was 27, Krishnamurti went through a series of mystical experiences. These, in his own words, made him understand that 'compassion heals all sorrow and suffering'. A few years later he dissolved the Order of the Star in the East. In a speech in 1929, he declared that religion cannot lead to truth and that his only concern was to 'set man absolutely, unconditionally free'.

From 1922 to his passing away in 1986, Krishnamurti travelled and lectured all over the world. His followers characterized him as more of a friend than a guru, a teacher whose discussions were based not on scholarship, but on deep insights into the human condition. His teachings revolved around everyday concerns – the individual's search for success and happiness, the corruption and violence of modern society and the inner burdens of fear, anger and

sorrow. He emphasized the need for each individual to develop self-awareness and meditative thought, without dependence on a prescribed path or teacher.

The organizations and schools run by his followers are spread over India, and also in the UK, USA, and Latin America. There are five Krishnamurti schools in India, located in Banaras, Chennai, Bengaluru, Pune, and Rishi Valley.

The following passage captures the essence of his philosophy:

…The first step is what matters because self-knowledge is not something you can learn from another. No one can teach you self-knowledge, you have to find out for yourself; it must be your own discovery, and that discovery is not something tremendous, fantastic, it is very simple… Just watch your thoughts, your motives, in the mirror of relationships, and you will see that the moment you watch, you want to correct, you say, "This is good, that is bad…" …Your approach is one of condemnation or justification, therefore you distort what you see. Whereas, if you simply observe in that mirror your attitude with regard to people, to ideas, and to

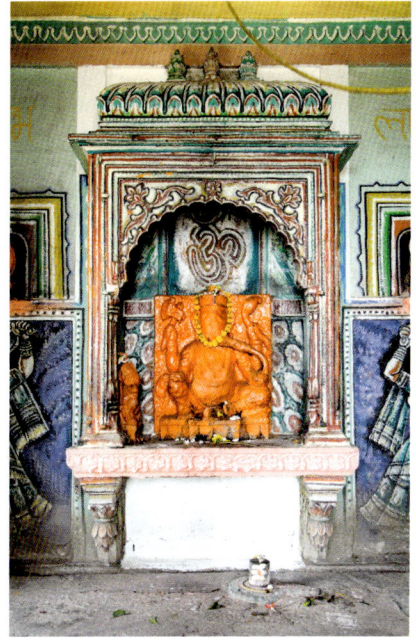

Chintaharan 'problem-solver' Ganesh at Adi Keshav Temple.

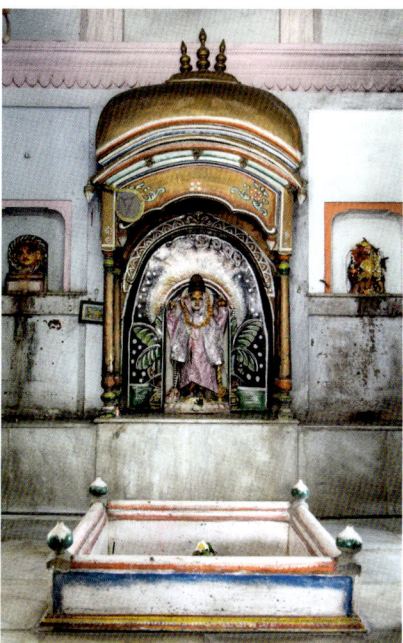

Vishnu at Adi Keshav Temple, flanked by Surya (left) and Durga (right) on her lion.

VISHNU'S PLOY

When King Divodas banished the gods from Kashi so that they would not interfere with his rule, Lord Shiva was sent to Mount Mandara. But Shiva yearned to return to his beloved Kashi. He asked all the gods for help, sending them one by one to Kashi to disrupt Divodas' perfect rule. First he sent a group of 64 goddesses called *yoginis*, then Surya the sun, then Brahma, and then his guardian deities the *ganas*.

Brahma challenged Divodas to complete ten exceedingly complicated horse sacrifices, reasoning that he would surely blunder while performing at least one of them. But Divodas successfully performed the ritual. In acknowledgement, Brahma installed the Sangameshvara *linga* at Adi Keshav.

The gods were unsuccessful at creating trouble in Kashi. Ashamed at their failure and relieved at being back in the luminous city, they settled down there. That is how Kashi came to be the home of three million gods.

The exasperated and lovelorn Shiva now turned to Vishnu, who agreed to help him. On the high bank of Rajghat, Vishnu bathed in the river Varana. That spot came to be known as Padodaka, meaning 'foot water'. It is said that drinking its waters provided instant liberation. Vishnu then sculpted an image of himself, which came to be known as Adi Keshav, the 'original Vishnu'.

Through his clever disguise and schemes as a Buddhist monk, Vishnu was able to spread chaos in Kashi. Divodas grew weary of his kingly duties and asked Vishnu how he could find release from the material world. Vishnu advised the king to establish a Shiva *linga* in the city. Despite his sin in banishing Shiva from Kashi, Vishnu told the king that he had proved to be a just ruler and remained in the great lord's heart. Divodas did as he was advised and was transported to heaven in a chariot. And Vishnu welcomed Shiva back to Kashi.

things, if you just see the fact without judgment, without condemnation or acceptance, then you will find that that very perception has its own action. That is the beginning of self-knowledge.

E ADI KESHAV TEMPLE
The 'original Vishnu'

→ *Directions from the Krishnamurti Foundation to the Adi Keshav Temple: Outside the Krishnamurti Study Centre, turn right down the road. At the end of the Krishnamurti Foundation buildings, a sandy path and a signboard to the right leads to the temple of Adi Keshav. A stairway amidst a cluster of homes leads to the elevated main sanctum.*

What to Know 'Keshav' is another name for Vishnu and 'Adi' means 'original'. The Adi Keshav Temple is unquestionably ancient. Similar to Lolark Kund in the south, it is a site mentioned in the Puranas. It is believed to have remained important until at least the rule of the Gahadvalas in the 12th century, who had their capital at Rajghat. Their inscriptions tell us that they regularly made donations to the priests of Adi Keshav and took ritual baths at the river here.

What to See The central pavilion houses a black, four-armed image of Vishnu. Beside Vishnu are Durga, Surya, the sun god, Narasimha, Vishnu's man-lion form, and Ganesh.

On the western (left-hand) side of the main sanctum, there is a smaller pavilion that houses an image of Gyana Keshav, 'the wise Vishnu'. To the opposite, on the eastern side, is a hallway, which directs visitors outdoors to the shrine of Chintaharan Ganesh, the 'problem-solver Ganesh'.

Along the two arms of the terrace are rooms belonging to Umakant Tripathi, the priest of Adi Keshav. A staircase on the western side of the terrace takes visitors down to the four-headed *linga* of Sangameshvara, 'lord of the confluence', celebrating the joining of the two rivers Ganga and Varana here.

F SHRINES & AKHARA

What to See Exiting the temple, turn right and walk along the wall of the Adi Keshav Temple. Notice the square spaces in the stones and the pipe-like structure jutting out of the wall. Umakant Tripathi, the priest of the temple, explains that after the mutiny of the British East India soldiers in 1857, the British occupied Adi Keshav and used the temple as a military outpost, because the river here was an important crossing-point for traders and messengers. The holes and pipes in the wall of the temple were used for rifles. After the threat of the mutiny had passed, they handed the temple over to the state of Gwalior. But

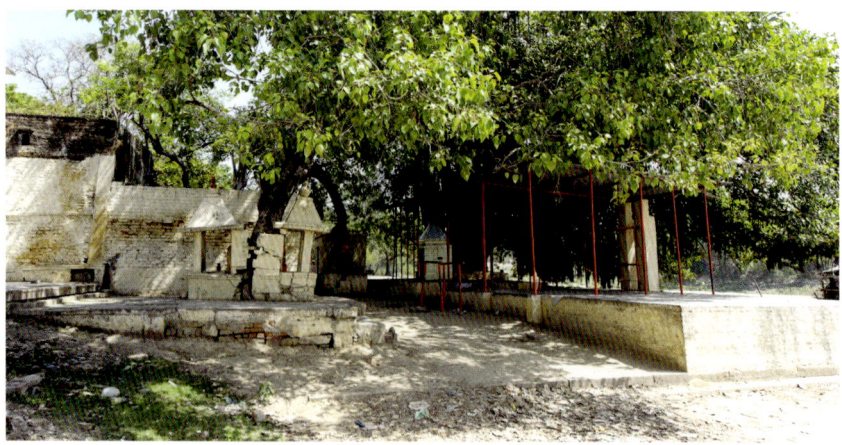

An akhara on the banks of the Ganga, near Adi Keshav Temple.

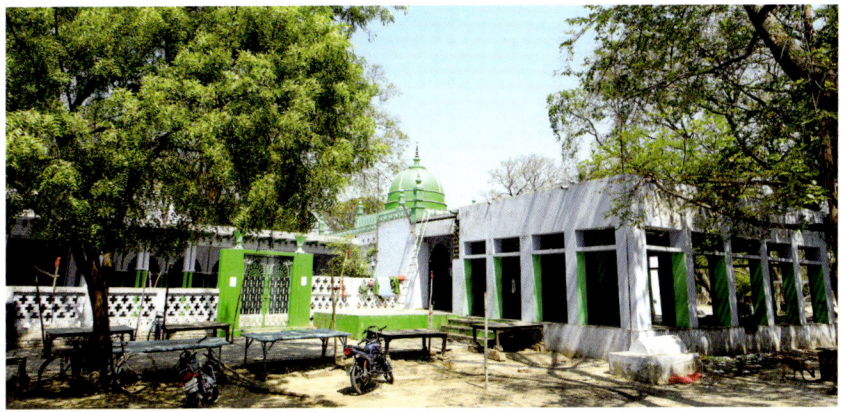

Chandan Shahid Ka Mazar, the tomb of a Sufi saint, popular with Hindus and Muslims alike.

since then the temple has fallen into a state of negligence.

To the left of the Adi Keshav building are the shrines of Vamana Keshav, Vishnu's dwarf-form and his fourth avatar, and the sage Dattatreya.

On the riverbank, an enormous banyan tree extends its gnarled arms over the clay bank and drops its thick roots to encompass an akhara. There is a large covered pavilion for working out. Parallel bars are fastened to the ground. The riverbank with its natural clay undoubtedly serves well as a wrestling arena. As is typical, the structures and weights are painted saffron. The bodybuilders, who work out during early mornings in summer and afternoons in winter, are lucky to have the old tree's shade and the river Ganga's water nearby.

Ⓖ CHANDAN SHAHID KA MAZAR
A fakir from far away

→ *Directions from Adi Keshav to Chandan Shahid ka Mazar: Go up the clay bank towards the road. Continue straight away from the river down the road that curves northeast. This road ends at the tomb of Chandan Shahid.*

What to See Chandan was a *fakir* or religious leader who travelled to Banaras from Kabul. His tinsel-covered tomb is housed behind the pillared verandah. A garden adjoins the verandah, bound by a wrought-iron gate. Along one side of the verandah is an office, where the *pir* (Sufi saint) has sittings with visitors to listen to their problems, which range from chronic headaches to marital conflicts. Anyone can come to receive the blessings and remedies of the *pir*.

CELEBRATIONS AT THE SHRINE

There are weekly and yearly celebrations at Chandan Shahid ka Mazar. Thursday is a special day for visiting the tomb, and every year an urs celebration commemorates the death anniversary of Chandan Shahid. Urs means 'wedding' and refers to the union of the soul with God. A fair called Chandan Shahid ka Mela is organized. On days of celebration, the tomb is scrubbed and sprinkled with sweet rosewater. Worshippers may offer a new chadar or decorated sheet, with which to cover the tomb. Others recite verses from the Qur'an, while many simply pray or tie threads on the wall or tree. In a line outside are balloon, candy sellers and 'holy beggars', those who look to the visitors for alms. Occasionally, qawwali groups also perform. Hundreds of Muslims and Hindus from Rajghat and the nearby weaving neighbourhood of Adampura come to celebrate. The mazar is a place not for religious worship, but for spirituality and celebration for Muslims and Hindus alike.

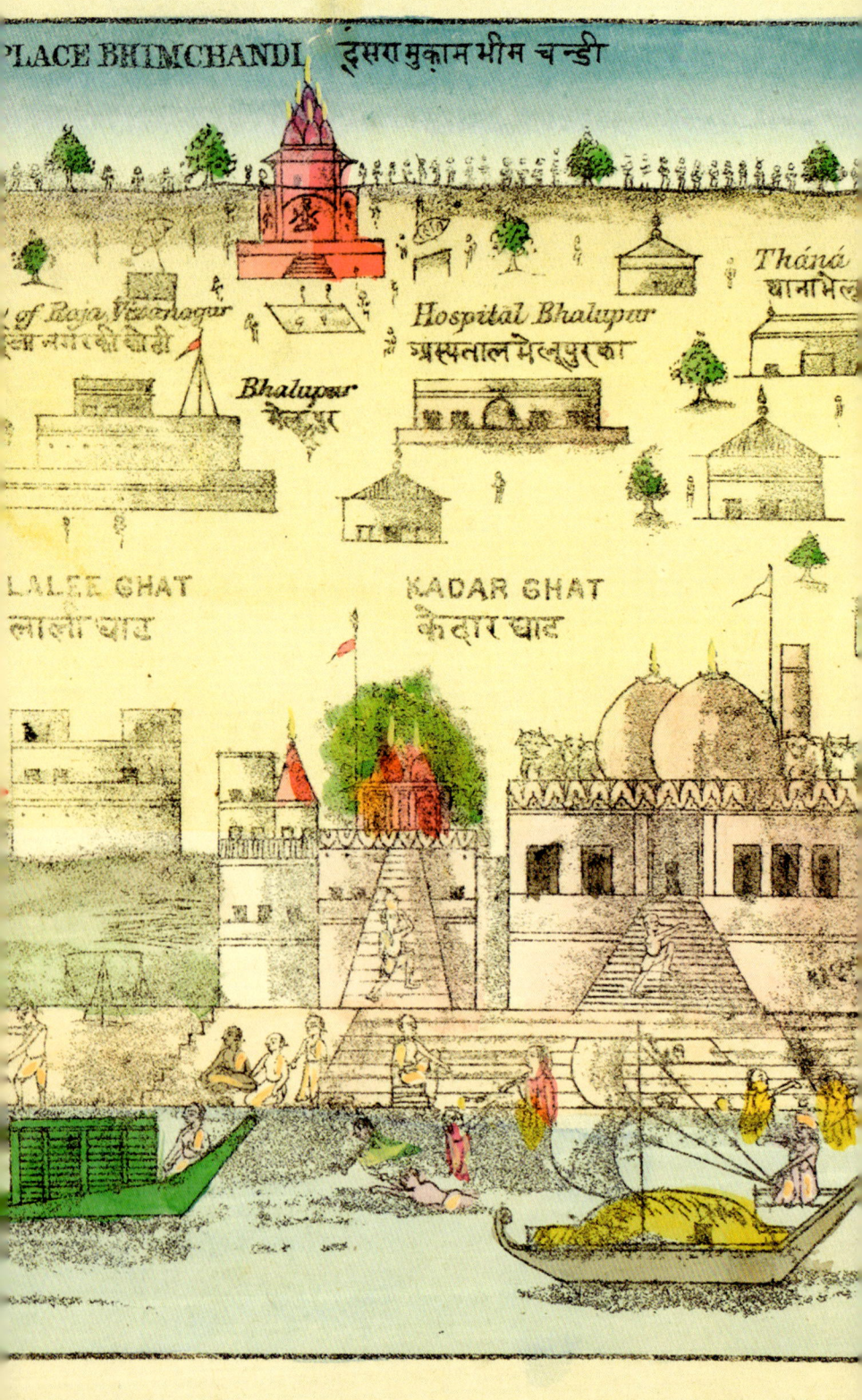

PLACE BHIMCHANDI दूसरा मुक़ाम भीम चन्डी

Thána थानाभैल

of Raja Visahagar जहाँ नगर की चौकी

Hospital Bhalupur ग्रस्तपाल मेलपुर का

Bhalupur मेलपुर

LALEE GHAT लाली घाट

KADAR GHAT केदार घाट

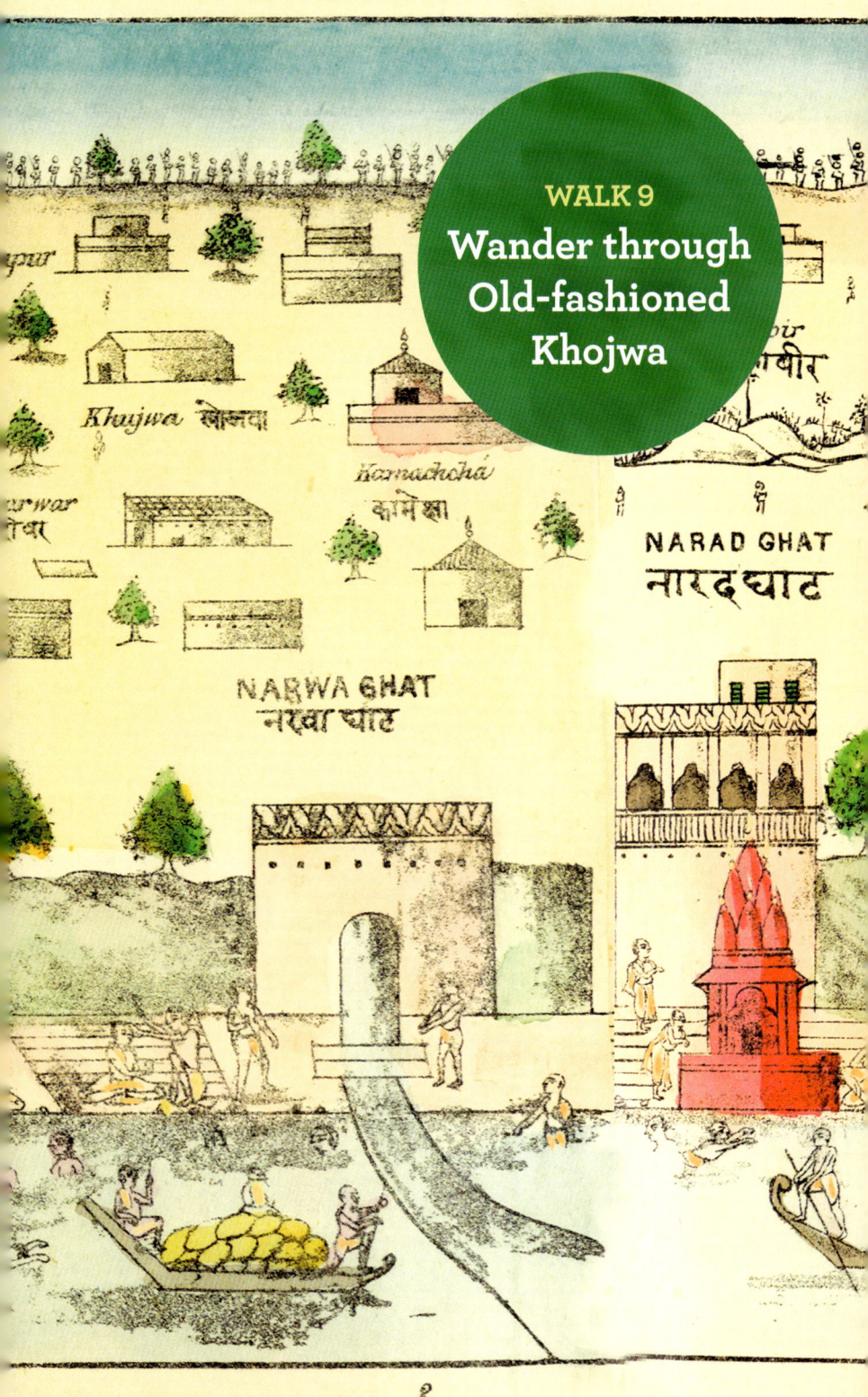

WALK 9

Wander through Old-fashioned Khojwa

Khujwa खोज्वा

Kamadhochá कामेश्वा

NARAD GHAT नारदघाट

NARWA GHAT नरवा घाट

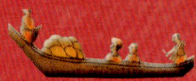

Explore a grain market, traditional artisans' workshops, an old reservoir and several shrines.

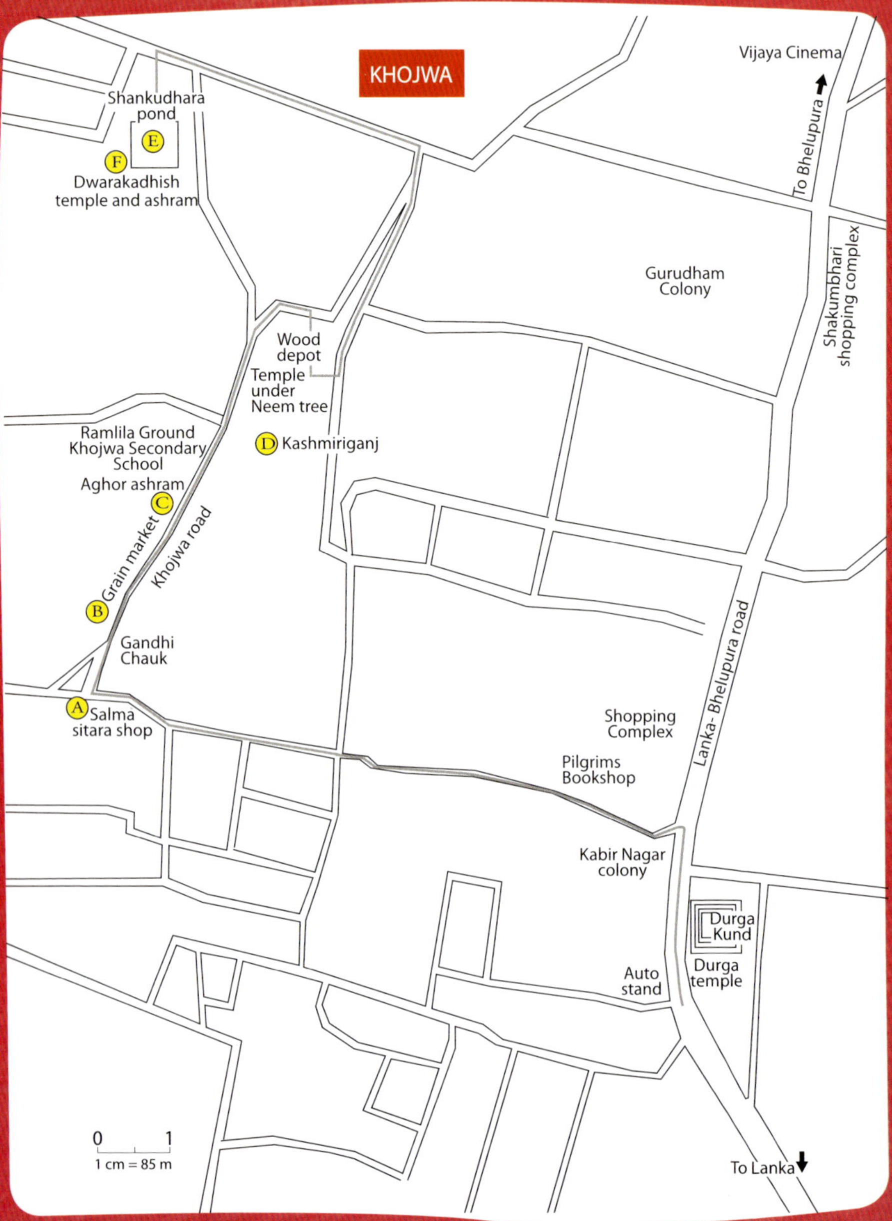

KHOJWA

Vijaya Cinema

To Bhelupura

Shakumbhari shopping complex

Shankudhara pond

Ⓔ
Ⓕ
Dwarakadhish temple and ashram

Gurudham Colony

Wood depot
Temple under Neem tree

Ramlila Ground
Khojwa Secondary School
Aghor ashram
Ⓒ

Ⓓ Kashmiriganj

Grain market
Khojwa road

Ⓑ
Gandhi Chauk

Ⓐ Salma sitara shop

Shopping Complex

Pilgrims Bookshop

Lanka- Bhelupura road

Kabir Nagar colony

Durga Kund

Durga temple

Auto stand

0   1
1 cm = 85 m

To Lanka

THINGS TO SEE

- A busy grain market
- Traditional embroidery, woodwork and weaving workshops
- An old water reservoir, an ashram and a 900 year-old Vishnu idol

WALK ITINERARY

Gandhi Chauk I Salma-sitara shop I Gandhi Chauk grain market I Aghor ashram & Ramlila grounds I Kashmiriganj I Shankudhara pond I Dwarakadhish Temple and ashram

ALLOW

Two to three hours

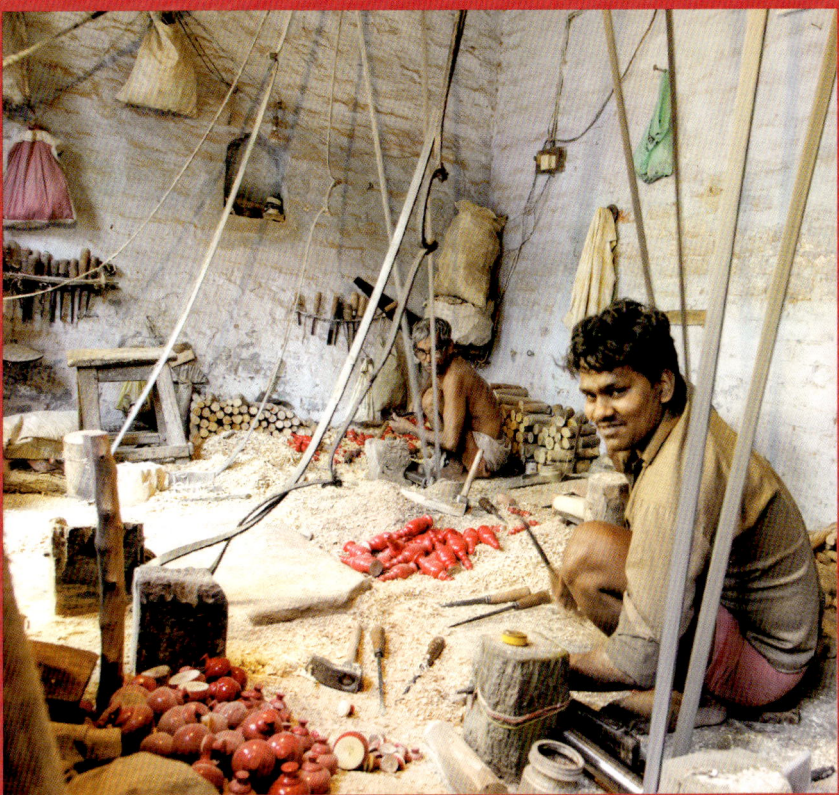

A traditional wood workshop in Khojwa.

GETTING AROUND KHOJWA

Khojwa is a large neighbourhood, bordered by new residential colonies on the Lanka-Bhelupura road. From Durgakund, Khojwa sweeps northward to Bhelupura, containing within it a vast network of lanes and homes. Khojwa can be entered from several points on the Lanka-Bhelupura road. The two main entry points are near the Durga Temple and behind Gurudham Colony.

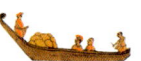

> **THE HISTORY OF KHOJWA**
>
> Khojwa is the main grain market of the city, and has been so for centuries. It is older than the northern grain market of Visheshwarganj. It is also a neighbourhood comprising of woodworkers, stoneworkers, embroiderers, weavers and others in the sari business, such as dyers. As you move through the lanes of Khojwa, pass the workshops where artisans work at looms or whirring, snapping machines, producing piles of toys and idols, as well as leftover raw wood pieces and puffs of stone powder.
>
> Until a few centuries ago, Khojwa was a quiet, rural neighbourhood on the western fringes of Banaras. It was the kaccha mahal, the antithesis of the dense, solid world of Chauk. In Khojwa, houses were cottages, not towering stone structures like the ones that lined the lanes in the urban heart of Banaras. The roads were unpaved and wide. Animal-drawn vehicles moved slowly down the roads, carrying sacks of grain.
>
> Khojwa has also become a neighbourhood of entrepreneurs and shopkeepers. In the past few decades, open spaces have been filled with concrete structures and lanes. Its rural charm has evolved into the ambience of a small town, an area that can be defined as neither village nor city.

→ *Directions from Durga Kund to Khojwa: Pass the auto stand, the Durga Temple, and the water tank called Durga Kund, adjacent to the temple. Turn left at Pilgrims bookstore. Walk all the way down through the residential neighbourhood until the road forks. At this fork on the left is a 'salma-sitara' or crafts shop. The right-hand fork leads to Gandhi Chauk and the Khojwa grain market.*

Ⓐ SALMA-SITARA SHOP
The jewels to decorate a sari
What to See This shop will surely fascinate those who enjoy crafts. It specializes in sequins and spangles (*salma-sitara*), gold and silver thread (*zari*), and sparkling tape (*gota*). Traditional *zardoz* embroiderers use these materials in decorating saris and stoles with a long hooked needle.

Ⓑ GANDHI CHAUK GRAIN MARKET
A centuries-old bazaar
What to See All along Gandhi Chauk road are wholesale shops of wheat (*gehu*), barley (*bajra*), millet (*jowar*), and oats

(*jau*). Enormous weighing scales occupy the central space of each shop. Carts loaded with sacks of grain pull up outside the shops. The shopkeepers sell to individual buyers as well as retailers. In Indian cuisine, grains make up the various breads that accompany lentils and vegetables. In Banarasi cuisine, wheat *rotis* (also called *chapati*s) are preferred.

Ⓒ AGHOR ASHRAM & RAMLILA GROUNDS
Asceticism and theatre
What to See On the left, under a large peepal tree, painted red, is the centre of Kinaram, the founder of the Aghor panth of asceticism, one of the most popular and beloved in Banaras. Kinaram preached that conventional categories are illusory, that nothing is 'impure', and hence no rules should bar anyone or anything in society.

Immediately after the Aghor centre, a lane to the left leads into the grounds of the Khojwa Secondary School, a government school, where several episodes of the Khojwa Ramlila are enacted annually.

Centuries ago, semi-precious jewels and real silver and gold were used to decorate the robes and saris of the upper class.

THE RAMLILA

The Ramlila is an enactment of the story of Lord Ram. In the 16th century, the poet Tulsidas adapted Valmiki's Ramayana into a vernacular version called *Ramcharitmanas*. He launched the Ramlila in Banaras, using his version as its basis. Tulsidas was a Vaishnava and a great *bhakta* of Ram.

Every north Indian village and city has its own Ramlila, but Banaras is special because at least 40 to 50 neighbourhoods put up their own productions every year. These neighbourhoods have 'Ramlila committees' that organize the production year after year. The committees comprise elderly men of the community who are *shaukin* or passionate about theatre andRam and who have acted in their youth, or who are skilled in make-up or music.

For those who perform and watch, the Ramlila is not simply theatre. *Lila* is a Hindu term that means, roughly, 'play' or 'sport'. The philosophy behind the Ramlila is this: since the divine is everywhere and in everything, we humans cannot describe the divine. The gods act, but we cannot know why or how. Perhaps then one way to understand their actions is as a kind of 'play' or 'sport.' The Ramlila is an enactment ofRam's 'play' or 'sport' on earth. The actors who play the gods are believed to be *swarups* and *patras* of the gods. *Swarup* means 'form' and *patra* means 'carrier'. Only pre-pubescent boys are selected to act because only they are considered pure enough to serve as 'carriers' for the gods. Through the boy-actors, we may glimpse the divine.

The Ramlila differs radically from Western realistic theatre. For one, the actors do not act out their characters realistically, but have blank faces and monotonous intonation. Perhaps this is because they are supposed to be 'carriers', more symbolic than 'real'. Then, the two directors, called *Vyasas*, stand prominently near the actors, prompting them with their dialogues and leading them to their positions. They are not invisible or 'offstage' as they would be in realistic Western theatre, but are very much a part of the *lila*.

The Ramlila is a spectacular theatrical genre. Each episode of the story is enacted at a different site in the neighbourhood. A street depicts Ram's capital Ayodhya. A water reservoir serves as the banks of the Sarayu river. These chosen sites are symbolic, like everything else in the production.

Close to the actors, a group of musicians, called *Ramayanis*, narrate portions of the text in song. They sing in full-throated voices, accompanied by the clanging of cymbals and the drumbeat of the *pakhawaj*. Flares light up the gods, who wear red robes and glittering crowns. Depending on the episode, giant bamboo and paper effigies of Ravana, the Lord of Lanka, and other demons tower over the scene.

The spectators can comprise a crowd from 50 to 5,000 people. They gather around the action, follow it as it moves, and react to each moment in each episode – the kidnapping of Sita, the cutting of the demon Surpanakha's nose, Ram's return home. As they do so, they become participants in Ram's story, a part of his lila. Sometimes they choose to sit by the musicians, or follow the dialogues in their own copies of the *Ramcharitmanas*.

The preparations for this spectacular production begin almost a year in advance. The Ramlila committee holds auditions, and five boys are chosen based on age, looks, and voice. The stage manager, called *Atma*, orders masks, costumes, and effigies and organizes sets and stages. Then a marvellous ceremony called *Mukut Puja* ('ceremony of the masks') takes place. Everyone involved worships Ganesh, the five boys, and the scripts, accessories, costumes, and tools that will be used in the production. After this, the boys become *swarups* and *patras* of the gods. Finally, the *Vyasas* train the children in declamation. Rehearsal lasts many months.

Each night of the Ramlila, the make-up artists spend hours on the boys' make-up. They use sandalwood paste, natural paints, glitter, and jewels to transform the children into idols devoid of their individual traits.

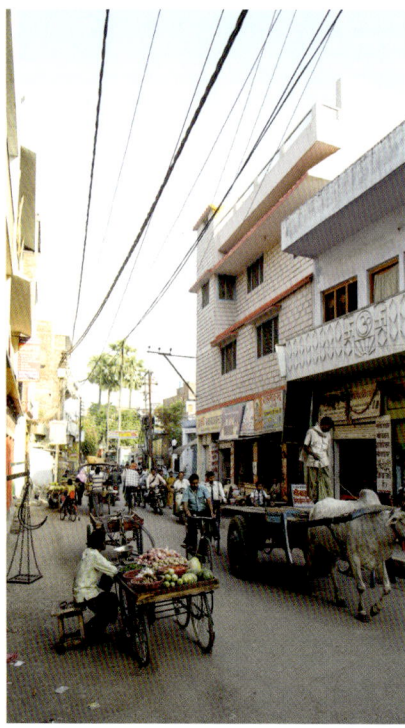

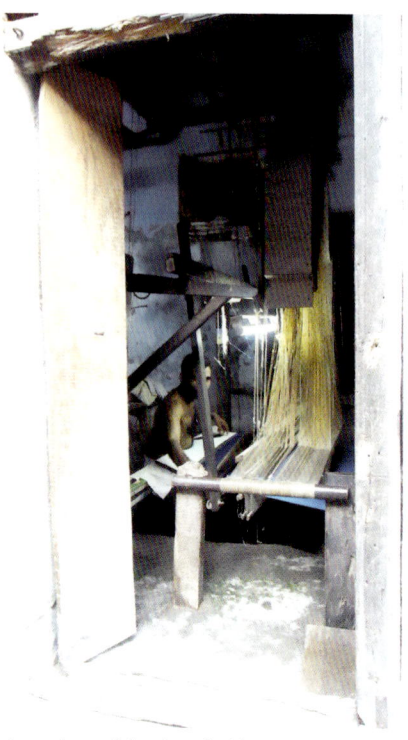

Gandhi Chauk grain market.

A weaving workshop in Kashmiriganj.

Ⓓ KASHMIRIGANJ
The world of Banarasi crafts

→ *Directions from Gandhi Chauk to Kashmiriganj: When the road diverges, take the right-hand road. When it ends in a T-junction, turn right again. This area is called Kashmiriganj. The shops and homes here belong mostly to artisans. Follow the road as it narrows, past a wood depot on the left and woodworking workshops, until you reach a temple in the middle of the road under a neem tree. Wind left around the temple and then left again at the road up ahead. Here we have the homes and workshops of weavers.*

What to See The small stone homes of Kashmiriganj, complete with a verandah and a courtyard, double as workshops of the artisans who live and work here. Walking through Kashmiriganj offers an insider's view of the world of Banarasi crafts. The population of Kashmiriganj mostly comprises embroiderers, weavers, woodworkers and stoneworkers.

Like the city's weavers and metalworkers, woodworkers and stoneworkers have a three-tiered system of production. Some work in others' workshops and are paid by piece. Others work partly independently, bringing their own raw materials to others' lathe machines. Finally there are independent artisans who own machines and raw materials. These artisans usually employ others. The artisans produce toys, animal and human figures, boxes, and idols all year round. During festival periods, they make specialized products. During Durga Puja, the festival of the goddess Durga, in Ashwin (September-October), machines hum from dawn past dusk.

What to Know The wood and stoneworkers of Khojwa describe themselves as Vishwakarmas. They are one among many communities that do so, including *lohars* or blacksmiths, *barhais* or carpenters, and *sonars* or goldsmiths. The

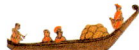

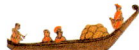

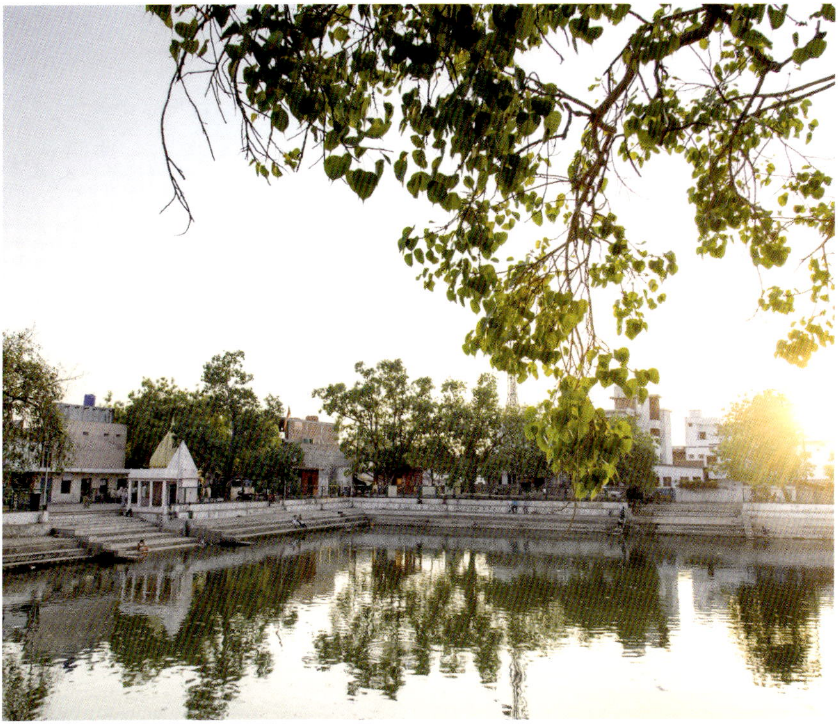

View of the Shankudhara Pond.

name 'Vishwakarma' refers to an aggregate of these artisans, and only means 'those who manufacture', such as the divine architect Vishwakarma did in exemplary fashion.

The wood and stoneworkers' homes in Khojwa are *kachcha* or unbuilt, unlike the homes of weavers and metalworkers in the more urban neighbourhoods. They are cottage-like, many still making use of thatch, tile, or clay. Women do any additional work they can get, like rolling biris (local cigarettes) and papad (lentil or potato wafers) and wrapping candies. Their domain is the interior of the house, while the outward-facing workshop is a male space.

Ⓔ SHANKUDHARA POND
One of the city's original ponds
→ *Directions from Kashmiriganj to Shankudhara Pond: At the main road, turn left. It will lead directly to Shankudhara Pond.*
What to Know Traditionally, kunds were not the man-made reservoirs we see in Banaras today. Many had natural clay banks, which were built up with stone steps in recent centuries. The Shankudhara *pokhara*, or pond, was one such: it was made solid in the mid-19th century by a wealthy resident.

What to See On the banks of the Shankudhara *pokhara* today is a temple, some shrines, and an ashram. Old trees shade the water and the paved spaces, which are cut-off from the traffic. The area is still open and quiet, and one can try to imagine what the atmosphere of ancient Banaras may have been like.

Ⓕ DWARAKADHISH TEMPLE AND ASHRAM
Dedicated to Krishna's city
What to Know The temple is named 'Dwarakadhish' after the city of Dwaraka, on the western coast of Gujarat. Dwaraka

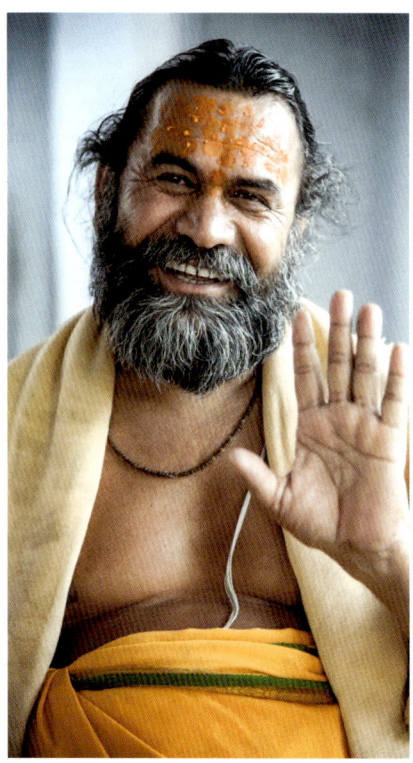

The head priest at Dwarkadish Temple.

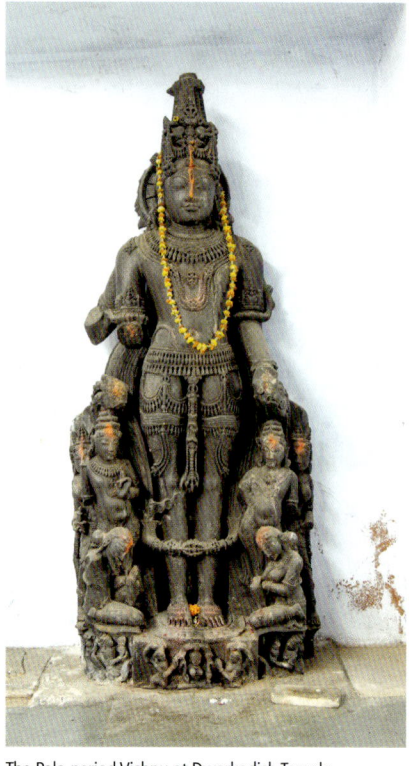

The Pala-period Vishnu at Dwarkadish Temple.

was the capital city of Krishna, an incarnation of Vishnu, in his princely days. Dwaraka is a *dhama*, one of the four 'abodes' of the gods located in different parts of India. In Kashi, which is said to contain all the *dhama*s of India, Dwaraka is situated in Shankudhara.

What to See The temple at Shankudhara, called Dwarakadhish, contains a Pala-period Vishnu image that is at least 900 years old. Other images accompany the black-bodied, wide-eyed Vishnu in the inner sanctum, including Lakshmi, Krishna-Radha, Ganesh, and Shiva. Two large images flank the main entrance to the temple with Hanuman on the left and Surya on the right.

There is some evidence that during Buddhist times, Shankha was a prominent serpent deity in Banaras.

In the adjoining ashram, gurus train young Brahmin boys in Sanskrit and the Vedas. They are taught in the tradition of the 15th-century teacher and follower of Vishnu, Ramanand, whose ashram is at Panchganga Ghat (see 'North of Chauk' page 104).

The multiple meanings of Shankudhara

As Diana Eck points out, there are two possible meanings of 'Shankudhara'. Literally, 'Shankudhara' means 'the salvation of Shankha'. In one myth, Krishna saves a demon named Shankha, and so 'Shankudhara' could refer to this demon. Interestingly, in Dwaraka, in western India, there is a shrine dedicated to

SHANKUDHARA MELA

During the monsoon months, several melas or fairs are organized around Shankudhara pond. The main fair is Shankudhara Mela, which usually takes place in September, in the season of Sawan. It is also called Katahriya Mela because of the tradition of selling *katahal* or jackfruit during that time. Even the Raja of Banaras attended this fair, travelling by boat and then elephant from his fort across the river. Every Banarasi musician and dancer who considered himself noteworthy wanted to perform at the mela. The fair continues today, in a shrunken form as do many of the city's fairs, but interesting to visit nonetheless.

Shankha. And so it is fitting that the temple near the Shankhudhara Pond in Banaras is called Dwarakadhish.

The other explanation is found in Buddhist texts, which refer to 'Shankha' as one of the four Nags (snake deities) who support the earth. There is some evidence that during Buddhist times, Shankha was a prominent serpent deity in Banaras. And the season believed to be important for pilgrimage to the Shankudhara Pond is monsoon, which is also associated with serpents.

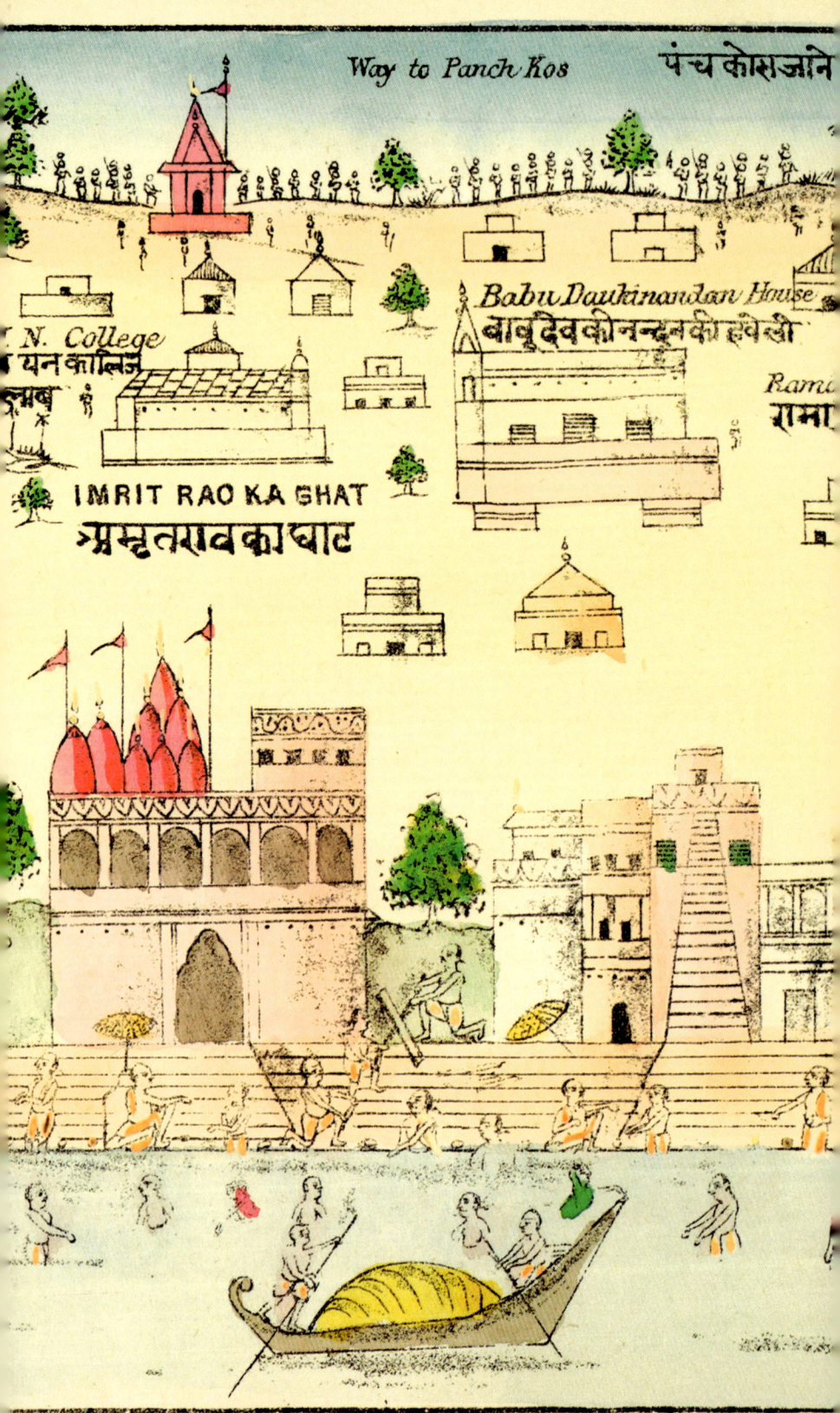

In the Footsteps of the Gurus at Laksa

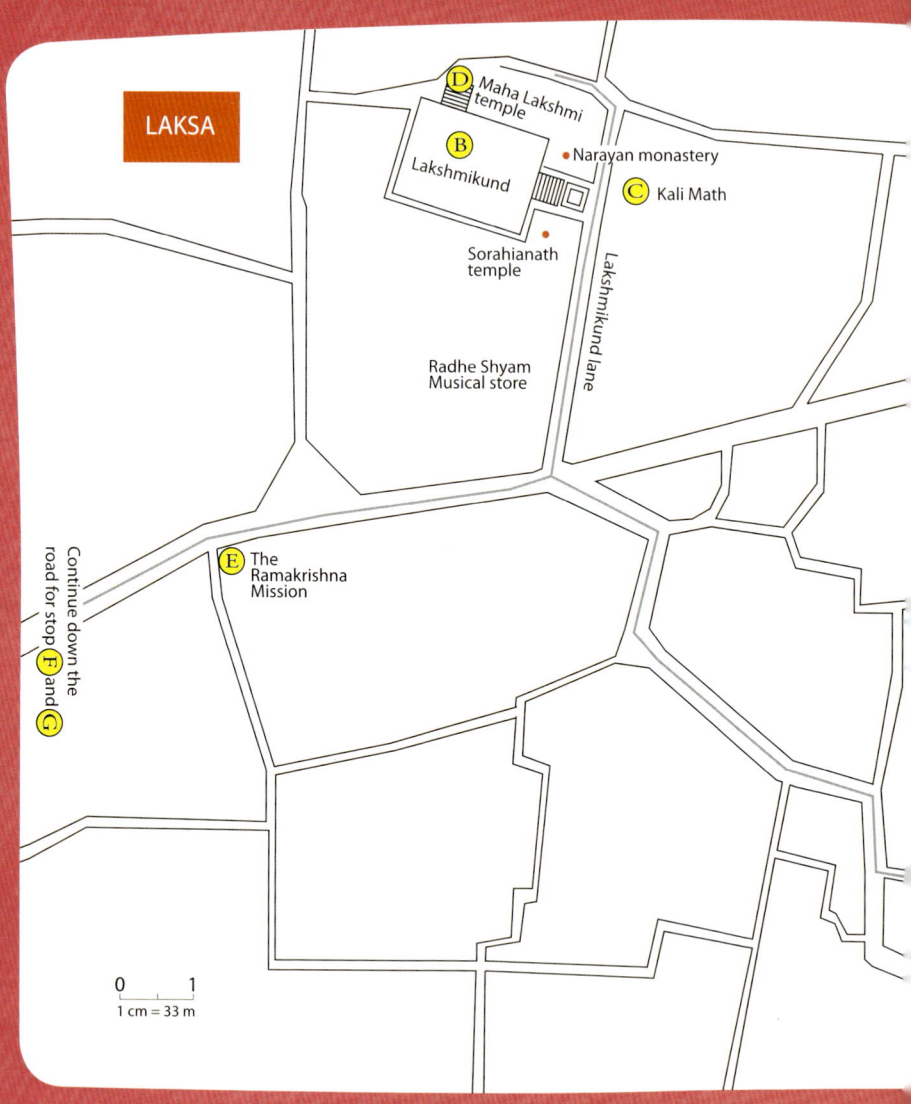

LAKSA

D Maha Lakshmi temple

B Lakshmikund

• Narayan monastery

C Kali Math

Sorahianath temple

Lakshmikund lane

Radhe Shyam Musical store

E The Ramakrishna Mission

Continue down the road for stop F and G

F and G

0 ——— 1
1 cm = 33 m

Stroll past famous musicians' homes in Ramapura and sit beside the old pond, Lakshmikund. Explore the peaceful lanes, temples and an old monastery dedicated to Kali here. Next, head back to the busy Laksa Road. Visit the historic campus of the Ramakrishna Mission and the city's main Sikh temple, while enroute to the Theosophical Society's national headquarters.

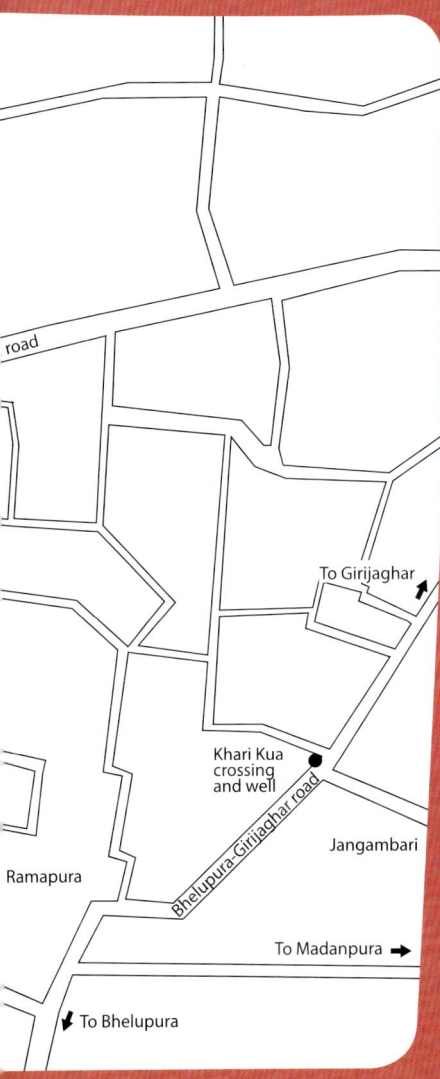

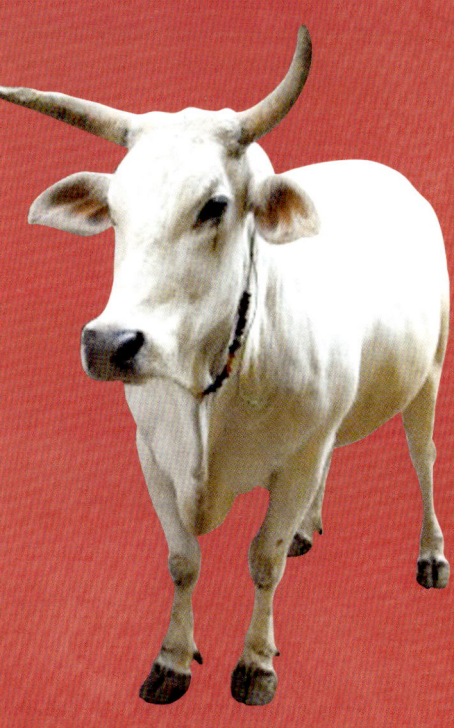

THINGS TO SEE
- The Lakshmikund pond
- Monastery of the wrathful goddess, Kali
- A Sikh Gurudwara
- Campuses of the Theosophical Society and Ramakrishna Mission

ALLOW: Two to three hours

WALK ITINERARY
Ramapura I Lakshmikund I Kali Math I Maha Lakshmi Temple I The Ramakrishna Mission I The Sikh Gurudwara I The Theosophical Society national headquarters

GETTING AROUND RAJGHAT
Laksa road connects the crossings of Godaulia and Girjaghar in the east, with Sigra in the west. On the northern side of this road are smaller neighbourhoods. 'Laksa' refers to the general area encompassing these neighbourhoods. To the south is Gurubagh, named after the large Sikh temple, which is situated at the Gurubagh crossing.

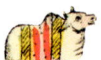

THE HISTORY OF LAKSA

Built during the British raj, the Laksa road was originally a narrow lane. Today, it has transformed into a wide street. On either side are the homes and shops of artisan families who have helped create Banaras over many generations. These families have recently switched their trade from traditional crafts to newer ones, such as the making of intricate electrical parts.

The larger area called Laksa is made up of small, busy neighbourhoods. The neighbourhood of Lakshmikund is named after an old water tank and a temple that hosts an annual fair in honour of the goddess, Lakshmi. Ramapura is home to the extended families of musicians and dancers, who are called 'Mishra,' many of whom are among India's most celebrated performers.

Historic institutions of social and political importance abound in Laksa. The area is also home to the city's only Sikh temple or gurudwara, where the active community of the Sikhs of Varanasi gather. Located here are also the national headquarters of the Theosophical Society, which was founded in Banaras by the British reformer Annie Besant to revive the power of Hinduism when it was under attack, and the Ramakrishna Mission, established by Swami Vivekanand, the disciple of the late 19th-century philosopher, Ramakrishna Paramahamsa. All of these institutions began and evolved as Hindu reformist attempts. Sikhism, the oldest, is today a major Indian and world religion. The Theosophical Society's schools and the Ramakrishna Mission's hospitals and schools continue to wield social and cultural influence.

A stroll through the busy street and quiet lanes of Laksa, gives visitors a sense of the remarkable spiritual diversity of Banaras and its innumerable popular practices and formal reforms.

Ⓐ RAMAPURA
The heart of music and dance

→ *Directions to Ramapura: A small Hanuman temple is located on the narrow road leading from Bhelupura crossing to Girjaghar church. The main Ramapura lane is located opposite the Hanuman temple.*

What to Know Ramapura is one of the two main neighbourhoods in Banaras that is home to the Mishras, the extended family of professional classical musicians and dancers. Settled here are the families of the late Mahadev Mishra, considered the Thumri *samrat* or 'Lord' of the Thumri, a playful and romantic genre of singing, especially popular in Banaras, and Ishwarlal Mishra, a senior tabla player who played solo and accompanied eminent artistes such as the late Ravi Shankar (himself a musician from Banaras). Some world-famous singers who belong to this family and continue their

'The whole world when I was born in Banaras was like an India as it existed two thousand years ago.' Pandit Ravi Shankar in his autobiography.

family's legacy are Girija Devi and brothers Rajan and Sajan Mishra.

What to See Take a detour from the main lane into one of the side alleys. Although the musicians' homes do not look special from the outside, you might catch the soulful strains of a sarangi or the sonorous rhythm of a tabla through a window. And you may pass a musician wandering in the lanes outside, dressed casually in a lungi, drinking a cup of tea or chewing pan.

Ⓑ LAKSHMIKUND
Small homes, simple lives

→ *Directions from the Hanuman temple/the start of the Ramapura lane to Lakshmikund: Turn left (west) down the Ramapura lane and follow it as it curves right (north), left (west) and right (north) to the broad Laksa road. Across the street is the lane leading to Lakshmikund.*

What to Know The small shops and homes here belong to stoneworkers, barbers,

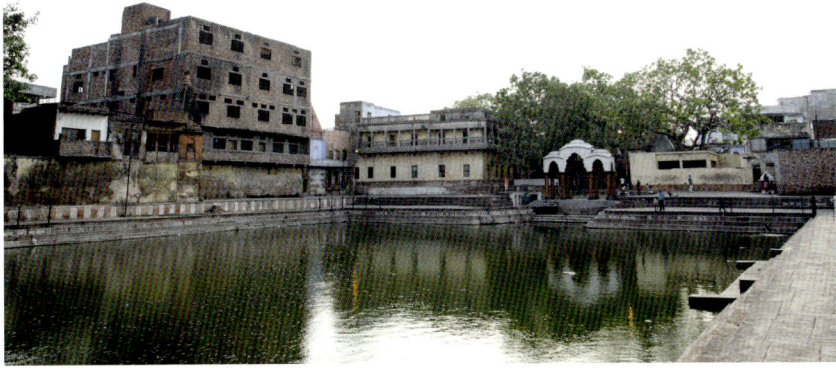

Lakshmikund with its arched doorway, seen from the opposite side.

tailors, mechanics and other artisans and businessmen. Old doorways allow glimpses into courtyards and stairways, which serve as spaces for cooking or bathing.

What to See On the left of the lane there is a shop that sells and repairs instruments, called Radhe Shyam. If you are lucky, you may find the owner repairing a sitar or harmonium inside.

The lane opens out into Lakshmikund, a wide reservoir surrounded by tall buildings and old trees. A stone plaque under the large peepal tree explains the Puranic significance of Lakshmikund. In translation, it reads:

Shiva sent 64 *yoginis* out in all directions in Varanasi. Chausatti Ma was sent to Chausatti Ghat where she established the Chausatti Ma Temple. Mayuri *yogini* was sent to Lakshmikund. She was also influential in establishing other temples in the city... (see Vishnu's Ploy page 117).

The three-storeyed old stone building, under the enormous peepal tree, houses the Narayan Monastery. The large Shiva *linga* and other images under the tree are fairly recent additions.

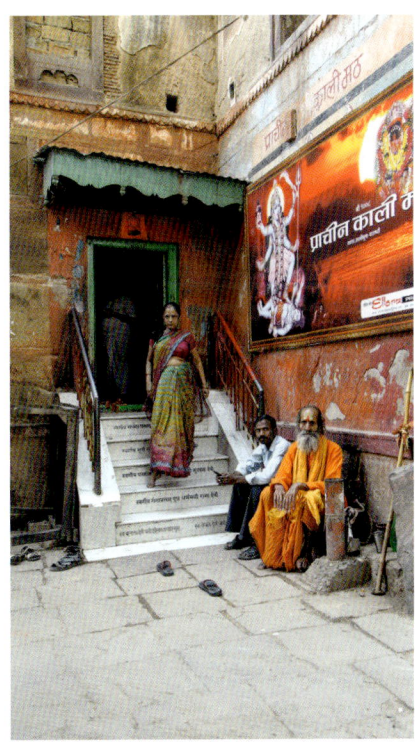

Entrance of Kali Math.

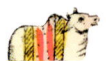

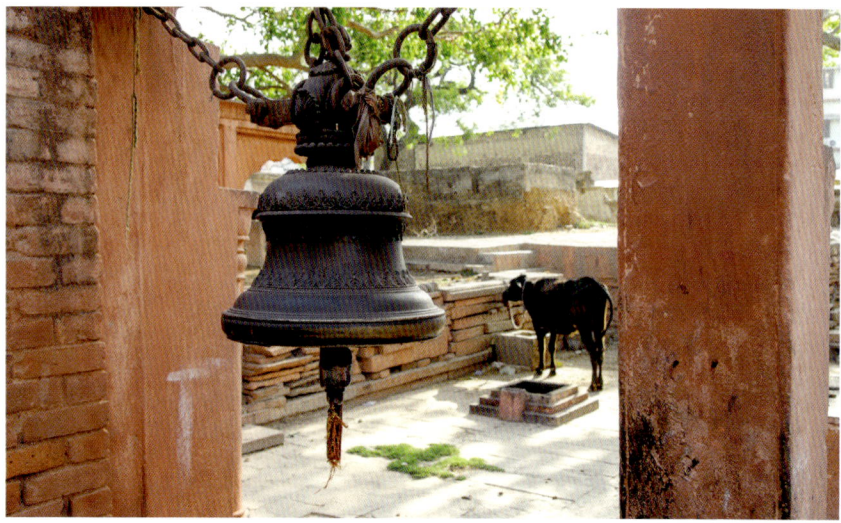
Glimpse of the Kali Math compound.

Adjoining the water tank is the temple of Sorahianath. The images and shrines within are from Puranic times, as the signboard outside states in Hindi. The temple houses four shrines: the first of the goddess Mangala Gauri and her two sons Ganesh and Kartikeya, the second of the goddess of smallpox, Sitala and the third of Sorahia Ma. The fourth and largest shrine at the far end is dedicated to Hanuman and the famous ascetic Sai Baba.

The old tree behind the Sitala shrine, whose trunk is swathed in red thread, has also been worshipped for years. The combination of an old tree and a cluster of images at its base, lovingly arranged and washed, is typical of any neighbourhood temple in Banaras.

Ⓒ KALI MATH
The wrathful goddess
→ *Directions from Lakshmikund to Kali Math: Opposite Lakshmikund is the crumbling building that houses the Kali Math. The entrance is framed prominently with a colourful sign and stairway.*
What to Know Kali, the fierce, fiery-eyed goddess, is a manifestation of Shakti or feminine power. Originally the building housed a monastery for ascetics belonging to the Dandi sect. The priests here recount an elaborate tale that describes how the monastery came to be a Kali temple (see How Kali Came to the Monastery, facing page). The story strikes one as funnily open-ended, but this represents how in Hinduism, origins are often obscure and tales popularly evolved and intricately intertwined. There are hundreds of such stories that Banarasis can narrate about their practices and the sites in their city.

What to See Inside the monastery, the main Kali image sits in the first room within a carved red canopy. Krishna stands on either side on a smaller throne. The painting above each wooden window is of Kali. In the second room, there are a few images of Kali framed in plastic and Shiva *lingas*. To the left, a stairway leads to a locked basement, where the original Kali image is believed to be stored.

Only two rooms from the original monastery remain intact. From the compound, at the back, one can view the ruins of the monastery. Two wooden clogs stand against the back wall. These belonged to a former head priest and are worshipped periodically.

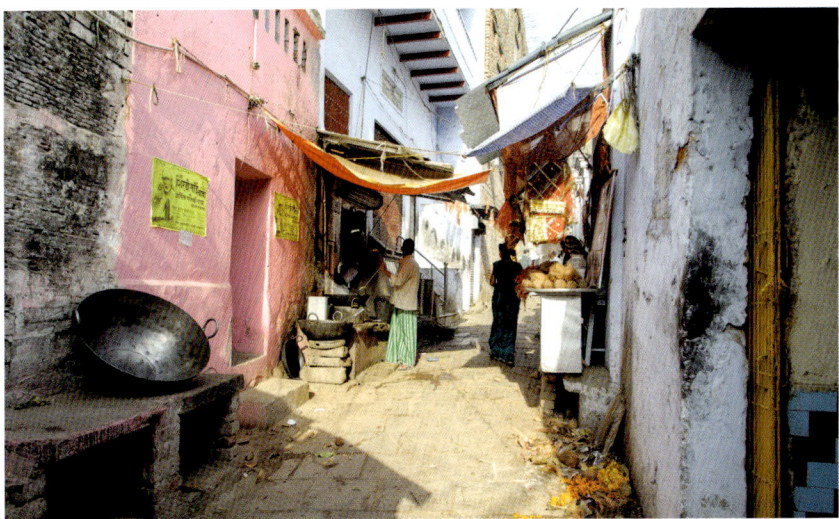

Shops of tea and of ritual items outside the Maha Lakshmi Temple.

The shrine in the middle of the compound is of Lakshmi, one of the most beloved among the goddesses. She is regarded as the patron goddess of wealth and prosperity. Every merchant and trader, in particular, have a shrine, however small it may be, devoted to Lakshmi in their shops.

There are several old wells and shrines in the compound, nestled among trees and overgrown grass. The shrines mark the spots where various priests took *mahasamadhi*, which is the act of consciously leaving one's body upon attaining enlightenment.

HOW KALI CAME TO THE MONASTERY

A long time ago, a businessman came to Banaras to sell idols. He stopped to rest by the river Ganga and put the idols down. One of them was of Kali and another of a lion. Incidentally, a Dandi ascetic had come down to the river to bathe at the same time. Seeing the idols, he wanted to purify them before purifying himself. So he splashed the lion with holy water from the river Ganga – and at that very instant, the lion came to life. It shook its tail and sat down beside the ascetic like an obedient dog. Next, the ascetic sprinkled the idol of Kali with the same water. Kali too came to life. The ascetic said, 'Proceed, Kali!' Kali began to walk away and the ascetic followed her, mounted on the lion. It is believed that Kali walked all the way to the monastery at Lakshmikund and established herself there.

One day, the head priest of the temple was resting in the Kali monastery. This was the time when Aurangzeb ruled India. Having heard of the miraculous powers of the Kali monastery, he decided to visit it. He entered the monastery and stood facing the old head priest, but the priest didn't get up from his restful position to greet him. A servant hurried up and tried to explain to the priest that the emperor had come on a visit. But the head priest only gestured to the servant to bring him an earthen pot kept in the corner. Mystified, the servant set the pot in front of the ascetic, while the enraged emperor looked on. The head priest closed his eyes and folded his hands in meditation – and the pot shattered into pieces. Aurangzeb is known to have destroyed hundreds of Hindu temples in Banaras, but he did not touch the Kali monastery after witnessing this miracle.

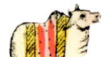

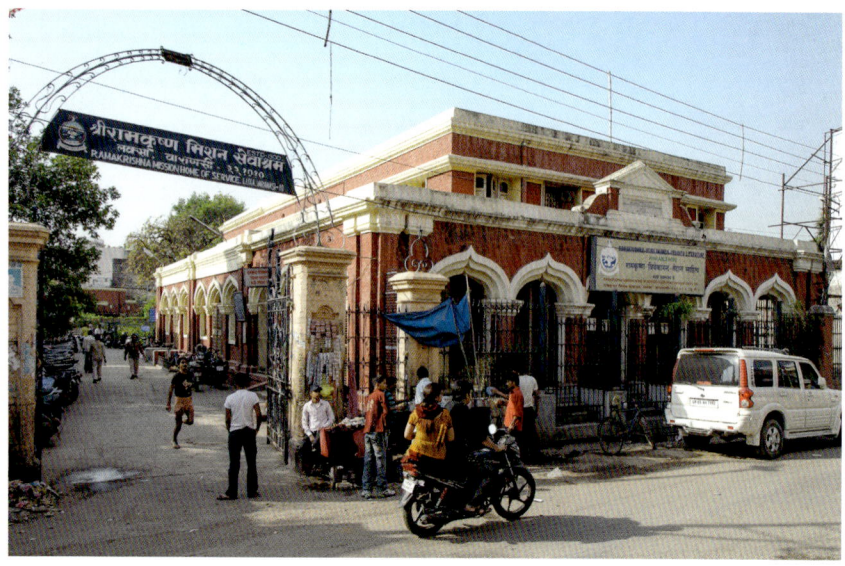

Ramakrishna Mission Hospital.

Ⓓ MAHA LAKSHMI TEMPLE
Poetry and painting

→ *Directions from the Kali Math to the Maha Lakshmi Temple: Turn right (north) outside the Kali Monastery and continue left along the side of the pond to the Maha Lakshmi Temple. Its elevated doorway will be on your left.*

What to See Moving clockwise, within this plainly constructed temple, notice the inner shrines that house images with marble faces and silver masks, which are forms of Devi, Vishnu, and Shiva. The walls are inscribed with artis or songs of worship to Maha Lakshmi. Colourful square paintings depicting Kali and other forms of the Devi encircle the altar at the back. Here also, a set of stairs leads to the waters of Lakshmikund. Easy access to water is a distinctive feature of the old Banaras temples.

The priests sit in a small canopy, near the front staircase, with their sacred books bundled in red cloth. Along with the *Hanuman Chalisa*, the priests' bundles contain poetry dedicated to various forms of Vishnu, Shiva, and Devi.

Ⓔ THE RAMAKRISHNA MISSION
The first modern Hindu missionaries

→ *Directions from the Maha Lakshmi Temple to the Ramakrishna Mission: Turn right (south) outside the temple. Go past Lakshmikund and the*

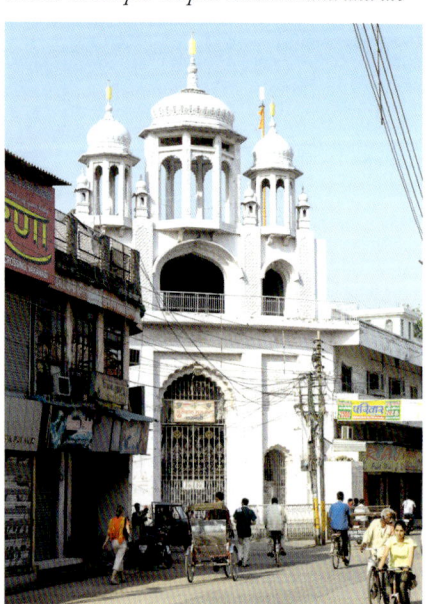

The Sikh Gurudwara at Gurubagh crossing.

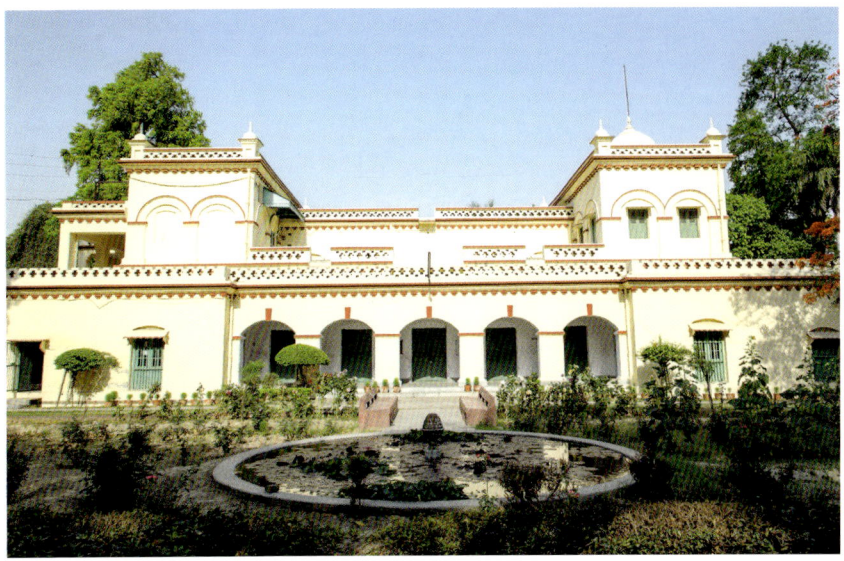

Theosophical Society headquarters.

music shop to the main Laksa road. Turn right (west) down Laksa road. Walk down it as it narrows. The Ramakrishna Mission appears on the left.

What to Know The Ramakrishna Mission Hospital is popularly called 'Cowria Hospital' from the time when cowrie shells were the lowest units of currency in India, implying that treatment here was so cheap, it was close to being almost free.

The Ramakrishna Mission, a premier service organization in India, was founded by Swami Vivekananda at the end of the 19th century in honour of his guru, Sri Ramakrishna Paramahamsa, a mystic from Bengal. This hospital, with its basic services, its old-fashioned interiors, and its monks, trained in both monasticism and medicine, is a model for a possible synthesis between the Indian notion of service, itself modernized by Vivekanand, and Western medical systems.

History of the Mission
Shri Ramakrishna Paramahamsa (1836-1886) is one of the most celebrated mystics of India in recent times. He was born Gangadhar Chattopadhyay to poor Brahmin parents in rural Bengal. He became a priest at the Kali Temple in Dakshineshwar in Bengal, which practiced the Bengali Shakta tradition.

Shri Ramakrishna experimented with Tantra, Vaishnav devotion, Advaita Vedanta or non-dualism and also other religions such as Islam and Christianity. Uneducated himself, he gained the support of the Bengali *bhadralok* or English-speaking intelligentsia. His prime disciple was Swami Vivekananda, born Narendranath Dutta, who became an influential figure in the Bengali Renaissance and Hindu revival in the 19th and 20th centuries. Swami Vivekananda is also credited with bringing Shri Ramakrishna's philosophy to the West.

Today, the Ramakrishna Mission is a large and well-funded organization that runs ashrams, temples and hospitals all over India and in many cities in Europe and North America.

Ⓕ THE SIKH GURUDWARA
The wise words of the guru
What to Know Sikhism was founded in the late 15th century by Guru Nanak Dev. He

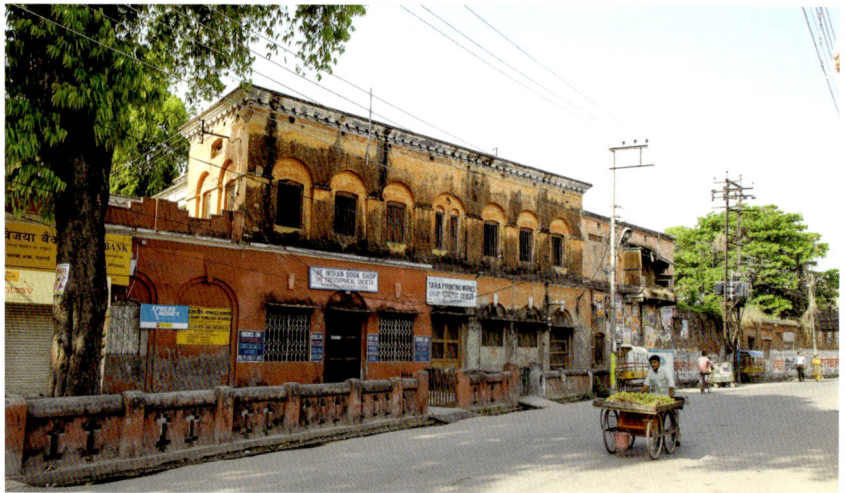

The bookshop at the Theosophical Society headquarters.

was the first Sikh guru in a line of ten. The writings of the first six Gurus were compiled into the sacred *Adi Granth* book by the fifth Guru Arjun (1563-1606). After Arjun was executed by the Mughal emperor Jahangir, Sikhism grew increasingly militant. The tenth guru, Guru Gobind Rai founded the militant fraternity of the Sikhs known as Khalsa that remains the principal Sikh order. After losing his sons, Guru Gobind Rai decreed the *Adi Granth* as the immortal guru. Sikhs believe in one non-anthropomorphic God known as *Waheguru* and are ordained to serve him through living their lives in accordance with the teachings of the *Adi Granth*, the ten gurus, and the qualities found in the *sant-sipahi* or 'saint-soldier', including those of valour, loyalty, and charity. Their system of religious philosophy is known as *Gurmat* or 'the counsel of the gurus'. The word *sikh* comes from the Sanskrit *shiksha*, meaning 'learning', and *gurudwara* means 'gates of the guru'. Sikhism is an amalgam of Islam and Hinduism. Sikhs also incorporate Hindu festivals in their celebrations.

What to See Inside the spacious Banaras gurudwara, the holy *Granth Sahib* or the *Adi Granth* lies under a silken canopy on an elevated platform, fly-whisked by a devotee on either side. The worshippers prostrate themselves before the holy book or sit before it, their heads covered, praying or singing along with devotional singers who sing hymns from the *Granth*. Sikhs believe in disciplined, personal meditation. On special occasions, a community meal called *langar* is served, which usually consists of *khichri* made with rice, vegetables, *dal* and prasad which is typically sweet *halwa* made with lentils.

The committee that runs the gurudwara also runs the nearby Khalsa Girls' College. This is typical of the old schools of Banaras, which are run by a regional or religious group. The girls of Khalsa Girls' College wear a green checked uniform, which is also typical, in that each school has a uniform and manages to find its own unique combination of colours.

Ⓖ THE THEOSOPHICAL SOCIETY NATIONAL HEADQUARTERS & CENTRAL HINDU GIRLS' SCHOOL
Reforms in education and religion

→ *Directions from the gurudwara to the Theosophical Society headquarters: Turn left (west) down the Laksa road. The Theosophical Society's national headquarters is on the left after the Central Hindu Girls' school.*

What to Know Annie Besant was a leading Theosophist and British reformer. She established the Theosophical Society in

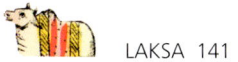

ANNIE BESANT – FOUNDER OF THE THEOSOPHICAL SOCIETY IN INDIA

In 1871, Madame H.P. Blavatsky and Colonel H. D. Olcott founded the Theosophical Society in New York. Six years later, in 1878, the Theosophical Society was established in India. Largely under the leadership of Annie Besant in India, it became one of the reformist organizations of the late 19th and early 20th centuries, targeting the repressive practices that had developed in religion, caste, education and women's conditions.

Born in Ireland in 1847, Annie Besant gained recognition in her home country as a social reformer and supporter of self-rule. It was when Besant reviewed Blavatsky's *The Secret Doctrine* that she sought a meeting with Blavatsky and Olcott. Soon after meeting them, Besant became a Theosophist and began lecturing and writing on Theosophy. She first travelled to India in 1893, where she was welcomed enthusiastically and began her famous Convention Lectures at the international headquarters at Adyar, near Chennai. She settled in Banaras in 1895.

It was with Besant that a new era of activism began in the history of the Theosophical Society. She not only was a proponent of Theosophy, but she also converted to Hinduism and became a leader of Hindu reform. In 1898, she established the Central Hindu Girls' School and in 1908, she founded the national headquarters of the Theosophical Society, both in Banaras. She supported the Indian movement for self-rule and is considered among the leaders of the nationalist movement in India.

Central Hindu School, with its space, resources and staff, was the initial nucleus of the Banaras Hindu University. When educationist and activist Madan Mohan Malviya initiated his petition for establishing the university in 1905, Annie Besant was a primary supporter of his petition. Their fascinating, unmatched experiment revolved around the idea that the best in Western learning could be synthesized with the best in Indian knowledge, to produce a curriculum that would be simultaneously 'Hindu' and 'modern'. Elsewhere, as in Aligarh and Delhi, the synthesis was sought for Islamic and modern education. The Central Hindu School was a noble experiment, with beautiful buildings, a faculty trained in both traditional Indian and modern subjects, and students who were imparted not just an academic education, but a cultural one as well.

Banaras as well as the adjoining Central Hindu School for Girls and Besant Primary School, which continues to be run by the Theosophical Society.

What to See The trees and gardens of the Theosophical Society campus make it a wonderful retreat from the street. But whether visitors are allowed to enter will depend on the guard at the gate. Today, the Society has over 200 members in Banaras. The quiet campus houses a bookshop, a lecture hall, a library, and the Besant Primary School. The library contains books on theosophy, religion, spiritualism, history and philosophy. Each Friday, the Society organizes lectures and meetings in the lecture hall. The library and bookshop are open to the public between 10am and 5pm.

> Annie Besant is considered among the leaders of the nationalist movement in India.

Exiting Laksa road: Turning left outside the Theosophical Society leads to the bustling Rathyatra crossing, which is the site of the annual Rath Yatra festival. From here, an autorickshaw can be taken south towards Lanka or north towards Cantt. Or turn right outside the Theosophical Society and walk or take a rickshaw to the Godaulia crossing. At the Godaulia crossing, autos are available for any destination towards Lanka, and rickshaws are available for any destination in the city.

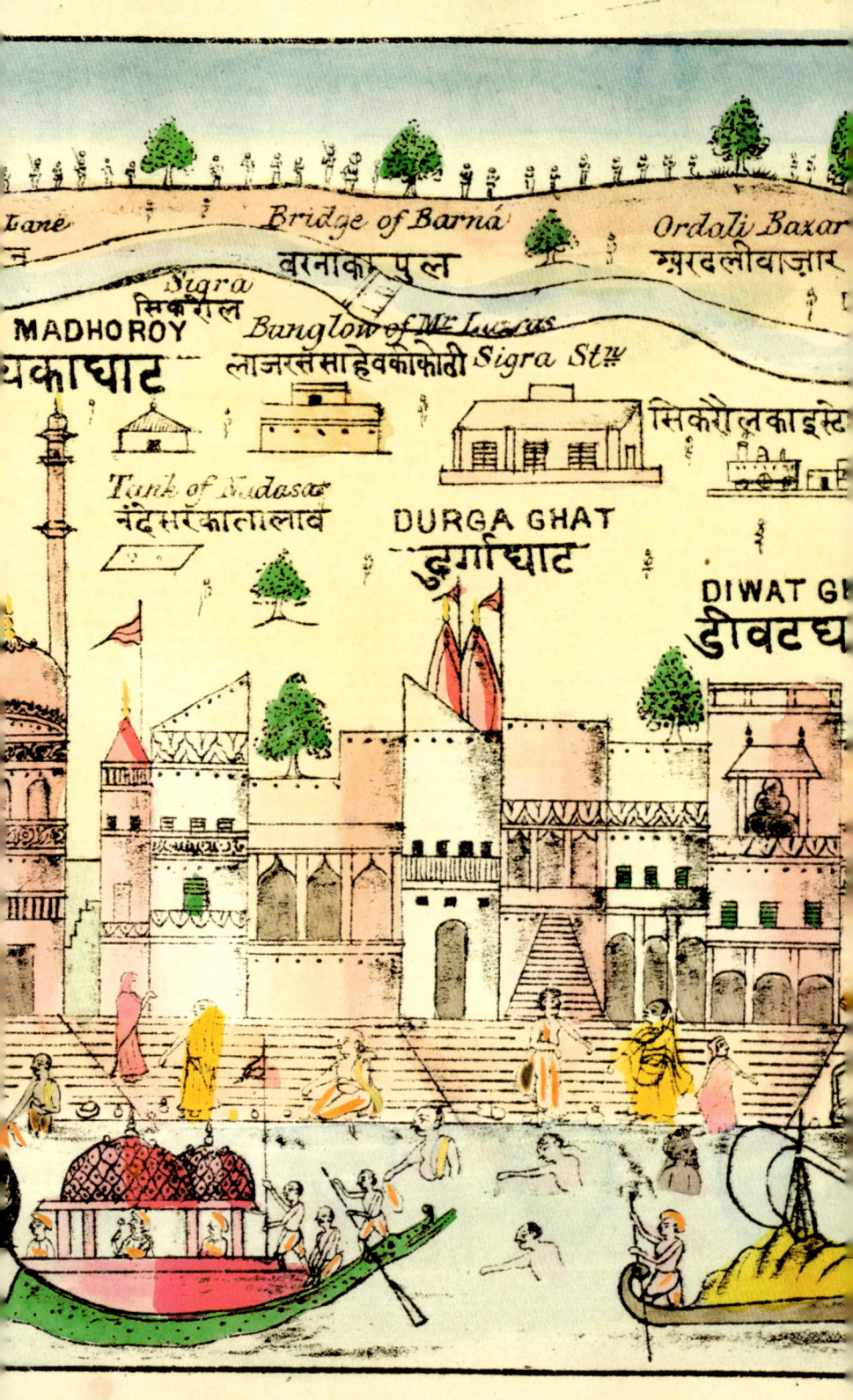

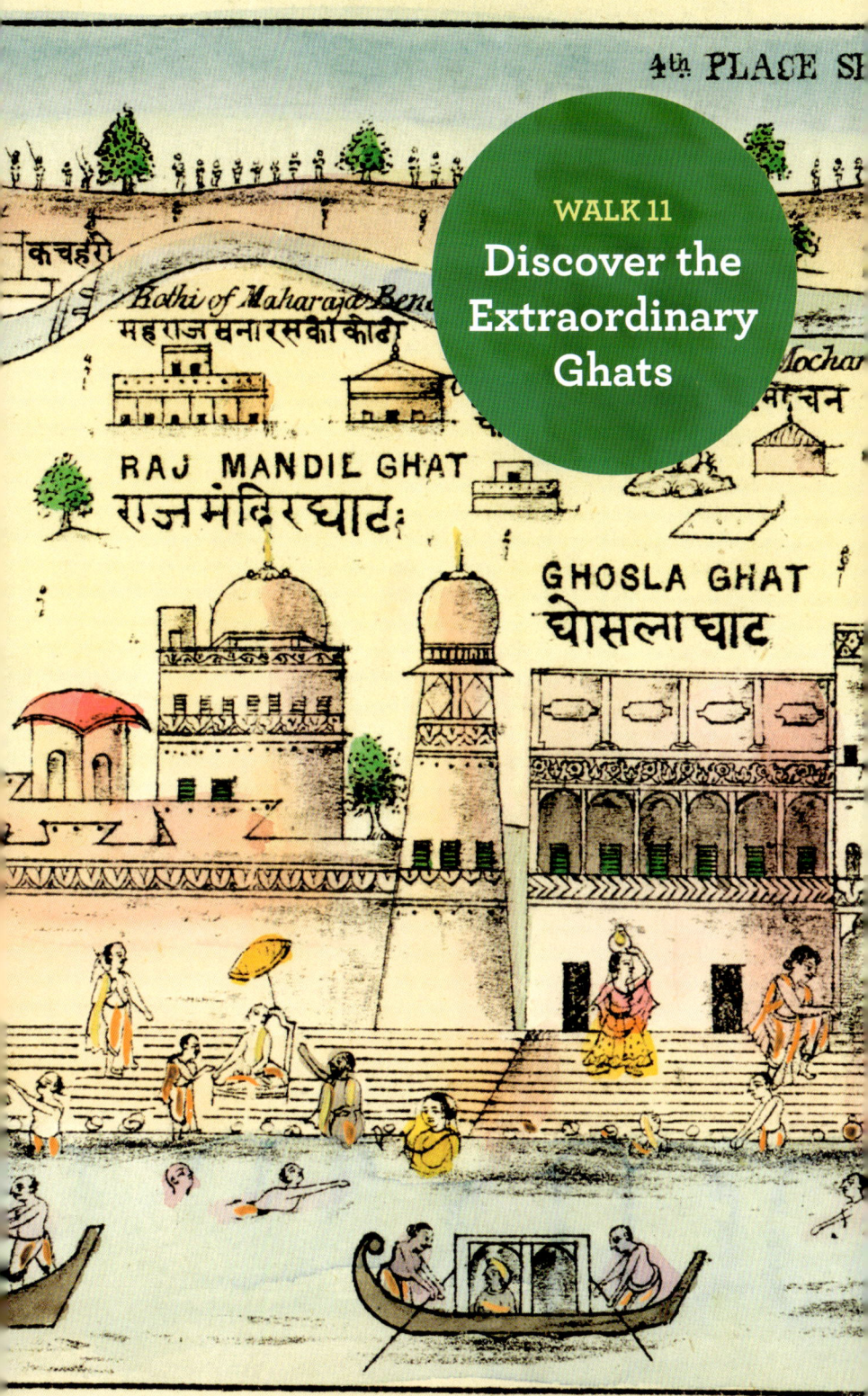

4ᵗʰ PLACE SI

कचहरी

Kothi of Maharaja Ben...

महाराज वनारसकी कोठी

RAJ MANDIL GHAT

राजमंदिरचाट:

GHOSLA GHAT

घोसलाघाट

Mochar

...चन

WALK 11

Discover the Extraordinary Ghats

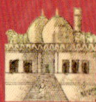 Walk along the famous ghats, built along the riverfront of Banaras.

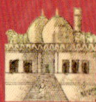

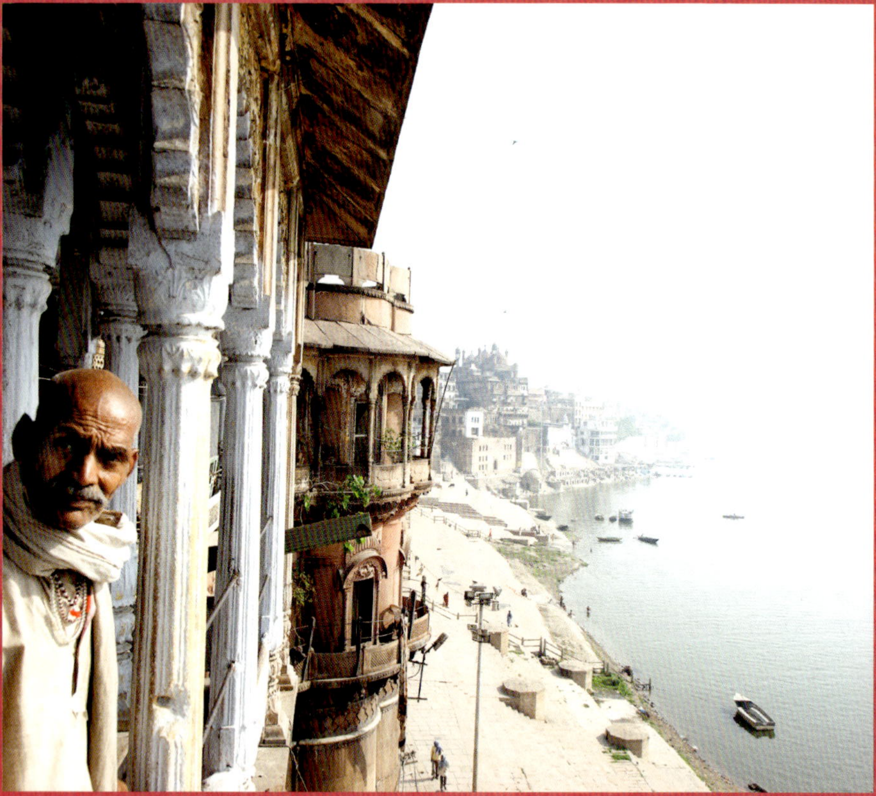

The 84 embankments of ghats along the Ganga are iconic of the city of Banaras.

THINGS TO SEE
- Palaces, historic shrines and reservoirs
- Alamgiri Mosque built by Aurangzeb

ALLOW
One to three hours

WALK ITINERARY
This walk can be done as a single three-hour walk from Assi to Rajghat or divided into separate walks – Assi to Dashashwamedh, Dashashwamedh to Panchganga, and Panchganga to Rajghat, each about an hour long.

GETTING AROUND THE GHATS
The 84 ghats of the city follow the curve of the river Ganga as it flows from south to north. The southernmost Samneghat and the northernmost Adi Keshav are not paved with stone, but remain the natural clay riverbank. So Assi is generally thought of as the southernmost ghat and Rajghat the northernmost, marking both ends of the built riverfront.

THE HISTORY OF THE GHATS

The ghat, or the unique embankment on the riverfront at Banaras, is regarded as the city's most celebrated image. For most, Banaras means stone steps, descending gloriously into the river, bamboo umbrellas clustered along the steps and narrow staircases winding up between temple spires.

Since the beginning of its long history, Banaras has been celebrated for its commercial and spiritual associations with the river Ganga. In around 800 BCE, the main city was located on the high northern bank of Rajghat, where the river Varana flowed into the Ganga. This point was a crucial dock, where the busy northern trade route passed the city on its way from Bengal to the northwestern regions.

Over the next two millennia, Banaras stretched southwards along the river. The city continued to thrive as a centre for commerce, culture, and religion. At the centre of all this activity was the river Ganga. Royal families who wanted to establish a presence in the glorious city paved ghats and constructed riverside complexes. Ships plied up and down the river, loading and unloading passengers and wares. Meanwhile, the *raees* or elite class of Banaras would sail in king-sized boats full-masted down the river. About 500 years ago, the riverfront at Banaras presented a splendid panorama, which was captured by painters of the British Company School. As Sandria Frietag describes in *Culture and Power in Banaras: Community, Performance and Environment, 1800–1980*, religion, commerce, and culture worked together to build Banaras in the 18th and 19th centuries. The river Ganga and its ghats were crucial to these developments.

Ganga in myth

The river Ganga has a long and rich history in Hindu mythology. The Vedas describe her as a celestial stream descending from the heavens to earth. In Hindu thought, the Ganga's pulsating waters are life giving. Every wave is a tirtha, a 'crossing place' from the earthly to the divine, bestowing liberation upon the bather. The ghats at Banaras were built based on this concept of tirtha, to provide access to the Ganga's sacred waters, and are themselves sacred.

For Banarasis, the Ganga is not just a goddess, but she is also *Ma* or Mother, a dear friend and constant companion. She provides entertainment in all seasons – boat rides, cricket matches, and picnics – and at any time of day, she is there with her majestic beauty, to soothe and inspire.

And just as Banarasis are attached to Ganga ji, she is attached to the city. It is said that as she flowed past Banaras, she was so charmed by the city that she nearly turned back: Banaras is the only point in her course that she flows from south to north.

Sagara's Saga

One of the most celebrated myths of Ganga's descent describes King Sagara, a just and mighty ruler who had 60,000 sons through practicing austerities. In order to fulfill his status as a great king, he undertook an *ashwamedh* or horse sacrifice. A horse was allowed to wander free for a year and Sagara would become ruler of any kingdom through which it roamed, unless he was challenged to war. As Sagara's horse wandered, one monarch after another gave up his kingdom. The watchful gods became fearful, for it seemed that Sagara's horse would soon approach heaven. They stole the horse and hid it away in Sage Kapila's hermitage. When Sagara learnt of this, he sent his sons to find the horse. After searching for many days and nights, they found it in the hermitage. In indignation, they charged at the sage, disturbing his austerities. But Kapila scorched them to ashes with one fiery glance. Then he sent a message to Sagara, that only Ganga's celestial waters would purify the ashes and allow his sons to find a place in heaven. However, many years passed and Sagara died without being able to call Ganga down from heaven. Finally, one of his descendants, Bhagiratha, managed to win the favour of Ganga through years of penance. Ganga agreed to restore Sagara's sons, but was certain the force of her waters would shatter the earth. Shiva promised to catch her in his tangled locks. Shiva kept his promise and Bhagiratha led Ganga onto the plains of north India, to the sea, and then to the netherworld, where she mingled with the ashes of Sagara's sons and purified them.

ASSI TO DASHASHWAMEDH
Pilgrimages, plays and royalty

Assi is one of the city's most spiritually important ghats. Some of the city's main pilgrimages, such as the Panchatirth and Haridwar, prescribe stopping here. According to ancient texts, 'Assi' was the name of a rivulet that flowed into the Ganga. Together, Assi and Ganga made a confluence auspicious for bathing.

Under the great peepal tree (Sacred Fig/ *Ficus Religiosa*) where boatmen sit, there is a Shiva *linga* and a Hanuman shrine of Puranic significance. Banarasis love Assi Ghat for its spacious landings and staircases and its views northward to Malviya Bridge and southward to the pontoon bridge. Everyday at dusk a festive atmosphere descends as families arrive to chat on the steps, take boat-rides, snack, and admire the river's beauty.

Riva Ghat, built by the king of Riva, is marked by his palace called Riva Kothi. Today, the building is a hostel for students studying music at the Banaras Hindu University.

It rises magnificently, with two pylons flanking a raised central doorway and two stories of carved balconies.

There are nearly 100 ghats in Banaras.

The next ghat is **Tulsi Ghat**, believed to have been built by the 16th-century poet-saint, Tulsidas, who is known mainly for his translation of the Sanskrit epic, Ramayana into an accessible version in the vernacular known as *Ramcharitmanas*. A great devotee of Vishnu, his incarnation Ram, and Ram's monkey-protector Hanuman, Tulsidas established a monastery, a Hanuman Temple, and an akhara above the ghat.

Every year in the season of Ashwin (September-October), Ram's fascinating story is enacted over several nights as the Ramlila. Neighbourhoods across the city have their own productions. Tulsi Ghat is one of the stage areas used for the performance.

Bhadaini Ghat is mentioned in late 11th-century inscriptions. It is marked today by one of the city's sewage point sources and a tall circular water tower.

Janaki Ghat with its pleasing symmetrical and steep staircases was built in the mid-19th century. Janaki is also another name for Sita, Ram's wife.

Anandamayi Ghat is named after the famous woman saint, Anandamayi Ma. Her ashram for girls stands above the ghat. '*Anandamayi*' means 'bliss-permeated'. She was known for her perpetual state of happiness and her ability to heal all kinds of physical and mental ailments through her aura of calm. She had scores of followers, including the former prime minister Indira Gandhi and the French filmmaker, Arnaud Desjardins.

Vachcharaj Ghat was built in the 19th century by Vachcharaj, a Jain banker who actively contributed to establishing Banaras as a centre of trade.

Above the narrow flight of stairs is the birthplace of Suparshvanath, the seventh *tirthankar* of the Jain tradition. The *tirthankars* or 'ford-makers' are also called *Jinas* or 'victorious ones', and were Jain spiritual leaders. The 24th in this legendary line was Mahavira, who lived in the 6th century BCE and was a contemporary of Lord Buddha.

The golden spire above the high wall indicates a Jain temple and a Jain Ghat. Jainism began to blossom in Banaras around 1,000 BCE, along with Buddhism.

Nishadraj Ghat is named after the mythical chief of the boatmen that helped Ram, Sita, and Lakshman cross the river Sarayu in the Ramayana. Nishadraj was adopted as the ancestral deity of fishermen and boatmen.

A small temple, dedicated to Nishadraj, sits high above the ghat, nestled among the homes of fishermen and embroiderers.

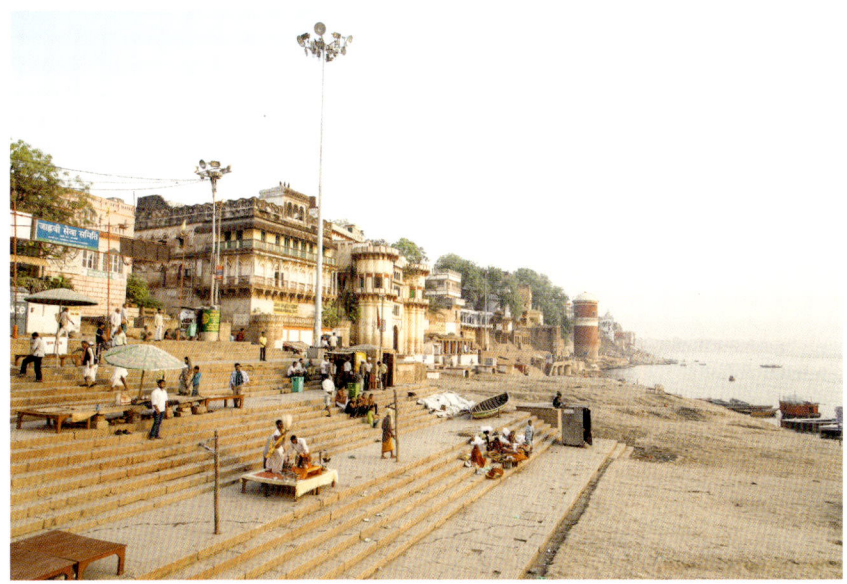
Greeting the morning at Assi Ghat.

Panchakota Ghat was built by the king of Panchakota in Bengal in the late 1800s.

Prabhu Ghat is named after Maharaja Prabhu Narayan Singh, who ruled Banaras from 1889 to 1931. He was the nephew and adopted son of Ishwari Prasad Narayan Singh, who was granted the title of Maharaja of Banaras by the British for his loyalty to the crown during the Indian Mutiny of 1857.

Chet Singh Ghat with its magnificent fort-like palace is named after Maharaja Chet Singh. Chet Singh was the illegitimate son of the first Maharaja of Banaras, Balwant Singh. He managed to secure his succession over Balwant Singh's grandson, Mahip Narayan Singh by bribing the Nawab of Awadh. A series of political squabbles with Governor General Warren Hastings followed Chet Singh's succession and in 1781, Hastings sent his troops to Chet Singh's fort. While his army was fighting the troops outside, Chet Singh let himself out of a window and down the high wall of his palace using turbans unravelled and tied together.

In quick succession after Chet Singh Ghat come **Niranjani Ghat** and **Maha Nirvani Ghat**, where according to legend the Lord Buddha bathed.

Shivala means 'abode of Shiva'. **Shivala Ghat** is named after the Shiva Temple above the stairs. Shivala is also the neighbourhood extending above the ghat, populated by a large south Indian community that migrated to Banaras over roughly the last two centuries for reasons of commerce and religion.

Apart from their homes, there are numerous south Indian monasteries and ashrams, temples and *goushalas* (homes for cows and buffaloes, belonging to milkmen) lining the lanes above the ghat.

Dandi Ghat is named after the Dandi ascetics who are known for carrying a stick (*danda* means 'stick'). They have their own monastery nearby.

Hanuman is Ram's monkey-devotee and helper and plays a significant role in the Ramayana. Under his supervision, the monkey-army built a bridge across to Lanka, where Ram defeated the ten-headed king of

Lanka, Ravan. **Hanuman Ghat** is named after Hanuman, but is known for its temple of Ruru, the dog-form of Bhairav, who is also one of the eight Bhairavs who assist Kal Bhairav. Bhairavs are the terrible, wrathful forms, evolved from the ancient deities called *yakshas*, *ganas*, *rakshasas*, and *bhairavs*. They gradually evolved into sons, assistants and forms of Shiva. Kal Bhairav, whose temple is in the northern neighbourhood of Maidagin, assumes the duties of the god of death.

Karnataka State Ghat was built by the southern state of Mysore or Karnataka as it is known now. The stately building extending over the length of the ghat is a guesthouse run by the government of Karnataka, open to all, but used mostly by visitors from the state.

The Juna order of ascetics has its *math* or monastery and its akhara here. One theory is that during Mughal rule, many orders of ascetics, such as that of the Juna sadhus, took to wrestling in order to protect Hinduism against Islamic proselytizing.

The Karnataka guesthouse provides a safe and appropriately distanced spot to view the cremations on **Harishchandra Ghat**, one of the two cremation ghats of the city.

People who work here will tell you that Harishchandra Ghat is the oldest

RAJA HARISHCHANDRA'S TALE

The sage Vishwamitra asked King Harishchandra for a ritual fee (*dakshina* or *daan*). Harishchandra generously gave the sage his entire kingdom. But Vishwamitra was not satisfied. Even after having accepted the kingdom he requested the king for his fee. Harishchandra had nothing left to offer. So, true to his word, he sold his wife and son into slavery and travelled to Kashi. Here he devoted himself as a worker at the cremation ground.

One evening, as he was toiling at the cremation ground, his wife arrived with their son in her arms. He had died of a snake bite. Harishchandra was stricken with sorrow, but he turned them both away, for his wife could not afford the cremation fee. The gods, watching carefully, were pleased. Harishchandra's strength of character was proven to them and his kingdom and family were restored to him.

Hindus associate his name with 'truth' or *satya*. In his autobiography, *My Experiments with Truth*, Gandhi recounts how he saw a performance of Harishchandra by a travelling troupe that won him over to the path of truth for all his life.

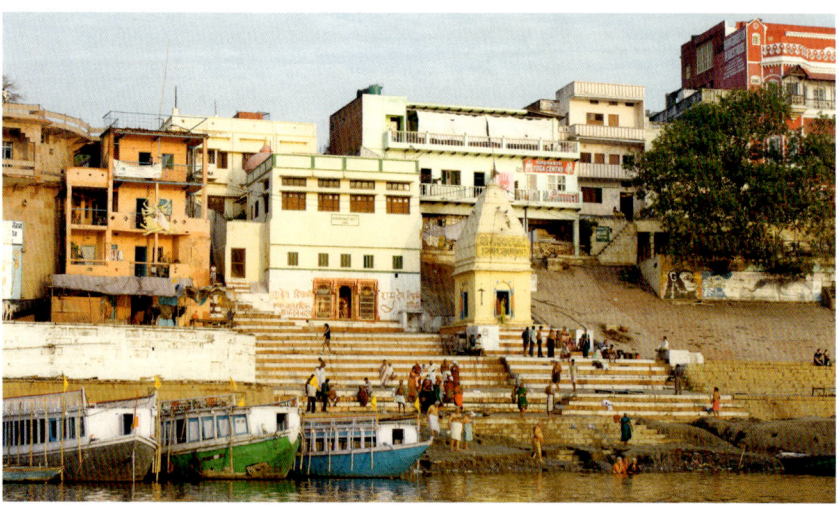

Pilgrims on the steps of the ghats.

cremation ground of Kashi, older than Manikarnika. Because of this, they sometimes call the ghat 'Adi Manikarnika' or 'the original Manikarnika'.

The ghat today has a large electric crematorium as well as traditional pyre funerals.

The wide, recessed stairs on **Chauki Ghat** have several convenient spots for chess games and naps. Chauki Ghat is also popular for its temple dedicated to Hanuman and *Nag,* the serpent deity, housed under a leafy peepal tree.

Sweet shops catering to Kedar temple-goers and authentic south Indian restaurants line the lane above the steps.

A quiet stretch of the riverfront follows. Washermen and women wash their clothes here and dry them on the steps. **Manasarovara Ghat**, built by Raja Man Singh of Amber (present-day Rajasthan), in the late 16th century, was named after the Himalayan lake, Manasarovar.

Narada Ghat is named after Narada, the divine sage, best known for the one-stringed *Ektara* instrument always tucked beneath his arm and his propensity to make mischief in the heavenly and earthly realms.

Raja Ghat was built in 1720 by a Maratha king Gajirao Balaji, while **Pande Ghat** was named in 1805 after the legendary wrestler of Banaras, Babua Pande, who established an akhara above the steps here. **Digpatia Ghat** is notable for its stately palace, built in 1830 by the king of Digpatia in Bengal.

Chaunsath means sixty-four, and **Chausathi Ghat** is so named after a temple of 64 goddesses, which is situated above the ghat. **Rana Mahal Ghat** was built by the king of Udaipur (present-day Rajasthan) in 1670.

The Darbhanga Palace towers over **Darbhanga Ghat**, an intricate and breathtaking structure. It was erected by the king of Darbhanga (Bihar) in 1915.

> Digpatia Ghat is notable for its stately palace, built in 1830 by the king of Digpatia in Bengal.

Built in the early 19th century, **Munshi Ghat** was named after Sridhar Narayan Munshi, a financial minister of Nagpur. **Ahilyabai Ghat**, built in the late 19th century, was named after Rani Ahilyabai of Indore, who built several temples in Banaras including the elegant Amethy Temple on Manikarnika Ghat and the famous Vishwanath Temple.

The 35th ghat is called **Dashashwamedh**, a stop for several important pilgrimages and often referred to by tourists and their guides as 'Main ghat'. It is the busiest ghat along the riverfront, followed by Assi Ghat.

All along Dashashwamedh Ghat, under bamboo umbrellas, sit priests called *pandas, ghatis* and tirtha *purohits,* who assist pilgrims in conducting various rites and rituals. Dashashwamedh's importance has grown in the past few decades thanks to the road that was built a century and a half ago linking the ghat to the city. Down this road a short distance away is the city's most important temple, Vishwanath Temple. Today an organization called Ganga Seva Nidhi conducts an elaborate arti to the river at sunset daily. The event, which has been designed as a religious spectacle, attracts hundreds of tourists and pilgrims to the ghat.

Dividing Dashashwamedh Ghat is **Prayag Ghat**, which represents Prayag or Allahabad, also a holy city in Hinduism for its location on the Triveni Sangam or confluence of the Ganga, Yamuna and the ancient river, Saraswati.

DASHASHWAMEDH TO PANCHGANGA
Music, temples and palaces

Dr Rajendra Prasad was the first president of the Republic of India, from 1950 to 1962. The ghat that bears his name lies immediately after Dashashwamedh. **Man Mandir Ghat** is distinctive for the palace of the Rajput king of Amber, Man Singh,

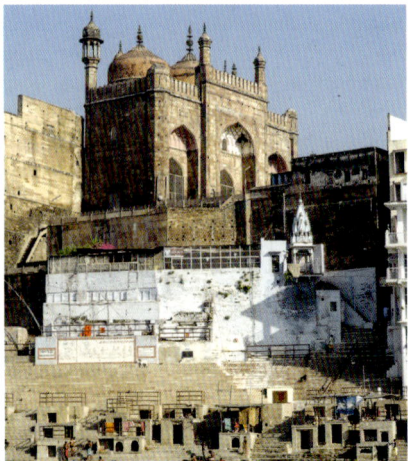

Imposing Alamgiri Mosque at Panchganga Ghat.

The temple is built on a square platform with a portal and three openings on each side. The pillars are carved with erotic images. An idol of Pashupateshvara, Nepal's most famous manifestation of Shiva, occupies the inner sanctum. The temple imitates the architecture and decor of the ancient Pashupatinath Temple that sits high above the river Bagmati, in the eastern part of Kathmandu, in Nepal. The triple-storeyed building beside the temple is a hostel for young Nepalese students who come to study the Vedas in Banaras. The neighbourhood behind Nepali Ghat, called Nepali Khapra, has a population dominated by Nepali nationals, old and new migrants to the city who come to work and study.

Visitor Information: The temple requires a modest ticket to enter.

Bauli, **Jalashayi** and **Khiraki** ghats follow in quick succession, leading to the city's second cremation ghat, **Manikarnika**.

The stretch of the city running north of Manikarnika along the river is called **Siddha Kshetra**, or 'field of fulfillment', so named because of the number of important shrines present here.

The ghats that follow are **Dattatreya**, **Scindhia** and **Sankata**, named after the temple of the goddess Sankata and Ganga Mahal. Ganga Mahal refers to the beautiful palace that is situated on the ghat.

which has rows of carved balconies. On its roof, not wholly visible from the ghat, there is an astronomical observatory, built by Man Singh's successor, Jai Singh.

Tripurabhairavi Ghat comes after, followed by **Mir Ghat** with a temple dedicated to Vishalakshi, the 'wide-eyed goddess'.
In the galis above can be found Dharma Kupa, the 'well of dharma'.

Mir Ghat was named in 1735 after Mir Rustam Ali, a popular tax collector whose name still appears in Holi and Chaiti, two forms of seasonal folk singing, which shows that he was a man of the people who took part in the festivities of Banaras.

Phuta ('broken') **Ghat** follows and then **Lalita Ghat**, famous for two shrines, one dedicated to Vishnu called Ganga Keshav, 'lord of Ganga', and the other to Ganga, called Bhagirathi Devi.

Nepali Ghat stands out for its Nepalese Temple with its overhanging tiled roof and the gilded spire. The Nepalese kings of the Gorkha dynasty built this temple at the beginning of the 19th century. At that time Banaras was popular with Nepalese royalty as a retreat.

A MUSICAL LEGEND
The legendary shehnai player Ustad Bismillah Khan played in Lakshmanbala Temple with his family for years, following the tradition of his ancestors. The shehnai is a long-stemmed wind instrument with a gentle bulge, similar in tone to the bagpipes. Bismillah Khan, who was born in the galis of north Banaras, is credited with single-handedly introducing the shehnai into Hindustani classical music. Sadly, he passed away in 2006.

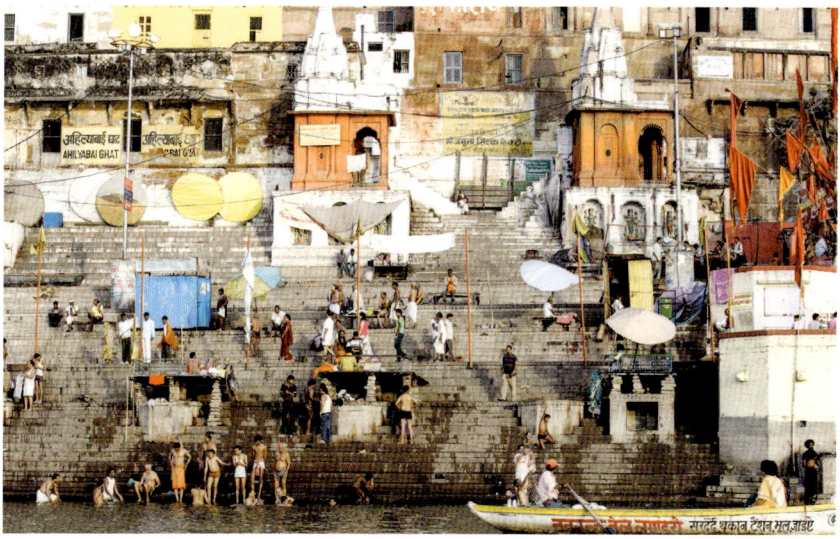

Bathers near Dashashwamedh Ghat.

The temple inside was built in 1865 by Queen Tarabai Raje Shinde, a Scindhia ruler from Gwalior. It is dedicated to Krishna and his consort Radha.

An imposing palace, built by the Marathas, stands on **Bhonsale Ghat**. The Maratha rulers of Nagpur (in present-day Maharashtra) built both the ghat and the palace at the beginning of the 19th century. These fierce horsemen from western India spread their influence eastwards to Orissa and Bengal. The palace uniquely combines might and grace. A commanding façade of sandstone, it rises to a breathtaking height from the ghat.

On either side of the palace, graceful pylons emerge, topped high above with *chhatris* or dome-shaped pavilions. The design is inspired by the hexagonal-sectioned, pylon-and-dome pattern of the Chet Singh Palace. The roof of the palace houses two ornate temples, dedicated to Vishnu and Shiva. The tall exterior was built not just to inspire awe for the Maratha

rulers and establish their presence, but also to protect it from flooding. Take note of the HFL or 'high flood level' marking on the palace wall, which indicates that this point on the river's course is particularly prone to flooding.

Naya means 'new' and **Naya Ghat**, was built by Peshwa Amrit Rao. The Maratha king dedicated this ghat to Ganesh, who is worshipped at the beginning of any new venture. The ghat was one of the main docks of the city.

Stairs lead up from the ghat to the widest lane in the area, called **Gola Gali**. *Gola* means 'warehouse', so in the past there must have been a wholesale market here. At the bottom of the stairs stands the haveli or mansion of Vachcharaj ji, a Jain banker who actively contributed towards establishing Banaras as a centre of trade in the 19th century.

Adjoining Gola Gali is Sula Tola, which means 'yarn market'. This bazaar was controlled by the Kherawals, who were originally Gujarati Brahmin bankers and jewellers. One

The neighbourhood behind Nepali Ghat, called Nepali Khapra, has a population dominated by Nepali nationals, old and new migrants to the city who come to work and study.

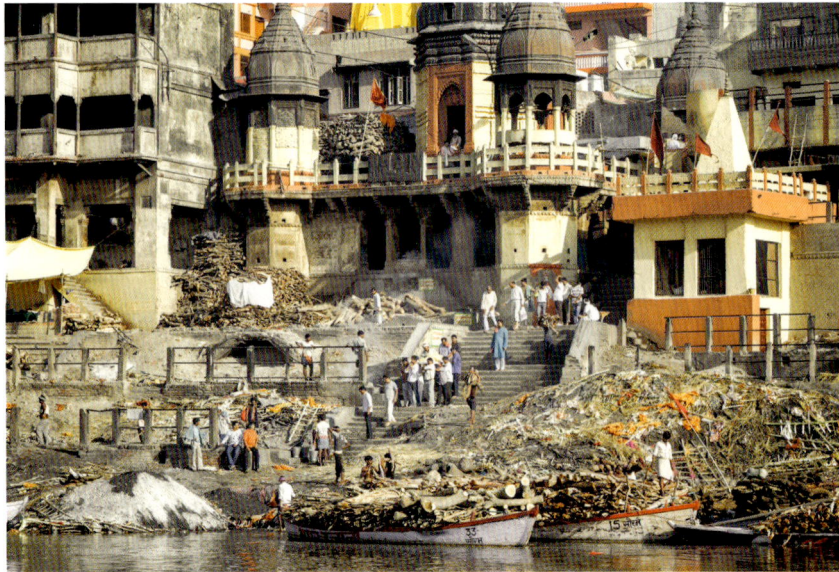

Temples and funeral pyres at Manikarnika Ghat.

story describes how the Kherawals of Sula Tola sold the Maharaja of Gwalior a pearl, the size of an ostrich egg. To their disappointment, the Maharaja used the enormous stone as a *farshi* or filter in his *hookah*.

Ram Ghat has been popular with bathers in the past. The Ram Temple here is small, but airy and serene. Ram is an incarnation of Vishnu, the hero of the epic Ramayana, and a popular Hindu deity.

The temple houses rows of brass deities that have vermillion *tikas* (sacred marks) shining on their foreheads. Ram stands on the highest row with his beloved companions, his wife Sita and brother Lakshman. In the story of Ram, when he was exiled from his kingdom for 13 years, Sita and Lakshman followed him devotedly into the forest.

Continuing north, Ram Ghat leads to **Lakshmanbala Ghat**, named after Ram's brother Lakshman. Lakshman is celebrated and loved for his loyalty to his brother. The partially collapsed Lakshmanbala Temple, dedicated to this

quiet hero, rests above the ghat. Originally, the temple belonged to the Maratha Peshwas, but it was passed on to the Scindhia rulers of Gwalior, who were known for their fabulous collection of jewels.

PANCHGANGA TO ADI KESHAV
Gods, myths and bridges

The ghats here are quiet and open, a contrast to the city's bustling ghats further south. Many have an akhara where well-oiled Banarasi men swing their *gadas* under the shade of enormous peepal or neem trees. Pass the ghats of **Durga**, named after the goddess Durga, **Brahma**, named after Brahma, one of the Hindu trinity, **Bundi Parkota**, **Shitala**, named after the goddess of smallpox, Shitala, whose main temple is on Dashashwamedh Ghat, **Lala**, **Hanumangarhi** named after Hanuman and finally **Gai Ghat**. Malviya Bridge crosses the river close to Gai Ghat, a shadow of steel and iron that periodically rumbles with a passing train.

On the ghat, Banarasis play chess, sing, talk, and swim. As the sun sets, this portion

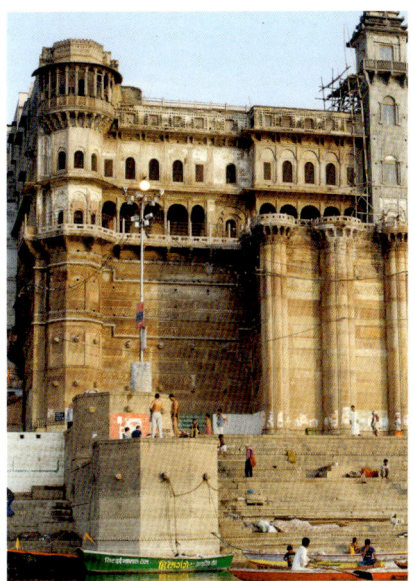

Darbhanga Palace on Darbhanga Ghat.

of the riverfront, where the Ganga has an extra bend northward, catches cool river breezes.

Badri Narayan Ghat was built by the state of Gwalior and named after the temple of Badri Narayan in the Himalayas.

Trilochan Ghat is named after its temple of Trilochan, the 'three-eyed' lord.

Beyond Trilochan, the ghats of **Nandikeshvara**, **Sakka**, **Telianala**, and **Naya** are much less elegant, some of them are still clay-banked. **Prahlad Ghat** was named after Prahlad, a character in ancient texts celebrated for his devotion to Vishnu.

In 1887 the Malviya Bridge was built on **Rajghat**. At that time, it was known as Lord Dufferin Bridge. When the ancient city occupied the elevated plateau here, Rajghat was an important dock for ferries engaged in trade and commerce along the northern road that is today called the Grand Trunk Road. This road continues over the bridge all the way to Kolkata.

The large white temple dedicated to Raidas is situated on Rajghat. Raidas (1418-1547) was one of the poet-saints of the Bhakti movement, who preached personal devotion without the aid of idols.

Further north beyond the bridge is the quiet ghat of **Adi Keshav**, marked by the Adi Keshav Temple with a Puranic Shiva *linga* and its black, four-armed image of 'the original Vishnu'.

HOLI, THE FESTIVAL OF COLOURS

Prahlad's father Hiranyakashipu did not want his son to be devoted to Vishnu so he tried everything possible to harm him. One day, Hiranyakashipu was inspired by the special fire-proof shawl that Prahlad's sister the demon Holika owned. Hiranyakashipu built a pyre and ordered Holika to sit in it with Prahlad in her lap, covering only herself with her shawl. As he sat among the leaping flames, Prahlad prayed to Vishnu. He was saved while Holika was burnt to death. This is celebrated as Holika Dahan on the eve of the festival Holi, during which large pyres are burnt. Holi is celebrated in the season of Phalgun (February-March).

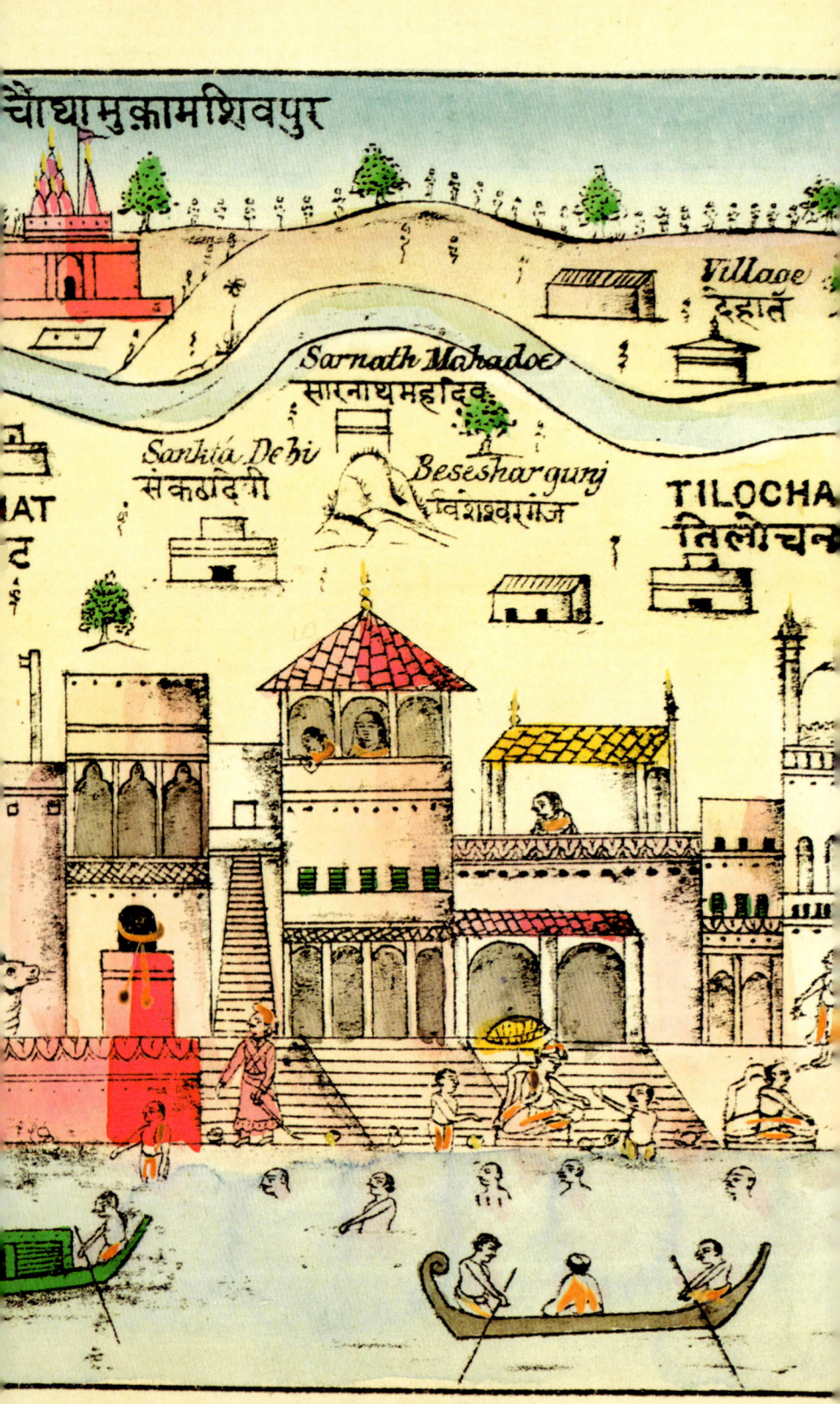

चौथा मुक्काम शिवपुर

Village दहात

Sarnath Mahadoe
सारनाथ महादिव

Sankta Debi
संकठादेवी

Beseshar gunj
विश्वेश्वरगंज

TILOCHA
तिलोचन

ᴀᴛ
ट

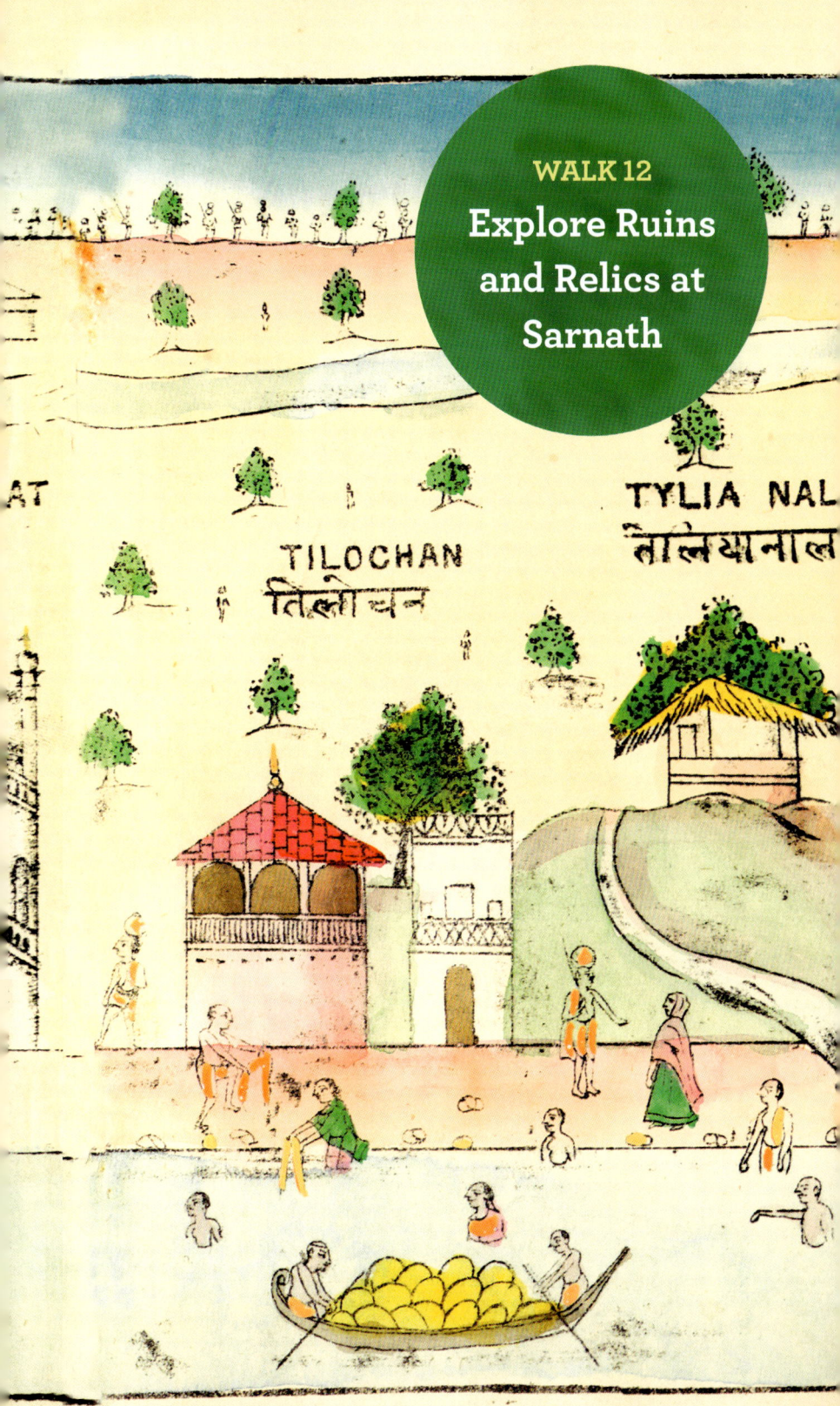

AT

TILOCHAN
तिलोचन

TYLIA NAL
तील्यानाल

WALK 12

Explore Ruins and Relics at Sarnath

Explore Buddhist monasteries, shrines, and stupas (monuments preserving relics) dating from the 3rd century BCE, as well as the shady deer park skirting the ruins. Visit the Archaeological Museum, featuring exquisite Gupta-period Buddha sculptures that were excavated at the ruins. End by visiting all or

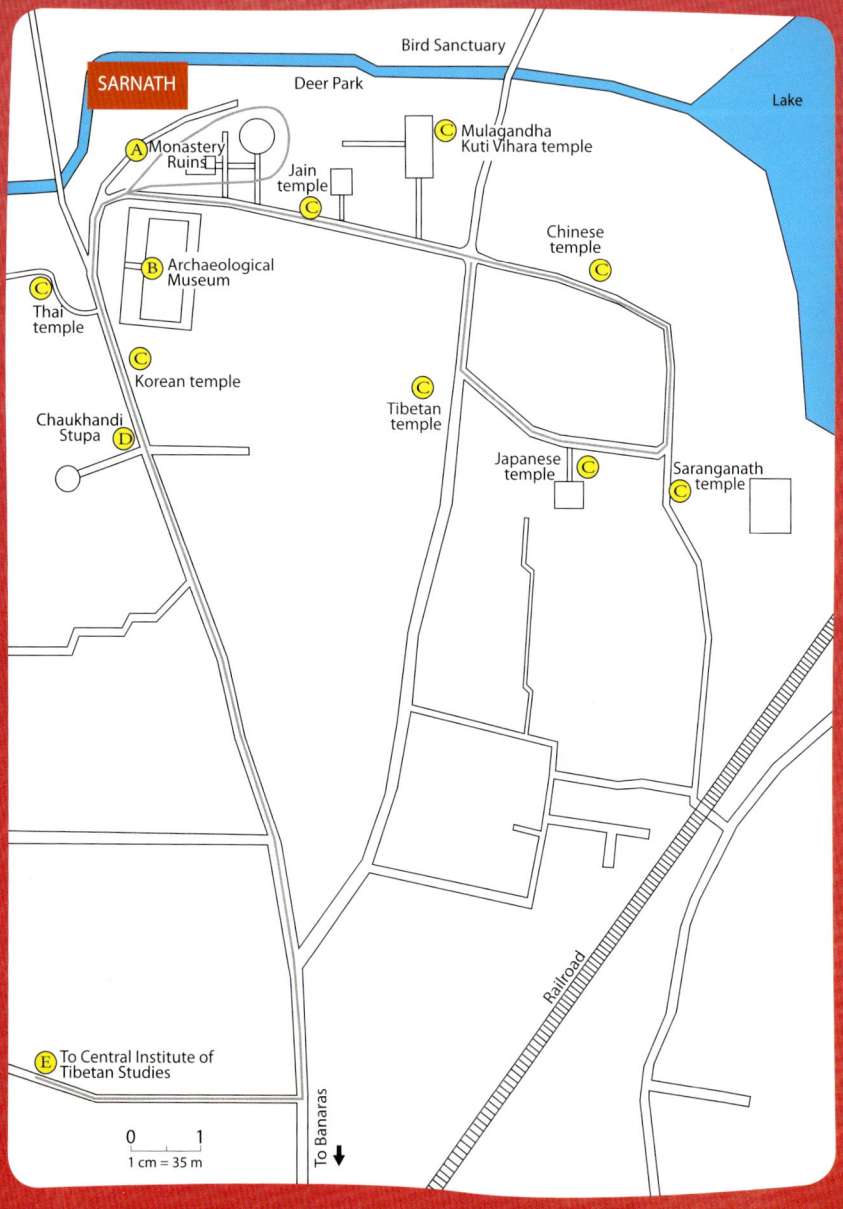

SARNATH

Bird Sanctuary

Deer Park

Lake

Ⓐ Monastery Ruins

Ⓒ Mulagandha Kuti Vihara temple

Jain temple

Ⓒ

Chinese temple

Ⓒ

Ⓑ Archaeological Museum

Ⓒ Thai temple

Ⓒ Korean temple

Ⓒ Tibetan temple

Chaukhandi Stupa Ⓓ

Japanese temple Ⓒ

Saranganath Ⓒ temple

Ⓔ To Central Institute of Tibetan Studies

0   1
1 cm = 35 m

To Banaras

Railroad

some of the temples built by Tibetan, Japanese, Korean, Chinese, and Sri Lankan organizations, including one Jain temple. Opt to visit the brick memorial to the Mughal emperor Humayun, the picturesque campus of the Central Institute of Tibetan Studies and the ancient Saranganath shrine to Shiva a little further away.

THINGS TO SEE

- Deer park
- Bodhi tree commemorating the Buddha preaching his first sermon
- Ancient 'Dhamekha' stupa
- The first Mauryan-period sculptures of the Buddha
- Ruins of monasteries dating from the 3rd century BCE Buddhist temples
- The headquarters of the Sri Lankan Bodhi Society
- Central Institute of Tibetan Studies

ALLOW

At least four hours

WALK ITINERARY

The monastery ruins at Sarnath I The Sarnath School of classical art I Archaeological Museum I Tibetan Temple I 'Mulagandha Kuti Vihara' I Thai Temple I Jain Temple I Mahabodhi Society Temple I Korean Temple I Chinese Temple I Japanese Temple I Saranganath Temple I Chaukhandi Stupa I Central Institute of Tibetan Studies

VISITING SARNATH

The Archaeological Museum requires its own ticket, as does the compound enclosing the monastery ruins and the Dhamekha Stupa. The temples do not require tickets. Spend a couple of hours, each at the ruins – stupa compound and at the museum. Take note of the museum timings and also the weather. Visiting the museum will not involve walking around outside, while exploring the ruins and the temples will involve plenty of walking. Plan your own walk tour accordingly.

GETTING AROUND SARNATH

Sarnath is a quiet town lying 13 kilometres north-east of Banaras. This walk will not cover the whole town, but the site within it where the Buddha delivered his first sermon. The site today features the ruins of monasteries, Buddhist temples, a Jain temple, a deer park, a museum, a stupa and the Central Institute of Tibetan Studies.

These sites are mostly arranged in a triangular route that can be covered in one single walk. The ruins, the Dhamekha stupa and the Deer Park lie within a grassy compound that occupies the length of one of the three roads making the triangle. On one end of this road is the ticket booth to the ruins and the museum, housed in a building opposite the ticket booth. On the other end, there are restaurants and public transport. The Tibetan institute is about a 20-minute walk south from the museum.

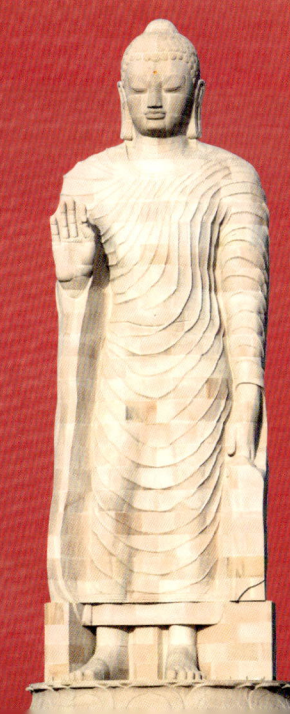

THE HISTORY OF SARNATH

Sarnath is one of the four most important Buddhist pilgrimage sites in the world, the other three being Bodhgaya (where Lord Buddha attained enlightenment), Kapalivastu (where Buddha was born), and Kusinagar (where he left his body). It is the nucleus of pilgrimage for 350 million people, or 6 per cent of the world's population. This makes it a staggeringly important place, comparable to, say, Mecca for Muslims.

Around the 6th century BCE, the old system of religion, with its emphasis on Vedic texts, the power of priests, the Sanskrit language, and elaborate rituals, began to be challenged by a plethora of new philosophies and sects all over north India. Banaras, with its reputation as a vibrant cultural and commercial seat, attracted new thinkers and was at the heart of this activity. Within its lush forests and the fortified city at Rajghat, ascetics and philosophers lived in secluded huts or busy ashrams, meditating and teaching disciples. This was the 'Establishment' that a new thinker needed to address.

One of the thinkers who made his way to Banaras was Gautam Buddha. He had been born to the king and queen of the Sakya kingdom (the present-day border of Nepal and Uttar Pradesh), and named Siddhartha Gautam. At the age of 29, Gautam left the royal palace and adopted a life of wandering and meditation in order to understand the nature of human suffering. After severe self-disciplining, he attained enlightenment. He travelled to Banaras to teach others the truths he had realized, and in a deer-filled grove outside Banaras called *Mrigadaya*, or Sarnath, he delivered his first sermon, setting in motion the wheel of Buddhist law (*dhamma*). The religion that he and his disciples founded, to be called *Bodh dharma* or Buddhism, was one of the philosophies born out of the spiritual questioning that took place during the 6th century BCE, that survived and flourished over the following centuries, along with Jainism, Tantrism, and Shaivism. Over the following two millennia, through ups and downs, fuelled by the work of monks and devotees and assisted by the patronage of kings, Buddhism grew into a powerful spiritual tradition. It spread from India in all directions as far as Iran, Sri Lanka, China, and Japan. Even while it shrank in importance within India, it greatly influenced Hinduism.

Exploring Sarnath, where the Buddha preached his first sermon, will reveal this story of Buddhism.

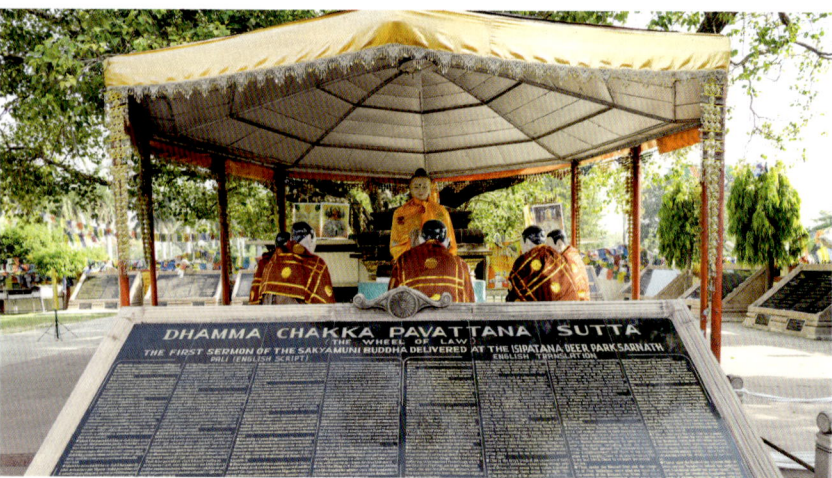

A sculpted memorial to Buddha preaching his five disciples.

THE LIFE OF THE BUDDHA

The Buddhist text *Tipitaka* ('three baskets' in Pali, means the collection in three parts of the Buddha's teachings) describes the story of the Buddha's life and death.

One night, Mahamaya the queen of the Sakyas had a vivid dream that a white elephant had pierced her abdomen and entered her womb. A few days later, Maya set off for her natal home in the neighbouring kingdom, Devadaha. On the way, in a beautiful grove called Lumbini, she gave birth to a baby boy. The Vedic sage Asita was summoned. By reading the bodily signs on the baby, Asita predicted that if the boy were never to leave the palace, he would become a supreme monarch. But if he were to leave, he would become a great spiritual leader, a Buddha.

Siddhartha's father, Suddhodhara, took every care to ensure that his son led a life of luxury within the palace. The prince had three different palaces all to himself, one each for summer, the monsoons, and winter. He was well educated and lavishly entertained. At the age of 16, he married a girl his age, Yasodhara.

Yet the young Siddhartha seemed uninterested in these worldly pleasures. Often, he would be found, by a friend or family member, lost in abstracted thought or fallen into a meditative trance.

When he was 29, Siddhartha took a series of carriage rides outside the palace walls, and saw for the first time, an old man walking with a cane, a man emaciated with illness, a corpse being carried away for cremation and an ascetic dressed in yellow robes. He was deeply disturbed by the suffering that he witnessed, and was struck by the ascetic's peaceful demeanor amidst all this. That very night, he decided to leave his home and family and to wander as an ascetic, trying to understand the meaning of human pain.

Siddhartha travelled south, crossing the Anoma river. At Vaishali, he met the ascetic Alara Kalam, who followed the Sankhya school of philosophy. He stayed at his hermitage for several weeks and mastered the 'sphere of nothing', the seventh stage of meditation. Then he travelled towards Rajagaha, the capital of Magadha. There he met King Bimbasara, who made him promise to return to Magadha after he had attained enlightenment. Siddhartha then studied with the famed Uddaka Ramaputta and mastered the 'sphere of neither-perception-nor-non-perception', a very high meditational state. But, not having attained ultimate release, Siddhartha was not satisfied, and left.

He travelled to the beautiful riverside Uruvela (near modern-day Gaya), where five companions joined him. Over the next few weeks, he and his companions began to undergo severe austerities. They would not eat, drink, or wash for days. Finally, Siddhartha fell ill and fainted. When he regained consciousness, he decided that such extreme penance would not lead to enlightenment. His companions, disgusted at his thoughts, abandoned him. Siddhartha regained his health slowly and travelled to Mrigdaya.

He meditated under a peepal tree, vowing to not rise until he had attained enlightenment. At night, the evil one Mara attempted to wrestle him out of his meditative state through a series of argumentative challenges. But towards dawn, Siddhartha defeated him. As the sun rose, he realized the Four Noble Truths and attained enlightenment, becoming a Buddha.

The Buddha was unsure whether anyone would be able to grasp such deep and subtle truths. He hesitated to preach them to others until the Sage Sahampati convinced him to do so. Then he sought out the five companions who had abandoned him. Near Banaras, at a deer-filled grove called *Mrigdaya* or *Risipatana* (named so because five-hundred ascetics attained enlightenment here), he preached his first sermon, the 'sermon on setting in motion the wheel of truth' or *Dharmachakrapravartan Sutra*, to his five companions. As his disciples, they became monks (*bikkhus*) and then 'perfected ones' (*arhats*), upon which the Buddha sent them out to teach others.

In three months, the Buddha gained 60 disciples. He then travelled to King Bimbasara in Rajagaha and his family in Kapilavatthu. All of them became his disciples. The Buddha spent the next 50 years teaching hundreds of individuals and establishing 'the three jewels' (*triratna*) of Buddhism, which are the Buddha, Buddhist law (*dhamma*) and the community of practicing Buddhists (*sangha*). These were also called 'the three refuges', as in 'I take refuge in the Buddha, I take refuge in the law, I take refuge in the community.' At the age of 80, he went north to Kasinara, where he fell ill. Reclining peacefully on his right side one day, he left his body, attaining *parinirvana*. A dispute arose among various states over his relics. Finally, they were divided into eight equal parts.

The Buddha's Teachings

The Buddha preached the Four Noble Truths, which are, all life is suffering, suffering is caused by desire, we may end suffering by removing craving and passion since all that we desire is perishable and changing, and we can get rid of craving and passion by methodically following a path. This Noble Eightfold path consists of correct views, correct aspirations, correct speech, correct conduct, correct livelihood, correct effort, correct mindfulness and correct meditational attainment. It is a 'middle path' advocating neither self-indulgence nor self-mortification.

The Four Noble Truths and the Noble Eightfold Path spring from the Law of Dependent Origination (*Pratityasamutpada*). According to the Law of Dependent Origination, all phenomena are embedded within a web of causality and conditionality. Every condition and mode of being, whether physical, social, or psychological, arises from a series of preceding conditions and modes. *Samsara*, as described by the Buddha, is not simply the material world but this web of worldly cause and effect. Human beings experience *dukkha* ('dissatisfaction' or 'sorrow') because they are unable to 'see' this natural characteristic of the universe and remain caught in causal action and consequence. According to the Buddha, reality is composed of microseconds or components called *dhamma*s (not to be confused with the *dhamma* meaning 'law'). The individual is like a flame, burning with the delusion of desire. In fact there is no ultimate self, soul, or ego. Everything, consisting of *dhamma*s, is transitory and evolving. The Pali canon treats the Buddha not as a divine being but as a kind of doctor who identified the problem or disease (the first and second Noble Truths) and prescribed a solution (the third and fourth Noble Truths and the Noble Eightfold Path). By pursuing a way of life different from the worldly life caught in the material world or *samsara*, that is by following the Noble Eightfold Path, one may 'blow out' the flame of the self and attain the ultimate goal of nirvana (sometimes translated as 'blowing out' or 'dying out') and the ultimate state of the Buddha (the 'enlightened' human being, no longer enflamed). Anyone can be a Buddha.

The Buddha is a title meaning 'enlightened one', and not a proper name.

Sarnath and the Historical Development of Buddhism

The Buddha outlined his teachings and established a framework for monastic life at Sarnath. After his passing, Sarnath flourished as an important site for the development of Buddhism and pilgrimage. Its ruins, temples, and museum today tell the story of the rise of monasteries, their subsequent decline, and the contemporary popular revival of Buddhism.

The Formation of Monasteries

After the Buddha's death in around the 4th century BCE, his disciples held many councils to discuss issues of faith. They compiled his teachings and composed

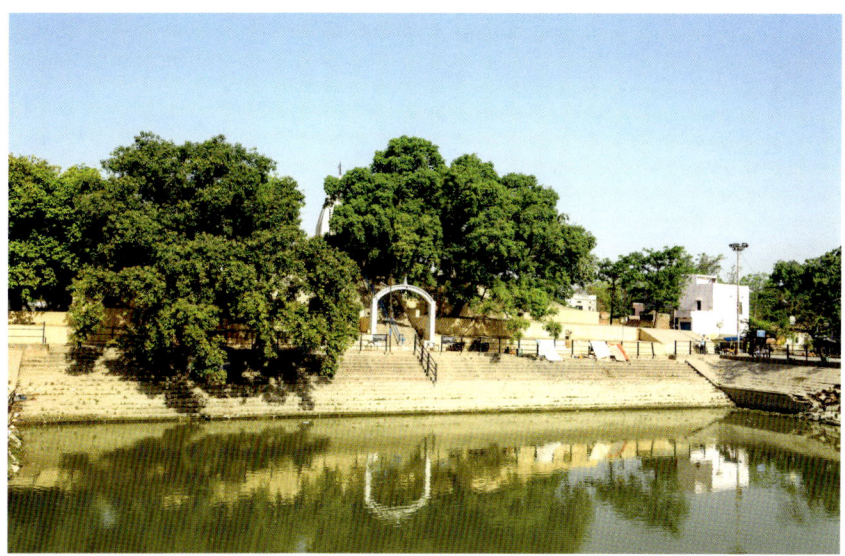

Saranganath Temple and tank.

the *vinaya*, which was the Buddhist constitution outlining monastic discipline. The *vinaya* may have been composed at a council at Rajagaha, but we cannot be sure that this is a historical fact. Another large council at Vaishali, which scholars generally agree happened, helped to form two schools that were distinct in their understandings of *vinaya*, *dhamma*, and the Buddha. These two schools or interpretations were called Theravada and Mahayana.

Understanding Theravada and Mahayana

The Theravada tradition was formed before the Mahayana school. *Theravada* means 'rule of the elders'. It was the more elitist and formalist of the two. It emphasized rules and regulations for the monastic community, meditative techniques and rituals. It viewed the *arhat* (the 'perfected one') as the ideal.

The Mahayana tradition was more relaxed in its interpretation of *vinaya*. *Mahayana* means 'great vehicle' or 'the means of salvation available to a larger number of

> In Buddhist thought, the world, consisting of *dhammas*, is transitory and evolving.

people.' It was formed in contradistinction to Theravada, even though both schools overlapped for centuries and shared certain basic principles and monastic rules. Mahayana Buddhists referred to Theravada as *Hinayana,* meaning 'lesser vehicle' or 'the means of salvation restricted to a smaller number of people'. The Mahayana school was more interested in the Buddha in human form and in the celestial forms experienced during meditation, in that the final goal of nirvana is the release from the material world. Mahayana upheld the *boddhisatva*, the Buddhist who has vowed to follow the Eightfold Path, as the ideal, not the perfected *arhat* or the non-worldly Buddha.

As such, the Mahayana school developed new ideas of relative and absolute truth.

One of the reasons Mahayana became popular among the laity was because it offered a wide array of methods by which any individual could be a devoted Buddhist and did not insist on anyone becoming a monk or nun. Out of the

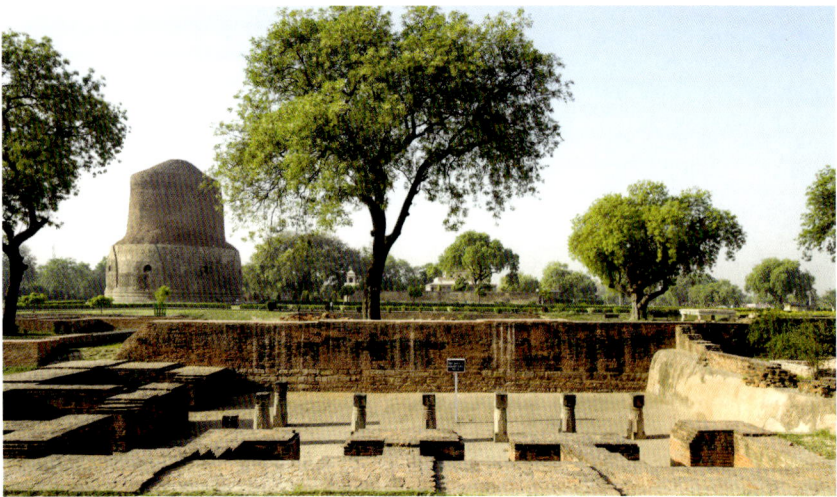

Monastery ruins with Dhamekha Stupa in the background.

transition from the Theravada to Mahayana schools emerged several sects, including the Sammatiya, Sarvastivadin, Vastiputriya and Sthaviravadin, all of which were important in differing degrees at Sarnath. The images excavated at Sarnath, today housed in the Archaeological Museum at Sarnath, reflect the stylistic influences of

EMPEROR ASHOKA AND BUDDHISM

Ashoka is remembered for his history of violence, but more so for his subsequent propagation of peace. The early part of his reign saw one bloody battle after another. From his kingdom of Magadha, he expanded the Mauryan Empire to cover nearly all of modern India, as well as parts of modern-day Bangladesh, Iran, and Afghanistan, making it the largest the subcontinent had ever seen.

In circa 265 BCE, Ashoka fought and conquered the neighbouring state of Kalinga (present-day Orissa), a feat unaccomplished by his predecessors and a victory he desired solely for that reason. However, he was supposedly filled with remorse by the suffering caused by the war and therefore he converted to Buddhism. His capital Pataliputra (modern-day Patna) was one of the places where the Buddha had preached and his kingdom Magadha was one of the regions where Buddhism was already becoming popular.

Ashoka spent the next 40 years of his reign advocating peace, secularism, and self-awareness. He sent Buddhist missionaries as far as Egypt and East Asia. On the basis of the Buddhist ideals of *dhamma* and *sangha*, he created a humane welfare state in which animals and humans alike, Hindus, Muslims, Buddhists, and Jains could live harmoniously. He had edicts advertising his law inscribed on hundreds of sandstone pillars and erected these all over his kingdom. The finest of these famous and remarkable 'Ashokan stone capitals' was erected at Sarnath and can be found in the museum today.

In the centuries following the rule of Ashoka, through the reign of the Sungas in the 2nd century CE, the Kushanas in the 1st century, and the Palas in the 8th century, monasteries began to join together to form influential monastic centres called mahaviharas. The most famous of these was the one at Nalanda (in modern-day Bihar), which trained young monks in Mahayana.

the Sammatiya sect. The Chinese Buddhist monk Hiuen-Tsang, who visited Sarnath in the 7th century, recorded that the only large monastery at Sarnath belonged to the Sammatiya monks.

During these centuries, the monks of various sects strove to elucidate their doctrines and elaborate their rituals and ceremonies. Rulers and rich devotees patronized them. A mutually beneficial relationship developed between the monastic community and the Buddhist laity. This relationship enabled small monasteries (*vihara*s) to form in North-eastern India and other areas to which Buddhism spread. During the reign of the Mauryas, Guptas and Palas, the monasteries gained wealth and influence, and both the monastic community and the laity increased in size and strength.

The third Mauryan emperor Ashoka, who reigned between 273 and 232 BCE, went on a pilgrimage to 32 spots associated with events from the Buddha's life, including Sarnath. At Sarnath, he built large monasteries, through which the township grew into an important monastic centre. He erected a stupa here, a Buddhist monument usually preserving relics, called the Dharmarajika stupa, and installed one of his famous capitals before it.

Present-day Hinduism evolved partly from the absorption of Buddhism into Vedic and post-Vedic teachings.

The Vajrayana sect
Vajrayana Buddhism was one of the major sects that developed under the umbrella of Mahayana between the 5th and 11th centuries CE. Some teachers (*acharya*s) at the monastic centre at Nalanda who were influenced by Tantric Hinduism and the Hindu Aghor ascetic tradition travelled to Tibet, where they incorporated elements of the Tibetan spiritual tradition (called Bon) into their Tantric-influenced Buddhism. Vajrayana Buddhism was born out of this synthesis of Tantra and the Tibetan spiritual tradition.

Vajrayana's emphasis on idol worship and ritual, including some extreme practices, resemble Shaivism. By contrast, Theravada, the oldest Buddhist tradition, reflects Lord Buddha's encouragement of self-awareness and self-discipline, over prescribed worship and ritual.

The Decline of Buddhism
In 1017, Mahmud of Ghazni, an Afghan ruler, raided Banaras and destroyed many of its temples, as well as the monasteries and stupas at Sarnath. Some scholars believe that Buddhism thereafter began to decline, because it had by then become mainly a monastic movement that paid little attention to the laity.

According to others, Buddhism declined because of the rise of Bhakti worship in Hinduism, around the 13th century CE. Bhakti was a movement propagating intense devotion by an individual towards a personal god. Bhakti arose in south India and spread remarkably over the subcontinent, spearheaded by poet-saints such as Meera in Rajasthan, Chaitanya in Bengal, and Tulsidas in Banaras, who sang of the futility of organized religion and the power of personal devotion.

The old Vedic system of religion had emphasized Sanskrit scriptures, ritual sacrifice and the power of priests. Buddhism was partly a challenge to this system.

According to scholars, during the Bhakti movement, Buddhism came to be absorbed into Vedic and post-Vedic practices. Adopting the Buddha as an incarnation of Vishnu, Hinduism incorporated into itself the Buddhist ideals of individualized devotion, independence from priests and texts, and the pursuit of release (nirvana in Buddhism and *moksha* in Hinduism), while retaining its love for ritual and systematized worship. Present-day Hinduism evolved partly from the absorption of Buddhism into Vedic and post-Vedic teachings.

THE STUPA

A stupa is a hemispherical or dome-like monument built out of brick or stone. From certain texts, it is clear that the custom of building stupas existed before the Buddha, although after him stupas acquired a specifically Buddhist association. Typically, a Buddhist stupa will have a low circular base surmounted by a square box (*harmika*). An elevated route that is sometimes fenced or walled, circumambulates the dome. An umbrella (*chhatra*) crowns the dome at the very top. One worships at the stupa by circumambulating the dome in the direction of the sun.

The origin of the stupa has been much contested by scholars over the years. One theory is that stupas commemorated pre-Buddhist burial mounds. The earliest Buddhist stupas were built both outdoors and indoors as monuments preserving relics of the Buddha or of his associates, commemorating an important event from his life or previous incarnations, or representing him in the final stage of nirvana. The stupas that were built indoors served as votive objects within rectangular halls called *chaitya*s. Ruins of such *chaitya* shrines from around the time of Ashoka exist at Sarnath and other sites. Gradually, as the Buddha began to be depicted in stone, the votive *chaitya* stupas were replaced by actual Buddha images.

According to art historian Vidya Dehejia, the inscriptions on stupas and relic caskets reveal that monks and lay worshippers understood the relic to embody the Buddha's presence and even contain his living presence. The worshipper visits the stupa in order to experience the Buddha's presence through the relic. Viewing the life-scenes carved on stupas enhances that experience, bringing the worshipper even closer to the Buddha's presence.

Unlike stupas elsewhere, however, the ones at Sarnath do not contain any relics. Their sacredness lies in their location, at spots associated with the Buddha's life.

Contemporary Buddhist Revival

After Ashoka's death the popularity of Buddhism waned. In a few centuries it was all but forgotten in India, even as it expanded overseas in other parts of Asia where Indian missionaries had popularized it. Since the mid-20th century, the number of Buddhists in India has been again increasing. This increase is in part due to the Chinese conquest of Tibet in the late 1950s, which resulted in a large influx of Tibetan Buddhists migrating to India,

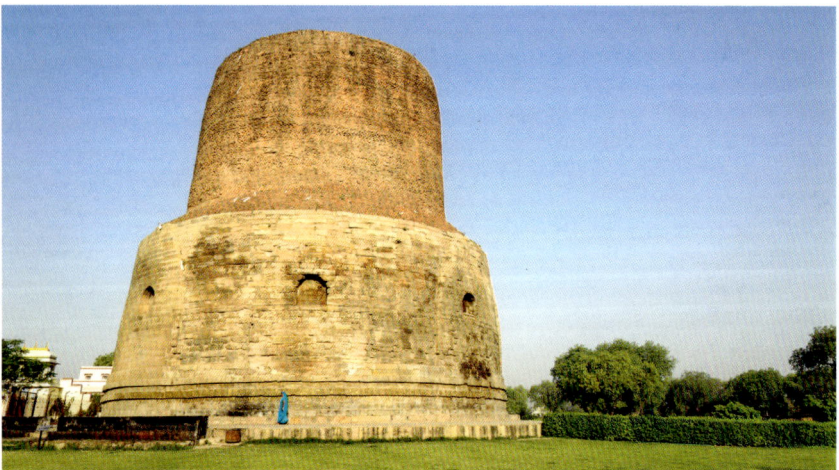

Dhamekha Stupa.

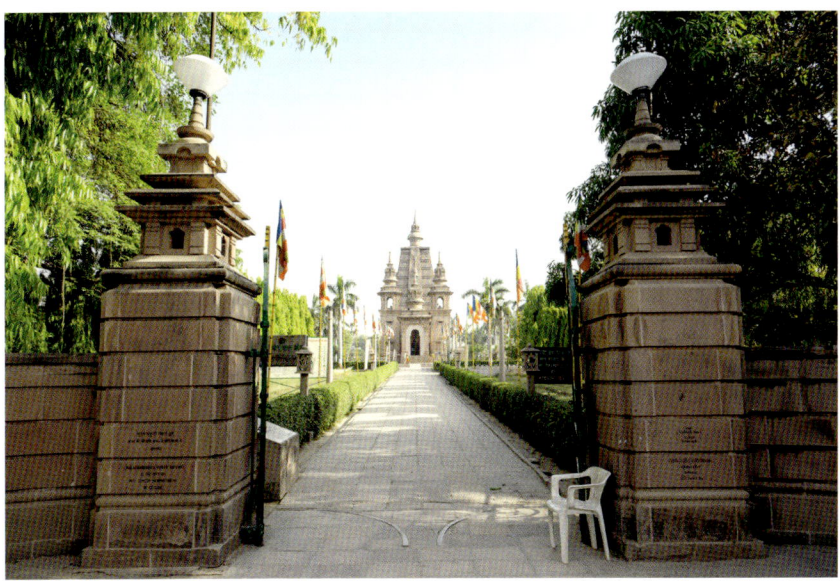

Mulagandha Kuti Vihara Temple.

the incorporation of Sikkim into India in 1975, and the mass conversion of Hindu 'untouchables' or dalits to Buddhism headed by Bhimrao Ramji Ambedkar in the 1950s. Ambedkar was the head of India's Constituent Assembly, responsible for writing independent India's Constitution.

Ⓐ THE MONASTERY RUINS – DHAMEKHA STUPA COMPOUND

The history of the monasteries

The monastery constitutes an important form of early Indian architecture. Typically, monasteries were built on a square plan, with a courtyard in the middle and rows of cells along the four sides. As larger monastic organizations formed, monasteries acquired more elaborate structures, often having several storeys.

According to archaeologists, the oldest ruins of the monasteries at Sarnath date from around 260 BCE. Ashoka's lion capital dates from his reign between 273 and 232 BCE, during which he had built several monasteries. Sarnath's monasteries flourished until Mahmud of Ghazni destroyed most of them in 1017. A century later, between 1114 and 1154 CE, the Gahadvala king, Govindcharan rebuilt and repaired most of the destroyed monasteries. His Buddhist wife, Kumaradevi built one of the largest monasteries here, perhaps the last of its size, called *Dharmachakra Jinavihara.*

One worships at the stupa by circumambulating the dome in the direction of the sun.

The monastery ruins at Sarnath
Monastery V

This monastery has an open courtyard, measuring 50 square feet, with cells all around, each measuring 8.5 by 8 feet, and a well in the middle of the courtyard. There was a central entrance with two guardrooms on either side. A terracotta sealing, engraved with the Buddhist creed in the characters of the 9th century, was found in one of the cells. The condition of the verandah pillars shows that it was destroyed during a fire.

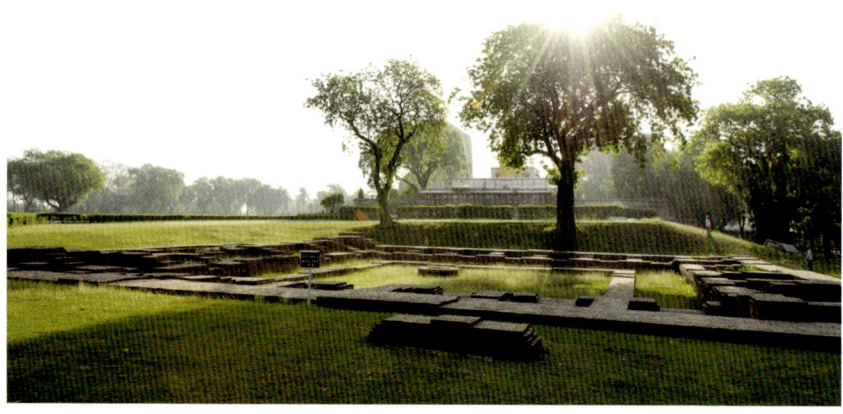

Monastery V

Monastery VII

This small monastery was built on the ruins of an older structure. It was destroyed by fire just like Monastery V. Its floor plan is typical, consisting of a courtyard, measuring 30 square feet, with a verandah and cells all around.

'Dharmarajika' Stupa and Ashokan shaft

Emperor Ashoka built the Dharmarajika stupa, of which only ruins remain today. He also had a capital erected before the stupa, of which the shaft remains on site west of the Dharmarajika stupa and the crowning capital is housed in the Archaeological Museum. Hiuen-Tsang recorded in 637 BCE that the capital was so lustrous with 'Mauryan polish' that it constantly reflected the stupa. A local king, Jagat Singh levelled the Dharmarajika stupa in 1794. When his workmen pulled down the stupa, they found a large stone box with a green marble relic-casket inside.

Excavations in the 20th century revealed that the stupa was enlarged six times over the centuries, first by the Kushan king, Kanishka in the 1st century and the last by Kumaradevi in the 12th century. It must have originally had a semi-circular shape and then been enlarged in an increasingly oblong shape.

Main Shrine/ Mulagandha Kuti

Judging by the thick walls that still exist, the original shrine was large. Hiuen Tsang's journals record it was over 200 feet high. It was built of bricks, plaster, and carved stones on a square plan, each side measuring 60 feet. The style of moulding dates from the Gupta period. At that time, the shrine housed an enormous metal image of the Buddha in *dharmachakramudra*, the posture of turning the wheel of the law.

Under the southern foundations of the shrine, archaeologists discovered a monolithic railing lustrous with the Mauryan polish of Ashoka's time. Scholars agree that it originally ran along the top of the Dharmarajika stupa. Two inscriptions on the railing mention teachers of the Sarvastivadin sect.

To the west of the main shrine is the stump of the Ashokan Lion Capital. It bears three inscriptions. The first and earliest is Ashoka's edict in Brahmi characters, in which the emperor warns monks against creating conflicts in the *sangha*. The second inscription refers to the 40th year of the Kushan king, Ashvagosha, whose capital was in Kausambi. The third inscription, in early Gupta script, mentions teachers of the Sammatiya sect.

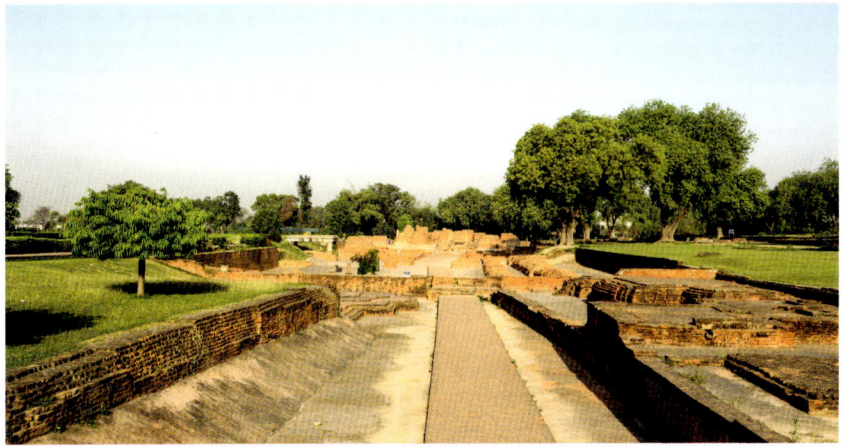

Chaitya hall ruins.

Chaitya hall/ Asidal Temple

The earliest stupas were often built as indoor votive objects within halls called *chaitya*s. West of the Ashokan pillar are the ruins of one such chaitya hall. It was 82 feet in length and 38 feet in width, with a semicircular section at the back. Archaeologists found antiquities dating from the Mauryan to the Gupta period here. Excavations revealed that the hall was ruined by fire in the post-Gupta period and a monastery was later built on its foundations.

Monastery I / Dharmachakra Jina Vihara

This enormous monastery was built by Kumaradevi, the Buddhist queen of the Gahadvala king, Govindcharan. The excavations, so far measuring 760 square feet, show that there was an open court on the west with cells surrounding it on the other three sides. The basement was built of neatly chiselled bricks decorated with elegant mouldings. There were two gateways on the east, 290 feet apart from one another.

An underground tunnel that is now closed leads west. Originally, it opened out into a small shrine.

Monastery II

Judging from the size of the bricks, this monastery dates from the early Gupta period. The central courtyard, measuring 90 square feet, was enclosed by 3-foot thick walls. The walls are believed to have supported the pillars of the verandah.

Monastery III

Monastery III resembles Monastery II in plan. The carvings on the pillars date from the late Kushan period. The thickness of the walls shows that the structure was at least two-storeys high.

Monastery IV

Archaeologists found a colossal, 12th-century image of Shiva piercing a demon with his trident here. Kumaradevi's inscription was also found nearby. Both pieces are housed in the Archaeological Museum.

Alongside the walkway leading from Monastery IV to Dhamekha stupa, one finds several ruined stupas and halls dating from the Gupta period.

Over 100 feet high and over 90 in diametre, the Dhamekha Stupa is believed to commemorate the spot where the Buddha preached his second sermon to his first five disciples.

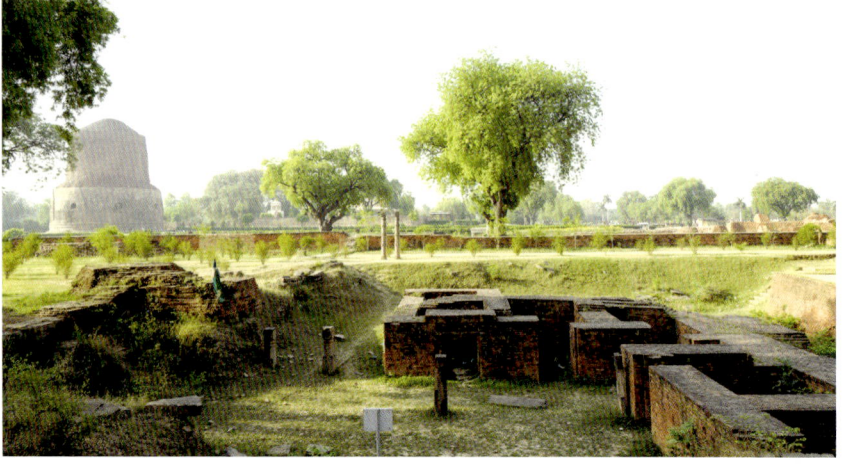

Dhamekha stupa, behind monastery ruins.

Monastery VI

To the west of the Dhamekha stupa are the ruins of what is believed to be a 'hospital', judging from the pestles and mortars found here.

Dhamekha Stupa

Scholars do not agree upon the derivation of the name *Dhamekha*. The name could mean 'the pondering of the law.' It could also be an abbreviation of *dharmopadeshaka,* which means 'preacher of *dharma*'. Over 100-feet high and over 90 in diameter, the Dhamekha stupa is believed to commemorate the spot where the Buddha preached his second sermon to his first five disciples.

In 1835, Alexander Cunningham, an archaeologist and British military officer who helped form the Archaeological Survey of India, bored a shaft into the stupa from its top in search of relics. He found instead a stone slab inscribed with characters from around the 6th century and some Mauryan bricks, which may have been the remains of an Ashoka-period stupa.

The dome and flat surfaces of the standing Dhamekha stupa are carved with scenes from the Buddha's life, geometric patterns, and, most strikingly, bands of lotus creepers. These motifs are acknowledged to be typically 'Buddhist' and found widely on other Buddhist images and monuments.

They are not, however, exclusively Buddhist but a characteristic of Gupta-period art. The life-scenes are illustrations of the Jataka tales, a widely-read Pali text that records episodes from the Buddha's previous incarnations as various animals.

John M. Rosenfield writes that the lotus motif, representing vegetative abundance and growth, may have emerged from the notion that material gain may be one fruit of following *dhamma*. Thus, apart from its decorative function, the lotus motif also served as an emblem of correct world order.

THE SARNATH SCHOOL OF CLASSICAL ART

From Indian folk deities to Buddha sculptures
From around the 1st to the 4th centuries CE, Mathura dominated as a centre of Indian sculpture. The images initially produced largely consisted of *yaksha*s, or ancient folk deities associated with fertility, as well as human heads, railing pieces, and secular images of birds and animals.

Little is known about the development of early Indian sculpture in general. For a number of reasons, including the rise of Mahayana Buddhism, the *yaksha* images of Mathura evolved into aniconic (symbolic) and then anthropomorphic (realistic) representations of the Buddha as well as the Hindu trinity. The first images of Lord

Buddha produced at Mathura were sturdy and voluminous, resembling the earlier *yaksha* images. These earliest images were sent out to other sites and centres of sculpture, including Sarnath, for installation outdoors and in shrines and for local reproduction. The other schools coexisted with Mathura, but produced much fewer pieces and were heavily influenced by Mathura in style.

Between the 4th and 6th centuries, during the reign of the Guptas, Indian sculpture moved into its classical phase. The earthy sensuality of the earlier work began to give way to constraint, elegance, and an abstract quality. The later images of Lord Buddha blended the sensuous and the spiritual, the physical and the psychological. They depicted not just the Buddha's form but also his contemplative inner state. During this period, the Sarnath school of sculpture began to surpass Mathura in achieving new levels of workmanship and in reflecting the psychological and spiritual values of monastic Buddhism.

As John Rosenfield describes, the Sarnath image possesses an extraordinary weightlessness and equipose. The plainness of the Chunar stone allows various parts of the body to blend into one another, resulting in an abstract quality. The facial expression is subtle, communicating both introspection and bliss. The earlier verticality of the body has been eased, and the figure now stands in a pose called *abhanga*, in which the weight is thrown onto the right hip and the body turns slightly at the knees, waist and shoulders, a pose that emphasizes the body's contours and imparts in it a sense of movement. As a whole, the Sarnath image of the Buddha conveys, as never before, a flawless spiritual state devoid of egotism or passion, just as the physical body possesses none of the blemishes of an ordinary mortal.

The Buddha sculptures housed in the Archaeological Museum at Sarnath reflect these qualities distinctive of the Sarnath School. They also reflect the distinctive qualities of the classical Gupta-period sculpture in general.

One quality of the Gupta-period sculpture is that it blends realism, symbolism and decorative art. For instance, along with the realism of figure and form that Gupta-period sculptors strove for, certain 'auspicious signs' were also included on the images of the Buddha. The auspicious signs include the half-closed eyes and cross-legged posture of a *mahayogi* (great ascetic), and the elongated earlobes, long arms and *chakras* (wheels) marking the palms and soles of the feet characteristic of the *chakravartin* ('lord of the four quarters') king. Gupta sculptors incorporated both types of signs on their Buddha images, thus depicting the Buddha simultaneously as *mahayogi* (great ascetic) and *chakravartin* king.

The scholarship of Vidya Dehejia and others also stresses the overlapping of realism, symbolism and decorative art in Gupta Buddhist art. Dehejia discusses how the common conception that prevailed was that the Theravada phase produced aniconic art, or art symbolizing the Buddha and his life, whereas the later Mahayana phase introduced the anthropomorphic icon, or images realistically depicting Lord Buddha

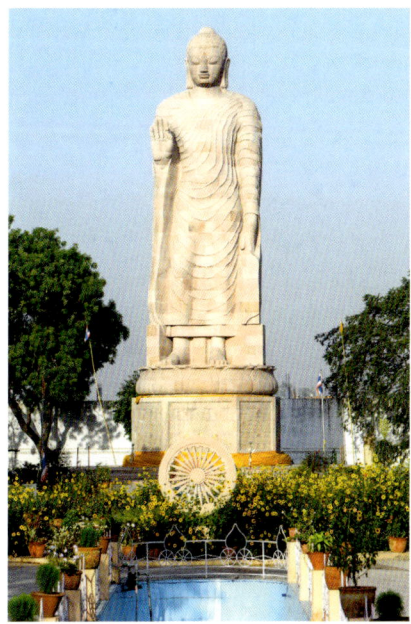

Buddha statue near Thai temple.

and his life. However, Dehejia points out that the Theravada and Mahayana schools overlapped, both chronologically as well as in their aesthetic concerns. Images and emblems were produced both to realistically depict the Buddha and his life, and to capture and communicate Buddhist teachings and values. The pieces are not singular in meaning, but multi-layered.

Little is known about the artists at Sarnath who produced the statues, steles and emblems contained today in the museum. A gorge in Sarnath discovered by archaeologists led them to conclude that there was once a rivulet that ran from the nearby quarry of Chunar to the stone workshops at Sarnath. Further excavations in Chunar led to the discovery that the sandstone was quarried in large round pieces. These pieces would be rolled down the hills onto rafts and ferried up the rivulet to workshops in Sarnath.

Only three of all the excavated pieces bear inscriptions with precise dates. The inscriptions reveal that the patron-donor of all three sculptures was one Abhayamitra, a monk who lived during the reign of the Gupta king, Kumaragupta. Rosenfield discusses how *bhikshu* Abhayamitra, about whom nothing else is known, may have funded the production of these sculptures to accumulate merit in his karma, in order to insure auspicious rebirth and, eventually,

liberation. The idea that merit can be accumulated through means other than austerities, such as by commissioning the image of Buddha, was essentially Mahayana and appealed to lay Buddhists. This idea helped Buddhism become a popular faith after Ashoka's reign.

The dates on the images and the level of workmanship displayed by them have led scholars to conclude that the Sarnath school matured rapidly at the end of the 5th century, a conclusion that says much about the creativity of the Sarnath masters. No sculpture that is 'pre-classical' in workmanship has till date been discovered at Sarnath.

The three dated images help us understand the late Gupta age during which the Sarnath style of sculpture flourished. They have also helped us understand the development of early Indian art as a whole, since very few of all the monuments excavated in the entire subcontinent are dated.

Ⓑ ARCHAEOLOGICAL MUSEUM

Fascinating galleries with historical relics

What to Know The Archaeological Museum at Sarnath is the oldest site museum of the Archaeological Survey of India. It was completed in 1910 under the guidance of Sir John Marshall, the then Director General of Archaeology in India, and James Ramson, the consulting architect to the Government

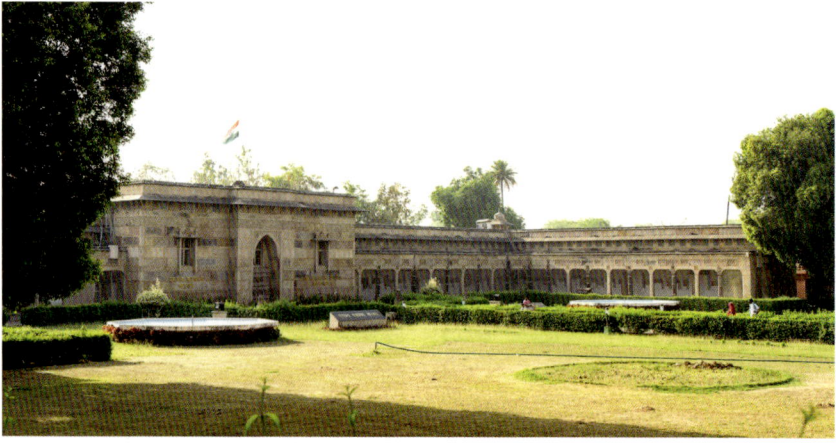

The Archaeological Museum at Sarnath.

of India. Ramson designed its floor plan to form half a monastery.

What to See The museum, small in size but fascinating in content, spreads over five galleries and houses over two thousand pieces. These comprise only 5 per cent of the museum's total collection, the rest of which is kept in storage.

Gallery 3
The Ashokan Lion Capital

One walks into the central Gallery 3 to confront the famous Ashokan Lion Capital of Sarnath, sculpted out of a single block of black sandstone from Chunar. Two and a half metres high, it originally crowned a monolithic column inscribed with one of Ashoka's edicts. The capital at Sarnath is just one of hundreds Ashoka had erected all over his vast kingdom, but it is considered the finest in workmanship. The lustrous polish of the capital was a speciality of the Mauryan period.

All Mauryan stone capitals consist of two parts, the shaft and the capital. The shaft is long, circular and slightly tapering. The capital consists of three parts, an inverted lotus or bell, an abacus, and a crowning sculpture. The plain surface of the shaft contrasts with the carved surface of the capital.

Forming the crown of the Sarnath capital, four lions sit back to back. Originally, there was a wheel balanced between their shoulders, but only fragments of the wheel remain today, which are displayed in a separate case against the western gallery wall. The wheel perhaps represented the Buddhist wheel of *dhamma*. The molding of the lions emphasizes their musculature and physical prowess. The details and realism, in the lions' muscles, manes, and jaws testifies to the sculptors' mastery. Interestingly, the lions roar, but do not look fierce.

The inverted lotus of the base is sharply ridged. Around the circular abacus are a lion,

Little is known about the artists at Sarnath who produced the statues, steles and emblems contained today in the museum.

an elephant, a bull and a horse, intercepted by *dharmachakra*s (wheels). These animals perhaps symbolize events from the Buddha's life or, together with the *dharmachakra*s, communicate the relentlessness of the turning of the wheel of law.

The Ashokan Lion Capital was adopted as India's national emblem when India became a republic on 26 January 1950. It is now reproduced on the gateways of many national buildings and on the currency notes of India.

Standing Boddhisatva

Behind the lion capital towers a giant nine and a half feet high red sandstone statue of a standing *bodhisattva* (an unenlightened individual who has vowed to become a Buddha). He stands in *abhaymudra* or the posture of fearlessness and security. The monk Bala commissioned the piece to be sculpted at Mathura in the Kushana period (2nd century CE). He then had it installed in Sarnath, between the Main Shrine and the Dharmarajika Stupa, sheltered by an accompanying carved parasol. The parasol is displayed separately on the northern wall of Gallery 1.

The piece was one of the first to be sculpted at Mathura, hence its heaviness of form as compared to the Sarnath pieces. Behind the statue stands the shaft that supported the parasol. It is inscribed with *bhikshu* Bala's inscription, which states that the piece was installed 'where the Lord walked'.

The other sculptures in the central gallery include several **Buddhas in *abhayamudra*,** the posture of fearlessness, with palms facing outwards. The piece standing between two others along the southern wall is one of the dated images of Abhayamitra. The inscription runs along the pedestal.

Along the eastern wall of the gallery are displayed the fragments of the wheel that originally crowned Ashoka's Lion Capital.

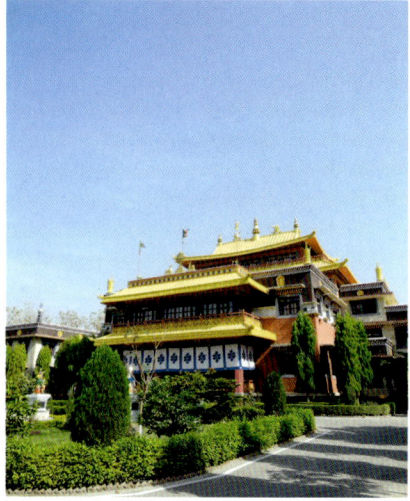

Tibetan temple.

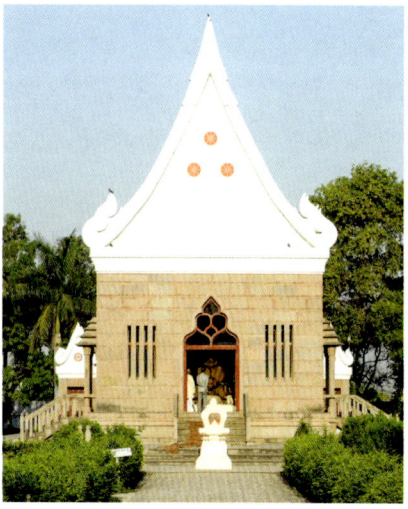

Thai temple.

Also featured in this gallery is an image of the **Buddha in** *bhumisparshamudra,* the posture of crouching and touching the earth with the fingers of the right hand, to call the earth-spirit to witness his enlightenment. This piece bears an inscription in the Gupta Brahmi script, identifying it to be the gift of Bandhugupta.

Featured here also is the goddess *Tara*, wearing elaborate jewellery. The piece dates from the late Gupta period (5th century CE). *Tara* could derive from the Sanskrit 'tar', which means 'to cross over'. She emerged when Vajrayana Buddhism developed, as the saviour and protector, comparable in many ways to shakti (female divine power) in Hinduism, of which Kali and Durga are two manifestations.

No sculpture that is 'pre-classical' in workmanship has till date been discovered at Sarnath.

Gallery 2
Two images of the mythical animal, the *leogryph* stand on either side of the doorway to Gallery 2. Along the eastern wall stands the voluminous *Tara*, wearing ornate jewellery and holding a pomegranate that bursts open to reveal a row of seeds.

The Buddha images include *Bodhisattva Padmapani* or Buddha holding a lotus and Buddha in *dharmachakra parvatan* (the attitude of preaching).

Jambhal, the pot-bellied god of wealth and prosperity, stands beside *Vasudhara,* his consort and the goddess of abundance.

Kumaradevi's inscription
The last piece along the eastern wall is Kumaradevi's inscription. Kumaradevi was the Buddhist queen of the Gahadvala king, Govindcharan who ruled over Banaras in the 11th century. The inscription refers to the construction of the large monastery she had built in Sarnath, called *Dharmachakra Jinavihara.*

There are also two steles dating from the 5th to 6th centuries. The first stele is called *Life Scene of Buddha* and depicts eight scenes from the Buddha's life, including his leaving home on his favourite horse, Kanthak to his *parinirvana* or final passing.

The second stele depicts *the great miracle,* in which the Buddha's body multiplied and appeared on top of lotuses in various poses. Also depicted on the stele are the ascetic Purana Kashyap, who converted at the miraculous sight, King Prasenajit on

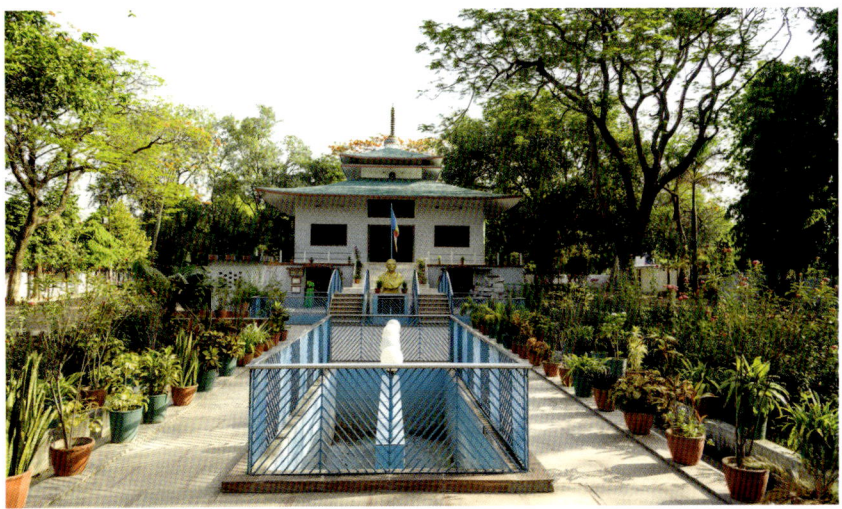

Mahabodhi Society temple.

his elephant, and the two *nag*s Nanda and Upananda, who presented the Buddha with his lotus seat.

The wall case displays Vasudhara, Aparajita (a form of Tara), Marichi (the goddess of dawn) riding her chariot pulled by seven boars, various Buddha heads, railing pieces, and steles.

Galley 1

Gallery 1 displays various standing Bodhisattvas and Buddhas, as well as a panel showing the Buddha's life.

Seated Buddha

One of the most exquisite pieces in the museum is of the Buddha seated. This piece is in superb condition and is displayed at the far end of the gallery.

The Buddha's delicate fingers are folded gently in *dharmachakramudra* (the gesture of turning the wheel of the law). He sits in perfect balance in *padmasana* (cross-legged in the 'lotus position' of meditation or preaching), while appearing to be utterly weightless. Above his aquiline nose, his slender eyelids are downcast. A slight smile plays on his full lips and seems to radiate onto his smooth cheeks. His

head is covered with dozens of ringlets that form a mound at the top. Two crocodiles and leogryphs flank him from above. Below crouch a mother with her child, six humans, and a deer. The entire piece exudes deep spirituality, introspection and bliss, and is sculpted with exceptional realism and delicacy.

This piece of the Buddha in *dharmachakra pravartan* is replicated in hundreds of clay pieces moulded by artisans, which are sold cheaply on roadside carts outside the museum.

> The emphasis on idol worship and rituals is representative of the Vajrayana tradition.

Gallery 4

Gallery 4 contains five wall cases. The first and second display secular pieces of birds and animals, human heads, carved Gupta-period bricks of different shapes, terracotta figurines of musicians and dancers, deities, humans and animals.

The third wall case contains terracotta pottery from the 10th century. The fourth displays iron implements and copper jewellery. The fifth wall case displays stone heads of deities such as Surya the sun, Saraswati, the demon-slaying goddess, Mahishasurmardini and the Jain *tirthankar,* Parshvanath.

Gallery 5

Gallery 5 displays Brahmanic sculptures, including Vishnu, Shiva, Parvati, Chamunda, and Ganesh, as well as Agni, the god of fire. Particularly noteable are two lintels depicting the nine planets or *navagraha*, an image of *Bhairav* (Shiva's aggressive form) and *Vishnu seated on Garuda.*

At the far end stands an unfinished, but spectacular image of *Shiva slaying the demon Andhak* with his trident.

Ⓒ THE TEMPLES OF SARNATH

Tibetan Temple
In the Vajrayana tradition

What to Know The temple was built in 1996 mainly with the help of donations by Tibetans. It follows the Vajrayana tradition.

What to See It has an elaborate inner chamber filled with idols of the Buddha, Mara, Maitreya, and other deities, as well as of the Reverend Tsong Khapa of Tibet and two of his followers. There are also prayer flags, bowls, drums, and rare scriptures that were translated into Tibetan between the 7th and 9th centuries. The emphasis on idol worship and rituals is representative of the Vajrayana tradition.

> Some scholars think that the name 'Sarnath' comes from 'Saranganath.'

'Mulagandha Kuti Vihara'
Exquisite frescoes

What to Know This is a Theravada temple run by the Mahabodhi Society of Sri Lanka. The Mahabodhi Society was set up by Anagarika Dharmapala (1864-1933). Dharmapala, born to aristocratic Buddhist parents in Sri Lanka, established the Mahabodhi Society in his home country. Today, it aims to preserve and develop Buddhist sites and popularize Buddhism, in both Sri Lanka and India. Since its establishment, the Society has built and revived many temples and monasteries in both countries. It is considered instrumental in reviving Buddhism in India.

What to See The frescoes inside the temple were painted by the Japanese artist, Kosetsu Nosu over four years between 1932 and 1936. The main image of the Buddha was sculpted at Jaipur.

Thai Temple
In the Theravada tradition

What to Know Badant Shashant Rashmi, a Buddhist monk from Maharashtra, built this temple in 1976. It follows the Theravada tradition and is therefore simple in its arrangement inside.

What to See The statue of the Buddha is in *bhumisparshamudra*, in which he calls the earth-spirit to witness his enlightenment.

Jain Temple
The 11th tirthankara

What to Know This temple was built in 1824 for the 11th Jain *tirthankar* ('ford-maker', Jain religious leader), Shreyamsanath. Paintings of the life of Mahavira line the walls of the temple. Mahavira was the 24th and last *tirthankar*. He outlined the central tenets of Jainism.

Mahabodhi Society Temple
A library and a museum

What to Know This Theravada temple was set up by the Mahabodhi Society in 1922. A golden bust of Anagarika Dharmapala, the founder of the Society, greets you at the entrance.

What to See Housed under the temple is a museum and library that preserves old photographs, journals, and books in languages including Singhalese, Japanese and Bengali.

Korean Temple
A Mahayana temple

What to Know Established in 1996, this is a Mahayana temple.

Chinese Temple
Sculptures and scriptures

What to Know This temple, also Mahayana, was established in 1939 by the abbot of Beijing

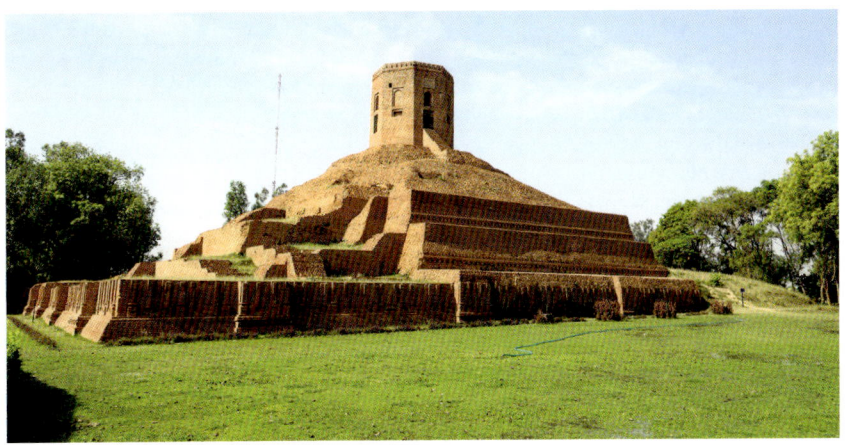

Chaukhandi Stupa, with Humayun's memorial on top.

Tao-Kai and the president of the Eastern Asian Buddhist association, Fa-Yuan-Tsu.

What to See The image of the Buddha inside was sculpted in Burma.

Japanese Temple
In the Mahayana tradition
What to Know This temple was built in 1986 by the Dharmachakra Indo-Japanese Society and follows the Mahayana tradition.

Saranganath Temple
The lord of the deer
What to Know This modest temple sits on a hillock adjoining a pond and is believed to occupy the site of an ancient shrine dedicated to Shiva as Saranganath, the 'lord of the deer'. Some scholars think that the name 'Sarnath' comes from 'Saranganath'.

Ⓓ CHAUKHANDI STUPA
A terraced shrine
What to Know Chaukhandi stupa, located outside the main compound of Dhamekha stupa, was destroyed when Mahmud of Ghazni destroyed the other stupas and monasteries of Sarnath in 1017.

The octagonal structure that rises above the ruins of the stupa was built in 1567 by Mughal emperor Akbar in memory of his father Humayun, who visited Sarnath in 1532. Akbar commissioned Govardhan, the son of his Hindu finance minister, Raja Todar Mal, to build it. Akbar is famous for his tolerance and secularism. He adopted the *Sulf-e-Kul* ('Peace to All') concept of Sufism as his religious policy.

The rising stepped terraces on the eastern side were revealed during excavations and show that during the Gupta-period, the stupa was a shrine built in a terraced form. Gupta-period sculptures were also found here, namely an image of the Buddha in *dharmachakramudra* and two bas reliefs of leogryphs and gladiators.

Ⓔ CENTRAL INSTITUTE OF TIBETAN STUDIES
Preserving language and culture
What to Know In 1964, in light of the Sino-Tibetan conflict of the fifties, the prime minister of India Jawaharlal Nehru and the Dalai Lama first discussed establishing a national institute for the study and preservation of Tibetan language and culture. Three years later, the Central Institute of Tibetan Studies was established at Sarnath for this purpose. It continues to be fully funded by the Government of India. The Institute offers regular BA, MA, M.Phil. (Masters of Philosophy) and Ph.D. degrees in a range of subjects related to Tibetan language, religion, culture and arts.

Other Places of Interest in Banaras

LAT MASJID

Location: The mosque is located in the far north, in Adampura neighbourhood, close to the railway track.

Lat Masjid is an old outdoor mosque, interesting because it shares its site with a Hindu temple. It is named after a pillar on the same site that Hindus worship as Lat Bhairav, a form of Shiva. On the festival of Id, the mosque gets spectacularly crowded with worshippers, perhaps the largest congregation for Id in the city. Near the shared mosque-temple site is the shrine of Maqdum Shahid, a legendary revered saint, where one may see men and women of the city 'get possessed'.

ALAIPURA & JAITPURA NEIGHBOURHOODS

Location: Walk to Alaipura and Jaitpura from the Jaitpura Police Station (Jaitpura thana), in the far north of the city.

The crowded northern neighbourhoods of **Alaipura and Jaitpura** are fascinating to walk through because of their preponderance of yarn dye workshops and shops selling weaving-related paraphernalia. Most of the homes here belong to weavers, interspersed with mosques, shops, shrines, and little open spaces where people socialize.

SAMPURNANAND SANSKRIT UNIVERSITY

Location: The University is located in the north-western neighbourhood of Chaukaghat. From the main Varanasi railway station, you can reach the university by going east on Station Road (Highway 29), by the bridge called Andhra Pul, and turning right at the Chaukaghat Electric Substation.

In 1791, Jonathan Duncan of the East India Company proposed the establishment of a university specializing in Sanskrit and related fields, to show British support for Indian education. The result was the Sanskrit University, to be housed in an amazing, ornate Gothic-style building. The university now named after a scholar called **Sampurnanand**, continues to focus on the study of Sanskrit, Indian philosophy, and Ayurveda, and affiliates hundreds of Sanskrit schools and colleges all over the country.

MAHATMA GANDHI KASHI VIDYAPEETH UNIVERSITY

Location: Kashi Vidyapeeth University is located in the north-west, on the road that links Sigra crossing with the city's main railway station popularly called just Cantt.

Mahatma Gandhi established **Kashi Vidyapeeth** in 1921, during the Non-Cooperation movement for India's independence. It was the first of a handful of institutions set up during the nationalist period that were outside British administration and were run by Indian nationalists and educationists. Kashi Vidyapeeth is one of the city's main universities today, with all the departments found in any university.

BHARAT MATA MANDIR

Location: The temple is located on the road linking the Varanasi 'Cantt' railway station with Sigra crossing, next to Kashi Vidyapeeth University.

The **Bharat Mata Mandir**, built in 1936, is dedicated to Mother India, a concept that took shape with the Indian independence movement in the late 19th century. Whereas Mother India is pictured as a goddess elsewhere, this temple in Banaras features a marble statue of Mother India as well as a large three-dimensional marble map of India sculpted onto the floor. It may well be the only place in the world where a map is meant to be worshipped! The walls are etched with texts in various Indian languages.

RAMNAGAR FORT

Location: Cross the river via the Pontoon bridge in the southern neighbourhood of Samneghat (down the road from Banaras Hindu University).

Visitors' Information: Museum timings 10 am to 5 pm. Tickets for Indians/non-Indians: Rs. 20/150

The **Ramnagar Fort** was built in 1750 by Balwant Singh, the first Maharaja of Banaras, and has been home to the royal family since. The current Maharaja of Banaras – a title that was abolished in 1971 – is Anant Narayan Singh.

Built in Chunar sandstone in Mughal style, it is not grand compared to India's other, larger forts but beautiful and interesting nonetheless. It features a temple overlooking the river, dedicated to Ved Vyasa, the author of the Sanskrit epic Ramayana. There is also a small museum that houses vintage cars, horse carriages, furniture, swords, jewellery, and costumes woven in special Banarasi brocade that belonged to the royal family, and includes a peek into the Durbar Hall, not in use today.

The fort and the Maharaja take on special importance during the Ramlila, in the season of Ashwin (September-October) in neighbourhoods all over Banaras. The Ramnagar town production is the most spectacular and famous of all. The Maharaja of Banaras, in keeping with tradition, attends each night of the Ramlila atop an elephant.

Outside the fort across the road are several shops that sell cups of the excellent lassi locally popular as the unmatched 'lassi of Ramnagar'.

BANARAS HINDU UNIVERSITY

Location: Banaras Hindu University occupies a large campus in the south of Banaras, its entrance marked by the large BHU Gate at the end of Lanka road.

One of India's largest and highly ranked universities, **BHU** was set up by Madan Mohan Malviya in 1916, as an Indian alternative to colonial education and a means through which to foster nationalism. It was special for the inclusion of departments such as Ayurveda, Indology, and Sanskrit, which continue to attract students today. BHU has a beautiful campus spreading over a thousand acres, with wide, tree-lined avenues. Its Vishwanath Temple, whose white spire can be viewed even far off in the city, is popular with students and tourists. The shops outside the temple serve tasty Indian meals, lassi, and cold coffee.

Bibliography

Corre, L. "Akhara and Naubatkhana". Ed. Pierre-Daniel Couté & Jean-Michel Léger. *Bénarès. Un Voyage d'architecture*. Paris: Edition Créaphis, 1989.

Darian, Steven G. *The Ganges in Myth and History*. Delhi: Motilal Banarasidass, 2001.

Dehejia, Vidya. "Aniconism and the Multivalence of Emblems". *Ars Orientalis*. Freer Gallery of Art, The Smithsonian Institution and Department of the History of Art, University of Michigan. Vol 21 (1991), pp 45-66.

Eck, Diana. *Banaras: City of Light*. New York: Columbia University Press, 1998.

Freitag, Sandria B. "State and Community: Symbolic Popular Protest in Banaras's Public Arenas." Ed. Sandria B. Freitag. *Culture and Power in Banaras: Community, Performance, and Environment, 1800 – 1980*. Berkeley: University of California Press, 1989.

Kapur, Anuradha. *Actors, Pilgrims, Kings and Gods: The Ramlila at Ramnagar*. Calcutta: Seagull Books, 1990.

King, Christopher R. "Forging a New Linguistic Identity: The Hindi Movement in Banaras, 1868 – 1914." Ed. Sandria B. Freitag. *Culture and Power in Banaras: Community, Performance, and Environment, 1800 – 1980*. Berkeley: University of California Press, 1989.

Krishna, Rai Anand. *Banaras in the Early 19th Century: Riverfront Panorama*. Varanasi: Indica, 2003.

Kumar, Nita. *The Artisans of Banaras: Popular Culture and Identity, 1880 – 1986*. Princeton: Princeton University Press, 1988.

Kumar, Nita. "Work and Leisure in the Formation of Identity: Muslim Weavers in a Hindu City." Ed. Sandria B. Frietag. *Culture and Power in Banaras: Community, Performance, and Environment, 1800 – 1980*. Berkeley: University of California Press, 1989.

Kumar, Nita. *Friends, Brothers, and Informants: Fieldwork Memoirs of Banaras*. Berkeley: University of California Press, 1992.

Lutgendorf, Philip. "Ram's Story in Shiva's City: Public Arenas and Private Patronage." Ed. Sandria B. Freitag. *Culture and Power in Banaras: Community, Performance, and Environment, 1800 – 1980*. Berkeley: University of California Press, 1989.

Lutgendorf, Philip. *The Life of a Text: performing the Ramcaritmanas of Tulsidas*. Berkeley: University of California Press, 1991

Parry, Jonathan P. *Death in Banaras*. Cambridge: Cambridge University Press, 1994.

Rosenfield, John M. "On the Dated Carvings of Sarnath". *Artibus Asiae*. Artibus Asiae Publishers. Vol 26, No. 1 (1963), pp. 10-26.

Rotzer, Klaus. "The Mosques." Ed. Pierre-Daniel Couté & Jean-Michel Léger. *Bénarès. Un Voyage d'architecture*. Paris: Edition Créaphis, 1989.

Rotzer, Klaus. "19th century building materials and construction techniques." Ed. Pierre-Daniel Couté & Jean-Michel Léger. *Bénarès. Un Voyage d'architecture*. Paris: Edition Créaphis, 1989.

Sherring, M.A. *Benares: The Sacred City of the Hindus*. Delhi: Book Faith India, 2000.

Singh, Rana P.B and Praveen S. Rana. *Banaras Region: A Spiritual & Cultural Guide*. Varanasi: Indica, 2002.

Singh, Rana P.B. *Cultural Landscapes and the Lifeworld: Literary Images of Banaras*. Varanasi: Indica Books, 2004.

The New Encyclopaedia Britannica, Vol 13, 15th Edition. Chicago: Encyclopaedia Britannica, 1991.

Index